New England NIGHTMARES

New England NIGHTMARES

True Tales of the Strange and Gothic

KEVEN McQUEEN

INDIANA UNIVERSITY PRESS

This book is a publication of

Indiana University Press
Office of Scholarly Publishing
Herman B Wells Library 350
1320 East 10th Street
Bloomington, Indiana 47405 USA

iupress.indiana.edu

The paper used in this publication meets the minimum requirements of the American National Standard for Information Sciences—Permanence of Paper for Printed Library Materials, ANSI Z39.48–1992.

Manufactured in the United States of America

Cataloging information is available from the Library of Congress.

ISBN 978-0-253-03470-0 (hdbk.)
ISBN 978-0-253-03469-4 (pbk.)
ISBN 978-0-253-03471-7 (web PDF)

1 2 3 4 5   23 22 21 20 19 18

Dedicated to Amber Rose Hughes.
(Uncle Kevvy hopes you won't be too badly spooked by the book
when you're old enough to read it.)

If you wish to read stories of the human will and heart, the best place to find them is the newspaper. In the book you read fiction; in the newspapers you find a record of life. . . . [Newspaper stories] would make good fiction, and as fiction they would be preserved in volumes. As it is, they are simply truths, and as truths they will be forgotten in a day.

—Editorial, *Louisville Courier-Journal*, February 3, 1907

CONTENTS

ACKNOWLEDGMENTS

They helped outright or inspired:

Drema Colangelo; Gaile Sheppard Dempsey; Eastern Kentucky University Department of English; Eastern Kentucky University Interlibrary Loan Department (Stefanie Brooks; Heather Frith; Shelby Wills); Amy McQueen and Quentin Hawkins; Darrell and Swecia McQueen; Darren, Alison, and Elizabeth McQueen; Kyle McQueen; Michael, Lori, and Blaine McQueen and Evan Holbrook; Lee Mitchum; Marilyn Sargent Oppenheimer; Carolyn Picciano; and Mia Temple. Also: the seer of all.

INTRODUCTION

WHAT KIND OF STORIES ARE IN THIS BOOK? A FAIR QUESTION!

These tales have one thing in common: they all originate from the northern part of the eastern United States, including New England. (For the geographically fastidious, I realize that New York, New Jersey, Delaware, and Pennsylvania are considered Mid-Atlantic states rather than part of New England.) The vignettes cover morally and spiritually uplifting themes, such as grave robberies, premature burials, ghosts, historical murders, idiosyncratic modes of death, body snatching, rat attacks, insane doctors, town eccentrics, cannibals, and sundry other topics.

Best of all, they are all true as far as I can tell. At least, they were originally reported as true. They are all part of a genre that I like to call "real-life surrealism" or "historical horror-comedy." Or, if you prefer, consider them anecdotes that chronicle the staggering wonderment and strangeness of life.

Reading this book should be like taking a pleasant, relaxing autumn stroll through a haunted cemetery. Who knows, it could even be historically useful and the reader might acquire a moral or two, such as, "Lock your doors at night" and "Don't do foolish things."

New England
NIGHTMARES

1

NEFARIOUS NEW YORK

Grave Robbers and Body Snatchers: New York

WE MUST MAKE A DISTINCTION BETWEEN YESTERYEAR'S BODY snatchers and grave robbers. Body snatchers *stole bodies*. Why would anyone want to open a grave by the light of the moon and the screech of the owl and steal the corpse, aware that armed and angry relatives might be lying in wait? Because medical schools were desperate to gain corpses for dissection; they were allotted a limited number of cadavers—usually prisoners who'd died of natural causes, the executed, and poorhouse occupants—but since there weren't enough to go around, there was a lively trade in the unlively.

Garden-variety grave robbers, however, had baser motives than body snatchers. Rather than steal a body for the ultimate benefit of science and humanity—and make a quick buck in the process—grave robbers were interested only in swiping valuables from their exhumed victims, as if performing a postmortem mugging. The northern states, like the rest of America, yield stories of intrepid ghouls who were not afraid of a little hard work and were not hampered with an irrational fear of the dead.

Ruth Sprague died at age nine in 1816 and was buried in Maple Grove Cemetery in Hoosick Falls, New York. Soon afterward, a medical student stole her body and took it to a doctor's office for dissection. Little Ruth's relatives located and reburied her remains and then erected a gravestone with the following epitaph, which records the outrage for posterity, names names, and ends with a piquant little quatrain:

> She was stolen from the grave by Roderick R. Clow and dissected at
> Dr. P. M. Armstrong's office in Hoosick Falls, N.Y., from which place her
> mutilated remains were obtained and deposited here.
>
> Her body dissected by fiendish Men
> Her bones anatomized
> Her soul we trust has risen to God
> Where few Physicians rise.

Judge P.'s family vault in Binghamton was noted for being one of the most expensive in the state. On the night of October 23, 1884, five thieves entered it and got so far as to open Robert P.'s tomb before grave watchers scared them off. Why were they out to snatch Robert? Some authorities speculated that they wanted to hold the body for ransom. There was a rival theory, according to the papers: "A suit is pending for $5,000, the amount claimed by a physician for embalming the body, and it is thought by some that persons interested in this suit sought to ascertain how far the embalming process had been successful in preserving the body." And the only way to do that, of course, was to encounter Robert P. face-to-face.

In July 1881, a former body snatcher in Syracuse regaled a reporter with tales of his exploits in which he and his cronies raided rural cemeteries to feed the need for cadavers suffered by the medical colleges of Syracuse and Rochester. He remembered especially the time they stole the body of "a young man belonging to one of the best families in Syracuse." The corpse was well dressed, and an impoverished but imminently practical medical student took the clothing. He wore the suit on graduation day.

Henry W. Livingston ("Fighting Harry") was a famous general; his widow, who survived him by many years, became known as "Widow Mary" because of her "undying fidelity to the memory of her husband." None of this made the slightest difference to the vandals who broke into the Livingston family crypt on the grounds of their Hudson manor on April 23, 1904. They opened nearly all the coffins within and scattered the occupants' bones about the vault—including the remains of the general himself, whose winding sheet had nearly crumbled to dust. Two coffins were carried away for whatever nefarious purpose. One was the casket of Mary Livingston, who had died in 1859.

⊱────⊰

As war clouds gathered in Europe in the late 1930s, bronze became a valuable commodity among Americans, who would sell the metal to munitions factories—hence the rise of ghouls in search of scrap metal. During the weekend of December 17, 1937, thieves made a big score at Rockland Cemetery in Sparkill by stealing a 3,500-pound bronze statue from the grave of Dr. Alexander Skene, once president of the American Gynecological Society and thirty-seven years deceased. They also broke into the crypt of Major General John Charles Fremont and swiped two bronze Mexican War–era cannon. To accomplish these feats, the unsubtle ghouls brought a derrick and a truck.

Body Snatching, Part Two: When Schemes Went Awry

On occasion, graveyard expeditions did not turn out well when the stealers of cadavers became cadavers themselves. Relatives understandably did not appreciate the idea of their deceased loved ones being snatched, and sometimes they took up arms and kept vigil at gravesites.

Such was the cause of the sensation that gripped Syracuse on the morning of May 18, 1882, when Dr. Henry K. was found dying near the county poorhouse's graveyard at Onondaga Hill. He had a bullet hole in his left side and a bag containing two shovels wrapped in old carpet (to muffle digging noises). The doctor also had a satchel filled with a bottle of whisky, a hook, a rope, a lantern, and a screwdriver. In addition, Dr. K. carried a dirk and two revolvers in his belt. The obvious conclusion is that he went to the poorhouse cemetery in the dark of night to procure fishing worms.

Had the doctor been assassinated by someone who resented his attempt to grab a medical specimen from the potter's field? Perhaps, but wagon tracks near the body suggested that Dr. K. had a run-in with a rival gang of body snatchers. In any case, the good doctor's wounds were fatal, so the expedition was the last time he tried to pilfer a pauper.

⊱━⊰

Some spoilsports objected so strongly to having their relatives' graves robbed that there was a thriving industry in planting booby traps along with bodies. In 1896, a "coffin torpedo" was patented. It was exactly what the name implies. If the unwary body snatcher tried to pry open the coffin lid, a spring would strike a percussion cap and explode a bomb that would send singed parts of the snatcher high into the air—and probably bits of coffin wood, tools, dirt, and chunks of the dearly departed too. Presumably workmen, coroners, undertakers, and the like were alerted beforehand if a coffin had to be exhumed for some legitimate reason. At least one celebrity shared her grave with planted explosives: Edith Whitney, wife of millionaire and former Secretary of the Navy William C. Whitney, who was buried in Zion Cemetery, Douglaston, Long Island, in May 1899. The *New York Herald* said the bombs were designed so that "their explosive force [would be] directed upward and to either side." Mrs. Whitney was later dug up, one assumes *very carefully*, and moved to Rock Creek Cemetery in Washington, DC.

I have been unable to find any documented cases of body snatchers being rent asunder by buried bombs, so perhaps the devices were effective deterrents.

⊱━⊰

Circa 1896, an inventor developed a veritable Chinese puzzle of a vault in which to place caskets. Its selling point was that it had difficult catches inside, so even if body snatchers unearthed the vault and hauled it away, they would be unable to get the prize within.

Sally Surprises the Shovel Men

Sally J. of the town of Whitehall, on the New York–Vermont border, died around 1850 and was buried in the old cemetery. Twenty-three years later, in October 1873, workers excavated the remains of Mrs. J. to transport her to the new burying ground. To their everlasting wonder, the casket and shroud had long since disintegrated, but the body itself was in superb shape. Her limbs were lifelike and resting at her sides; her fingers and toes were in fine condition, including the nails; her face looked natural except that her eyes, hair, and the tip of her nose were missing. Onlookers noticed an indentation across Mrs. J.'s chest where the bottom of the coffin lid had lain.

Obsequies for the Obese

Elizabeth C. of Fleming was five feet one inch tall at the time of her death in February 1879 but weighed over three hundred pounds. As one might imagine, her dimensions caused the undertakers some trouble. They had to produce a coffin six feet long, nearly three feet wide, and twenty-one inches deep, supported with iron braces. Wrote a reporter, "It would easily have accommodated six persons by placing them one upon another, three abreast." Of course, the outer box intended to contain the gargantuan coffin had to be even larger. The coffin was too big to be brought into the house, so Mrs. C. had to be carried outside and placed in it. The reporter quoted above said her grave resembled "a miniature chasm."

The Miracle Face

An article that made the rounds of America's newspapers in October 1895 reports on a "miracle face" that had appeared on the back of a large marble shaft in Oak Hill Cemetery at Stony Brook, Long Island. The face was not the work of a sculptor, but rather had appeared naturally, "formed by a peculiar grouping of the clouded veins and dark spots characteristic of first-class imported stone." The "face" was roughly the size of a human countenance and was indistinct when viewed closely, but "at a distance of from thirty-five to fifty feet it is as plain as though done with an artist's brush." The face had hair, eyes, a nose, cheeks, a mouth, and a chin, and appeared to be looking downward at the grave of the person for whom the monument was built. Unfortunately, the report did not provide the person's name, but feel free to search for it.

Spirit Son

A widower identified in the unsympathetic press in 1878 only as "a Brooklyn idiot"—and who presumably was a Spiritualist—was informed by the spirit world that if his late wife had lived a little while longer, she would have borne a son. The BI took this news so seriously that he had a monument erected to his "spirit son," whom he touchingly named Charles.

Premature Burial: New York

We moderns have medical technology that tells us when clinical death has occurred, and we also have embalming. Lucky us! But our ancestors were not so fortunate. They lived in times when medicine was in its infancy and embalming was not common. An untold number of them revived in their caskets after a hasty burial. Old wills often include stipulations that the deceased be kept aboveground until signs of decomposition set in. For example, Dr. William D. of Jersey City so feared premature burial that his will directed that a surgeon cut his radial artery, for which he was to be paid thirty dollars. The doctor passed away on October 20, 1909, and his orders were carried out.

People worried enough about the possibility of being buried alive that Edgar Allan Poe devoted a story, "The Premature Burial," to the phenomenon and began it with several instances drawn from real life. Newspapers from the era also include numerous examples—such as the following case.

Emma R. of Syracuse caught a bad cold in mid-March 1889. It settled in her lungs, and the seventeen-year-old died on March 22. Neighbors who dressed her for burial were surprised that she remained warm to the touch even four hours after she'd stopped breathing. She was buried in Geddes Cemetery on March 24. Her father, Edward—who also happened to be the cemetery sexton—dug her grave himself.

As the days passed, Edward became obsessed with the notion that Emma had been buried alive. A month after her interment, Mr. R. could stand the suspense no longer and strode to Geddes with a sense of determination and a spade in hand. Without assistance he dug up the coffin. Then he removed the lid, and this is what he saw:

> The body of the young girl [was] lying turned over on one side. He says that her hands were clasped over her face and her brown hair was tangled up over her eyes, as though it had been torn in dreadful agony. Mr. R. says that there were fingermarks on her face. He said he was nearly paralyzed with terror, and hastily replaced the cover, shoveled the dirt back into the grave and ran from the place.

Mr. R. was nearly driven insane by the experience, which proves the old truism: sometimes you really don't wanna know.

><del>·►·+·0·◄·◄·

In 1881, a New York City undertaker recalled his adventure when he was requested to embalm the body of a Union officer who fell in battle at

Fredericksburg. When the mortician opened an artery to pump in his chemicals, he was splattered by a stream of blood that indicated the "corpse's" heart was still pumping. After medical treatment, the unnamed officer recovered, fought in two additional campaigns, and worked on a Southern railroad after the war. The undertaker remarked, "I met him at Washington last winter and spoke about the matter, but all he would say was that he had many close shaves in battle, but that one beat them all."

⊢━◆━◦━◆━┤

Elderly Mary C. of 4 Delhi Street, Syracuse, passed into the Great Beyond at 8:00 a.m. on August 2, 1889. Within an hour, friends and relatives were mourning at the house. Her body was washed and dressed; her limbs were cold and her eyes glazed. Around noon the mourners got the scare of their lives when the dead woman turned over on her side and asked when lunch would be served. Given that people who died in the heat of summer generally were buried in haste, Mrs. C. was fortunate indeed to have revived when she did. The papers didn't record what she had for lunch.

⊢━◆━◦━◆━┤

Walter E. died at his home at 110 Berry Street in Williamsburg, New York City, on December 13, 1889. His heart stopped beating and his face took on an ashy pallor. The undertaker showed up with the tools of his trade, including an icebox, and performed the "usual services," such as straightening out Walter's grimace. Suddenly the dead man's eyes flipped open and he said, "What are you going to do with me?" "Nothing at all," stammered the undertaker, who packed up his shroud and icebox and left, having been cheated out of his fee. A reporter noted that Walter was "highly indignant at the manner in which he has been treated."

⊢━◆━◦━◆━┤

A sadly undetailed news report from New York, datelined December 13, 1901, reads: "A 'corpse' sat up in a coffin and barely escaped burial."

Devices to Prevent Premature Burial

A journalist writing in 1895 estimated the odds of being buried alive while cataleptic to be a comforting "one in ten million." Those odds weren't good enough for many jittery persons, and inventors assuaged their fears with devices designed to rescue the prematurely buried.

For example, in that same year, the *New York Herald* mentioned the inventor of a "grave signal," a tube stretching from the surface of the earth to the inside of the coffin. An individual could breathe and shout through the tube; the slightest movement in the coffin would trigger a signal aboveground.

One wonders if the invention were actually tested by a brave soul willing to be planted six feet deep. Sarcastic undertakers who objected to the device suggested that the inventor try it out on himself. He countered that they hated his brainchild because it would render embalming obsolete.

The inventor wasn't particularly original; several contraptions intended to thwart live burial were patented, most having as common features the long tube reaching the surface and some means of signaling that all was not well below. One device sent up a red flag if the "corpse's" hand twitched.

The ingenious so-called grave annunciator operated like this: "A disturbance in the coffin closes an electric circuit and springs an alarm in the watch-house of the cemetery. The superintendent takes note of the number of the grave indicated by the alarm." Then, it is to be presumed, he would shout something like, "Grab the shovels, boys, and head for grave number 32, section P!"

Another device with a tube extending from the surface to the casket had an interesting variation on the usual idea. The tube was open at the coffin end and sealed at the top, but if the occupant woke up, a spring catch opened the tube end that was on the surface—thus allowing oxygen in but trapping the stink if the inhumed one actually were dead. At the same time, the device set off an alarm bell if necessary.

Some opted to have a glass case placed on the grave, with wires within that reached the presumed corpse below. If the body moved, needles indicated so in the glass case—and then the victim of premature burial had only to pray that some passerby would happen to notice that the needle had moved.

For those who liked jewelry, one patented invention featured a ring placed on the corpse. Movement of the hand caused a clockwork gadget to set off an alarm and turn on a fan, which forced air down a tube. A second tube provided a lamp and a mirror. Folks on the surface could look down the tube and enjoy the frightened expression on the person below, as reflected in the mirror, and then provide help if they had nothing else to do.

Then there was the inventor who suggested dehydrating bodies to about a third of their original weight and storing them in a mausoleum with compartments like a bank safety deposit vault. These compartments were to have an iron outer door and a glass inner door—not unlike an apartment building for the dead, or a corpse condo. Relatives would have private keys with which they could drop by at their leisure and gaze upon the shriveled departed. Also, "a system of electric alarms would give notice in case any person prematurely desiccated should come to life." But perhaps this creative genius wasn't entirely serious.

Almost as Bad as Premature Burial

It is difficult to imagine our ancestors facing a worse predicament than being buried alive, but there is a conceivable runner-up: once technology made it possible for undertakers to place bodies in cold storage, people feared that—well, you can guess.

The *New York Sunday News* ran a story about this dreadful possibility in January 1881: "The physicians nearly all claim that persons still alive are frequently taken by undertakers and placed on ice, thereby making death certain, whereas if the body was kept until the first signs of decomposition set in, all uncertainty would be dispelled." The author mentioned a recent case in which a physician left a patient on her sickbed and then returned in the morning to find that she had been seized in the night without his approval and packed in an icebox. The doctor expressed the opinion that she could have been living when spirited away by an undertaker who might not have checked closely for vital signs.

An embalmer told the *Sunday News* of a case in which an undertaker friend was called in to prepare a lady for burial. She was dressed in robes, placed in a first-rate casket, displayed in her house's parlor, and surrounded by floral tributes. The next day her grieving friends and relatives paid their respects and heard a touching address by the minister, after which the crowd filed by the coffin to take one final look at her face. But one of the woman's friends took the undertaker aside and insisted that she saw the corpse's eyelids flutter.

"You must be mistaken, madam," said the mortician, pointing out that the young woman had been dead two days. But he took a closer look— and, surely enough, the eyelids twitched and the dead woman proved to be more alive than she seemed. A doctor applied restoratives, and the woman who was only minutes away from going to her tomb made a full recovery. The embalmer's unspoken moral: the woman had had a close call to be sure, but if she had been stuffed in an icebox when she seemed to be dead, she could not have survived the adventure.

A while later, the same undertaker made another house call where he recommended the subject of his visit be placed on ice immediately. A woman at the residence forbade it, exclaiming that the deceased should not be frozen until decomposition set in.

"That's impossible, my dear woman," replied the mortician. "Do you not see the lady is dead?"

"No, sir! She only looks dead, as I did once, and is in just the same position, and you know it too."

The undertaker took a harder look at the insistent lady and recognized her as the woman mentioned above, whom he had nearly buried alive some time before. Presumably he deferred to her prior experience.

So did thousands of our forebears slip into comas, only to freeze to death slowly in undertakers' iceboxes? The reader will notice that while the *Sunday News* article explored the harrowing possibility, it did not provide a single confirmed case. Let's hope it was an overblown fear—though it certainly was not a groundless one.

For the record, embalmers also were upset over iceboxes; they pointed out that their art cut the risk of premature burial to zero, because no comatose individual could survive the process. But they had another, less altruistic reason to adamantly oppose icebox technology: it rendered their jobs obsolete. If bodies could be frozen for days and then taken straight to their graves, embalmers would lose work.

The Joke Was on the Doctor

A woman who lived in Greenpoint, Brooklyn, had a bizarre keepsake that she showed to a *New York Sun* reporter in January 1883: a silver coffin plate reading, "Clara M., Died June 3, 1864, Aged 16 years."

The woman in question was Clara herself, and she had a story about the time she was nearly buried alive. An uncle in Chicago kept her casket as a conversation piece. "I kept the plate," said Clara, "which I seldom allow anyone to see, for the recollections it awakens are not pleasant." Nevertheless, the remarkably untraumatized woman thus entertained the reporter:

As a young girl, Clara often fell into epileptic trances in which she was unable to speak or stir but was cognizant of everything going on around her. A doctor warned her that she might be mistaken for dead someday and buried alive. Poor Clara eventually became afraid to sleep or take catnaps.

As time passed, the trances became less frequent, but the doctor opined that her epilepsy was only "mustering its forces" for a major attack. This diagnosis frightened the girl so badly that she caught "brain fever" in the summer of 1864. She conquered the fever but was so weak afterward that the doctor—who really needed to learn a thing or two about bedside manner—predicted that she would never rise from her sickbed. "She may go out like the snuff of a candle at any minute," the patient overheard him say.

Usually, Clara snapped out of her trances in ten or fifteen minutes. But on June 2, 1864, she did not. She slipped into a waking coma, aware of all stimuli but unable to react to them. A nurse entered the room, examined her, cried out in alarm, and urged Clara's mother and sisters to hurry. That pessimistic doctor was called in; he took her pulse, touched her forehead, peered into her eyes, and announced: "I feared it. She is going fast."

Years later, Clara remembered: "On the morning of June 3, my body was cold and stiff, and while my mind was active as ever, I knew that I looked like a corpse." She heard friends and relatives crying. The doctor said, "Yes, poor creature, she is gone," and pulled the sheet over her face.

(It was not lost on Clara that this was the same physician who had warned her that she might be mistakenly assumed dead one of these days, and she felt great indignation that he failed to do more to determine whether death had actually occurred.)

Clara spent the next two days motionless on the bed. People placed fragrant roses near her; she overheard acquaintances who obviously were firm believers in the adage "Of the dead, say nothing but good" extravagantly complimenting her: "Friends came to me, and reminded each other of good qualities in me that neither by myself or others had ever before been suspected."

The "dead" girl spent the night of June 4 lying beside her open coffin, into which she was placed for burial in the morning. Unable to move, she heard people reading aloud her coffin plate and commenting: "Poor girl, so young to be called away! But she was always delicate!" No one, not even the doctor—*especially* not the doctor—seemed to notice that the body had lain in the summer heat three days without showing any sign of decomposition.

The undertaker's assistants stood by, waiting to screw down the lid, when Clara's elderly aunt Jane elbowed her way to the front of the line. She had come all the way from Albany. Clara took some relief from her feisty aunt's presence, "for we loved each other so well that I could not think it possible that she would allow me to be buried alive."

Clara's trust was not misplaced. Aunt Jane noticed something that everyone else had missed: "Why, her nose is bleeding!" *Even* the doctor knew that corpses can't leak fresh blood, and he ordered her removed from the coffin.

The sheer relief of the moment shattered Clara's mental barrier, and she was able to speak again. She said, charmingly, "Thank you, doctor. How are you, Auntie?"

Clara never slipped into another trance. She told the reporter nearly twenty years after the harrowing incident that the doctor was still alive in Greenpoint and that whenever he ran into her, he always made a point of saying that while she was lying on her deathbed and in her coffin, he suspected that she *might* be alive after all—a statement his former patient refused to believe.

Extraordinary Epitaphs: New York

It was reported in 1872 that a gravestone in Ithaca read: "She is in Heaven (I hope)."

⊢•⊹•◦•⊕•⊣

On William Reese (d. 1872), in Westernville: "This is what I expected but not so soon."

⊢•⊹•◦•⊕•⊣

The inadvertent humor in one epitaph resulted from a typographical error. For many decades the tombstone of Susannah Ensign (d. 1825) in Presbyterian Churchyard in Cooperstown read: "Lord, she is thin." The stonecutter meant "thine." At some point in the midtwentieth century a final *e* was added to the line and a great absurdity was spoiled.

⊢•⊹•◦•⊕•⊣

On John Young (d. 1836), Saint Andrew's Churchyard, Staten Island: "Those that knew him best deplored him most."

And Harry Edsel Smith's Epitaph That Wasn't

To show how much work I am willing to do to find out something that interests me, and to prove once and for all that I don't have a life, here is the story of my search for the gravestone of Harry Edsel Smith, which is reputed by many sources to bear a hilarious epitaph.

1. I first read about Smith's epitaph years ago in *The People's Almanac*, and later saw it turning up in forwarded emails concerning funny gravestone inscriptions. All sources claimed that his gravestone reads: "Harry Edsel Smith. 1903–1942. Looked up the elevator shaft to see if the car was on the way down. It was." The sources stated that Smith was buried near Albany, but none provided the name of the cemetery.

2. I mailed an inquiry to the New York State Department of Vital Statistics, which confirmed that a Harold E. Smith who had been born on August 10, 1903, died in Albany on September 9, 1942, at age thirty-nine. I decided that had to be *the* Harry Edsel Smith, since the name, town, birth year, and death year all matched the story about the alleged tombstone inscription. But again, the records did not name the cemetery where he was buried.

3. Through interlibrary loan I got a microfilm reel of the Albany *Knickerbocker News* of September 1942. There I found the obituary in the September 11 issue: "SMITH—Sept. 9, 1942, Harold E. of 628 Broadway. He is survived by a wife, Gertrude McKinney, a father, Howard Smith, a brother, Irving Smith. Funeral services Sunday 2:30 p.m. at Garland Brothers Funeral Home, 143 Orange Street." Drat—still no cemetery name. No mention of cause of death, either (i.e., squooshed by descending elevator).

4. I wondered idly if the Garland Brothers Funeral Home could still be in business many decades after Smith had died. If so, maybe they would still have the interment records on file? Using the Yahoo Yellow Pages, I looked through the Albany directory and found that they *were* still in business! I wrote them a nice letter asking if they knew where Harold E. Smith was buried.

5. Garland Brothers Funeral Home responded, telling me Harold E. Smith was buried in Albany Rural Cemetery in Menands, New York. I now knew the name of the cemetery!

6. I went back to the Yahoo Yellow Pages, looking up Albany cemeteries. Another snag: there was no listing for Albany Rural Cemetery. However, there was a listing for an Albany Rural Chapel, located on Cemetery Road. I checked a map of Albany and found that Cemetery Road was located very near the suburb of Menands. Could this be it? Getting the address from the Yellow Pages, I wrote another letter, this time to Albany Rural Chapel, asking if they had a Harold E. Smith who'd died in 1942.

7. After mailing the letter, I reflected that lots of people out there probably think I'm a total nut.

8. A few days later: success! Now who's nuts? Albany Rural Chapel is in fact located in Albany Rural Cemetery. Their records showed that Harold E. Smith is there along with a few other family members, including his father Howard (see #3 above), who died in January 1971. The records also showed that this Harold E. Smith died on September 9, 1942, at age thirty-nine. They sent a map, so now I knew the plot number: lot 17, section 207. By the way, Smith shares the cemetery with President Chester A. Arthur.

9. I wanted to get a copy of Smith's death certificate to see if he really had been killed in an elevator accident. The State of New York Department of Health sent me the requested document. He died of coronary sclerosis. I also learned that he was born in Valatie, New York, was black, was separated from his wife at the time of his death, and—get this—his occupation was *elevator operator* at Albany's Kenmore Hotel!

10. I wrote back to the Albany Cemetery Association at Albany Rural Cemetery and asked if they would please go look at Smith's gravestone and tell me if the famous epitaph is really there. They responded with the disappointing news that there is no such inscription. Alas, the legend of the epitaph must die, like all beautiful things, and I was its reluctant slayer.

11. But if the gravestone bears no such inscription, how did the story of the epitaph originate? My guess is that, inspired by his occupation, the dying Smith had his relatives put the astonishing epitaph on his tombstone as a final joke and that it was later removed after attracting unwanted attention. Harry Edsel Smith—who must have had a twisted sense of humor—has moved to near the front of the line of people I wish I could have met.

An Urban Golgotha, or: Rolling the Bones

A few days before Christmas 1884, New York City's Board of Health Commissioners received an anonymous letter guaranteed to get any bureaucrat's attention. "Dear Sirs," it read. "There is a perfect graveyard in an attic room of the house at No. 11 West Third Street. It is filled with bones from different parts of the body."

The note sounded like the work of a crank, but when police checked out the old four-story frame dwelling, they found that the accusations were only too true. An attic room contained a pile of bones "in all stages of moldiness."

The sanitary inspector and a *New York Journal* reporter were greeted by the house's owner, Herman G., who lived on the lower floor. He spoke forthrightly: "Yes, there are some old bones up in the attic. Would you gentlemen like to see them?"

The inspector and the reporter said yes—of course they would! Herman led them upstairs, where they saw not only a heap of decaying bones but also nine skulls on a fireplace mantel lined up like bowling balls. The homeowner told the story of how they came to be there:

> Well, they have been here for nearly twenty years. About that time a gambler occupied this room. Then there was a graveyard next door, but a few days after he came here the then health officers ordered all the bodies to be dug up and removed to a larger burial ground in Jersey. This was done, but my gambler lodger, thinking to secure good luck by doing so, stole those nine skulls which you see before you. He would fill them in turn with marbles of variegated colors, and after shaking them up would turn them out on the table. If the first color out was red he would play red cards all day; or, if black, the latter would be his favorite shade in cards. He was killed in a faro bank in Brooklyn about sixteen years ago and, of course, left his skulls behind him. That's all the mystery in the old heads.

Then Herman asked the authorities a question about what was *really* bothering him: "But how did you come to hear about them?" When told about the anonymous letter, the landlord of the private charnel house replied: "I can't imagine who would try to injure me by sending such a letter, unless indeed it was a woman who was lodging in this house for two years until a week ago, when I put her out for coming into this house intoxicated. She asked me on one occasion who owned the skulls and I refused to give her any explanation. I think she wrote the letter through spite."

That is to say, Herman G. was the sort of upright, respectable landlord who had no problem with piles of rotting human remains upstairs but would not tolerate having a drunk on the premises. Although Herman explained the presence of the line of craniums, he did not tell how the other bones got there; presumably the unnamed gambler stole entire cadavers and brought them home, but as he was only interested in the magic powers of good luck conferred by their skulls, he lazily tossed the other parts in a pile and let nature take its course.

The story does not redound to the credit of the New York health officers of the 1860s, who didn't notice that someone had stolen nine bodies from the old cemetery right under their, uh, noses. The story also does not speak well of their counterparts in 1884 who, amazingly, decided to let Herman the landlord keep all his souvenirs despite the potential health hazards they might wreak. But then, it *was* Christmastime.

Evicting the Dead

Rose D. was in need of some cash and so desired to evict eight of her relatives from their dirt dormitory in Brooklyn's Green-Wood Cemetery so she could sell the land. In May 1939, a Supreme Court justice ruled that she could *not*.

What Smelled Up the Sunday School Library

The congregation of New York's Fourteenth Street Presbyterian Church gathered for Sunday services on August 7, 1881. Things got off to an unusual start when the sexton, J.B.O., did not show up to unlock the church, so that duty had to be fulfilled by the organist. Matters got stranger, not to mention disgusting, during the sermon. The odor of gas, combined with something worse, slowly filled the church on that humid summer day. The reek increased as services continued, and at last became so overpowering that some of the less hardy parishioners got up and left.

After the sermon, it was realized that no one had seen a trace of the sexton since the previous Wednesday. The stink appeared to be coming from the Sunday school library, and when police opened the door, they found the nearly nude remains of Mr. O. resting on a cushion in the center of the room. The *other* offensive odor was coming from a broken gas pipe.

Cementation and Paperweights

Theodore H. was no run-of-the-mill crank: he had been a justice of the Niagara County, New York, court for several terms. But he was perhaps a bit eccentric on the topic of disposal of the dead. In 1886, he spoke at a convention of the American Association for the Advancement of Science about his idea to make embalming and cremation obsolete: cementation!

The process consisted, as the reader has probably guessed, of making veritable statues of perishable things by sticking them in cement. He proudly displayed blocks containing fruit and dead animals that he had created in 1874. A report describes the objects thus preserved: "They were changed into a substance closely resembling stone, and the original colors were preserved to a remarkable degree." Theodore explained that the gases emitted by a decomposing body escape through cement very slowly, leaving a perfect statue of the remains. If only Moses had been subjected to cementation, he said, every college in the world could have had a copy of his body.

Theodore asserted that he was willing to advance the cause of science by cementing the bodies of his own loved ones when their time came. Two of his late daughters had expressed reservations because being lodged forever in a block of cement "would be pretty close quarters," so instead he had their caskets immersed in the substance. His own will directed that his body be encased in cement, and it appears that some of his neighbors at Niagara Falls thought highly of Theodore's idea and hired him to bury their bodies in the building material.

On September 29, 1886, Theodore addressed the Sanitary Board of Buffalo on the topic of cementation. Needless to say, his idea never caught on. Too bad, since we should do everything possible to foster a love of the arts among the younger generation.

><>-0-<><

Circa 1896, an inventor in Canandaigua patented a similar idea for doing something practical with human remains. Just have your loved ones cremated, he said, and mix the ashes with silicate of soda and whipped into a paste. Mold it into a bust of the dearly departed, which can be electroplated with copper, silver, or gold, thereby becoming sufficiently beautiful to put on proud display in your home—in effect it would be a bust of your favorite uncle, made of your favorite uncle. In fact, the ashy paste could be molded into many shapes, and the inventor suggested that your favorite uncle might make a good paperweight. Curiously, this idea never caught on either.

An Unorthodox Filing System

Robert W., cofounder of a carriage manufacturing firm, died in Buffalo in 1877. Immediately a legal problem arose: although he often had told his four children by his first wife that they would be provided for in his will, no such document could be found. His affairs were settled according to the law: the widow—Robert's second wife—was appointed administrator of his estate, to which she was entitled to a third. Her stepchildren each got a share of the remainder. The widow herself died in 1884, leaving a bequest to a daughter by her first husband and her children by Robert, but entirely cutting out her stepchildren.

In January 1885, a person searching for Robert W.'s will had an inspired idea: why not dig up the body and see if perchance he was buried with it? The exhumation was performed and there it was, right between his shirt and vest.

No Dignity for the Dead!

Wards Island, located on the northern end of the East River between Manhattan and Queens, was for generations one of New York City's least pleasant locales. Over the course of the near-century between 1840 and 1930, the island was used variously as a cemetery for bodies relocated from other city graveyards, a hospital for impoverished immigrants called the State Emigrant Refuge (1847), an insane asylum (1863), and a more enlightened psychiatric hospital (1899).

This story concerns the hospital's "dead house," where patients who passed away at the institution were taken for storage before burial.

In mid-December 1886, the Wards Island Committee of the Board of Emigration Commissioners got an anonymous letter declaring that the hospital's doctors were ill-treating dead patients. In the course of the ensuing investigation, they called a witness named Peter K., who had been the island's cemetery sexton and undertaker for a year, and who'd been an orderly in the hospital for two years before that. Under oath, Peter pointed out that everyone who died on the island was subjected to an autopsy by the doctors. Fair enough! But when the committee asked if there had been cases in which the dead were unnecessarily mutilated or subjected to indignities, Peter had plenty to tell them:

Patrick F. died on November 13, 1885; his brain and stomach were removed.

Catherine F., stillborn on December 31, 1885, was skinned and boiled. Peter performed these procedures himself under direction by a staff physician.

Julia R., age twenty-one, died on March 5, 1886; her head was removed, skinned, and given to a doctor.

Claus B. committed suicide on May 23, 1886; during the autopsy, the top of his head was sawn off and his brain removed. Peter K. was told to "fix" the body before the coroner arrived. Peter's novel solution was to take the top of a second cadaver's head and attach it to Claus. The coroner didn't notice.

Gustav F. died June 9, 1886, and was locked up in the dead house. When Peter returned a few hours later, the body was missing both eyes. Adding to the mystery, the right eye of a second corpse also was gone. When Gustav's widow found that cotton wads had been stuffed in his vacant eye sockets, she "kicked up an awful row," in Peter's words, and one feels that she was entitled to. (One of the doctors later said that the cadavers' optics fell prey to famished rats.)

Sexton Peter remembered another case in which a doctor cut off part of a corpse's leg; another, in which the doctor removed the upper half of a skull and an eyeball; and several cases in which organs were removed from bodies, after which the missing parts were carelessly stuffed into coffins alongside their already stitched-up owners.

Peter K. admitted that he had not reported these activities because he was afraid he would lose his great job if he did.

Keep Did Not Keep

Charles D. Keep, owner of the *Wall Street Daily News*, died at Elberon, New Jersey, on June 9, 1887, and afterward was buried in Calvary Cemetery in Long Island. Somehow his widow Mary became convinced that Charles was alive and a dummy buried in his stead—or, if actually dead, that he had been murdered.

Mrs. Keep beseeched the coroner to have the grave opened so she could see for herself. That beleaguered official finally agreed. The coffin was exhumed and moved to a receiving vault on January 17, 1888. It was opened in the presence of the coroner, Mrs. Keep, and a very fortunate Associated Press reporter. Said a news account: "Though the body was evidently in an advanced state of decomposition, the features were perfect almost as in life, and Mrs. Keep immediately recognized the body as that of her deceased husband."

Mrs. Keep admitted the error of her theory concerning her husband's liveliness, but she still wasn't sure he'd died of natural causes and requested that the body be kept in the vault until she could get the case reopened. She fainted after making this request.

The case was not reopened, and Mr. Keep's friends were so upset over the coroner's "unlawful procedure" that they made formal charges against him to the governor. The coroner issued a groveling apology on February 24, in which he told the governor that he regretted his action and "was imposed upon by the statements and affidavits submitted to me." In other words, he got swept up in Mrs. Keep's weird theories. The dead man's friends felt this act of contrition was sufficient and pursued no further action.

Sometimes Cigars Are Good for You

Philip Z. spent a lot of time in cemeteries, since he was an assistant to his father, a Brooklyn florist. One day in February 1889, Philip went to Green-Wood Cemetery to place flowers in a large, ornate vault.

When Philip entered the mausoleum, the bronze door slammed shut behind him and locked with a click. And it was almost the cemetery's closing time, so no groundskeepers were within earshot.

Philip shouted for help. Some women heard him but naturally mistook him for a ghost and ran screaming to the front gate. The elderly gateman thought them fools and did not investigate.

Therefore, the florist had no alternative but to spend a cold winter's night pacing back forth in the inky blackness of a cemetery vault surrounded by the unanimated. Luckily, he had a pocketful of cigars with him, and by smoking them one after another he had a faint, glowing light to help him keep his mind on cheerful things.

The cemetery superintendent helped Philip out of his amusing predicament the next morning.

A Vandalistic Vortex

Tornados are rare in New England, but they do happen sometimes. A tornado with a strange disposition struck just south of Norwich on June 17,

1889, and spent its entire fury on the village cemetery, touching down just as it entered the grounds. It moved along a path about five hundred feet wide, uprooting trees and bushes and damaging or overturning hundreds of monuments, some of which weighed between five and twenty tons. The only notable damage it did outside the confines of the cemetery was toppling a few trees.

The Grateful Dead Sing, and Other Strange Recordings

When Thomas Edison invented the phonograph in 1877, it was cutting-edge technology just as the MP3 player is in our time. It wasn't long before people thought of unusual—even borderline macabre—reasons to record their voices. One such was Rev. Thomas Allen H. of Larchmont. Before he died in February 1890 at age seventy-seven, he recorded his own funeral sermon so mourners could hear the voice of the gone away as well as peer at his remains.

The funeral was held in Rev. H.'s dining room and parlor. As it began, the assembly heard a female voice singing a hymn:

> A few more years shall roll,
> A few more seasons come,
> And we shall be with those we love,
> In the land beyond the sun.

The mourners were seriously creeped out when they recognized the voice as that of Mrs. H., who had died eight months before her husband. They regained their equilibrium when they realized the voice issued from a phonograph. (By the way, this incident occurred so early in the history of recorded sound that the machine played wax-coated cylinders rather than records.)

The reverend's nephew Charles replaced the cylinder with a second one, and the mourners heard the voice of the preacher himself. "It sounded so weird," wrote a reporter, "that two ladies fainted and had to be carried out." Rather than praise himself, Rev. H. listed his own personal flaws and asked the assembly to pray for him. The nephew put on a third roll, on which the reverend listed the virtues of his late wife and broke down weeping at one point.

The grand finale came when the nephew placed two phonograph players side by side on the table—one containing a cylinder of Rev. H. singing, the other with a recording of Mrs. H. singing. When they were played simultaneously, listeners heard the dead couple reunited in an unearthly duet.

Augusta B. was a big baby, to use an understatement. At the age of a year and a half, she weighed ninety-two pounds. She was put on exhibition in a tent near the Sea Beach Palace Pavilion on Coney Island. But the child was sickly, and in August 1895, she died of pneumonia.

There was a problem: preachers need a vacation every now and then like everyone else, and there wasn't one to be found to do a funeral service for Augusta. Luckily, an absent minister had recorded one for such an emergency. The deputy coroner just happened to have a phonograph on which the canned obsequies could be played, a gadget described as having "a trumpet as big as the head of a drum and a deep sonorous voice." A facetious reporter added, "It was a reverent machine . . . and never in its life had it ground out a dance tune or a music hall ditty."

Augusta's mother insisted that her child be given the proper church rites. The deputy coroner told her that the recording was in some ways better than having a live preacher: "I've got a religious phonograph which can go through the service without a hitch, for I've tried it. No hemming and hawing and turning of leaves, either."

The services lasted thirty-five minutes and required five changes of cylinders. The first was the Lord's Prayer, "recited in a slow, impressive manner." The second consisted of the Amphion Quartet singing "Nearer My God to Thee." The other three cylinders played a sermon and the benediction.

The newspaper account ends: "The mother silently wept and the friends bore the body away to its last resting place in the old Gravesend cemetery."

Edith S. was engaged to be married soon and she wanted her father, a minister, to perform the ceremony. But Rev. S. took fatally ill and, realizing he might not live long enough to fulfill his daughter's wishes, recorded his voice reciting the wedding ceremony. So it came to pass that although he had been dead several weeks, the reverend married his daughter to Frank M. via phonograph in Binghamton on February 24, 1900. "The bride and bridegroom answered the questions that came like a spirit voice from the machine, and the spectators were strangely affected," said a contemporary account.

The Less-Than-Successful Cremation of Percy R.

Percy R., a New York baker and confectioner, desired to be cremated after he passed from substance to shadow. Friends and family obliged him by taking his body to the crematorium at Fresh Pond, Queens, on August 14, 1892. Smoke billowed from the chimney, indicating that the facilities were ready. Pallbearers drove the hearse to the back door, removed the casket, and carried it inside, followed by the mourners. They lifted Percy's body from his coffin, wrapped it in a shroud soaked in alum, and placed it in an iron cradle. This device was raised with a block and tackle and set on a high table. The idea was to push the cradle along the tabletop into the furnace, close the door, and let the inferno do its work.

The furnace door was opened; the men commenced pushing the cradle containing Percy's body into the flames, which burned with the incandescence of hell. And then it was that human error intervened.

One pallbearer was so terrified by the intense heat that he hesitated. The table tilted. Percy's upper half was inside the oven, but his lower half was outside and resting on the table! Flames belched from the open furnace door and licked about the remains—then the shroud ignited, and the mourners witnessed the phase of cremation no one is supposed to see: "There was a vision then of black burial garments, as the shroud shriveled away, a sight of the white face and the hands folded over the breast, with the flames playing wildly about the face and body." The smell was probably not reminiscent of a nosegay, either.

Women screamed; men stared in horror; one man fainted. The pallbearers mustered their courage and shoved the rest of Percy into the oven. The furnace's inner door slammed shut and the awful spectacle was no more. The superintendent of the crematorium got too close to the heat when attempting to help push the body and sustained a burned hand and blisters on half of his face. Had Percy known what excitement his last wishes would engender, he might have opted instead for a less spectacular disposal of his remains, like being shot from a cannon.

But even Percy's botched cremation went better than another one on record, which took place in New Haven, Connecticut, on February 18,

1902. A woman who saw the body burning became so terrified that she died of fright.

Would You Like Flies with That?

In the summer of 1899, someone had the great idea of opening a restaurant in the office of New York City's Washington Cemetery, located between Gravesend and Coney Island. That someone was the cemetery's proprietors. They soon came into conflict with the board of health, which found the very idea unseemly.

A Profusion of Problems

The P.J.H. family, who lived in a two-story house on Montgomery's Island in the Hudson River, faced a number of unenviable problems in March 1903. The first came when they ran out of food. The second came when Mr. H. died of pneumonia on the night of the twenty-third. The third came the same night, when a flood trapped the survivors on the island along with his body. The eight children and Mrs. H. were rescued by tugboat the next day, after what must have seemed an eventful night.

Brokenhearted Businessman

Jonathan R., a retired Brooklyn businessman, took his wife's 1898 death hard. Jonathan asked officials at the Cemetery of the Evergreens for permission to place a cot in her tomb so he could stay there around the clock. Naturally, they told him no. Jonathan circumvented their rules by furnishing the crypt with all the comforts of home so he could stay there every day from dawn until closing time. He followed his ritual every day for seven years—and often was overheard having decidedly one-sided conversations with his dead wife—until he suffered a fatal apoplectic stroke in the tomb on March 23, 1905.

Very Still Life Photography

Trainman Henry B. hated having his picture taken! Thus it was that when Henry died at age fifty-seven in December 1907, there were no photographs of him in existence.

After Henry was buried in the Bronx's Woodlawn Cemetery, his widow was annoyed because she had no pictures of him. Somehow she inveigled the Health Department to issue a permit to have her husband exhumed.

Henry was dug up on December 26, twenty days after burial. The coffin was opened under a photographer's tent and that professional took two presumably flattering portraits.

Death's Deed

Jay W.'s death in 1911 was followed by years of squabbling between his niece, Mrs. John W. of Fairmount, and other family members. She claimed that her uncle had given her the house in which she lived, with the transfer becoming permanent effective upon his demise. Unfortunately, she had no deed to document the promise. The late Mr. W.'s relatives insisted she vacate the house; she insisted on remaining.

Matters came to a head in July 1915 when Mrs. W. suddenly remembered seeing some papers in her uncle's hand as he lay in his coffin. Could one of them have been the deed? She hired a man to help with the dirty work, and together they exhumed Uncle Jay's casket, opened it, and pried the long-lost deed from his cold, dead hand. The triumphant Mrs. W. maintained that her nefarious relatives had buried the document in an intentional effort to defraud her.

Keeping Them Around: New York

Twenty families lived in the tenement at 319 East Sixtieth Street, New York City. Over the course of several successive days in May 1889, they noticed a smell that became an odor, and then a reek, then a stink, then a stench. At last, on May 28 the unwholesome miasma became so unbearable the building's janitor complained to a policeman, who investigated and found that the putrescent smell was coming from the room occupied by the widow Bridget H. and her eighteen-year-old son, John. The officer burst down the door and was greeted by a starving John H. staggering toward him as though drunk or insane, or an insane drunk. In a back room the policeman found Mrs. H. lying on a bed, deceased about five days and black from decomposition. The body was removed and the board of health disinfected the premises. Young John was carted off to Bellevue, a psychiatric hospital. I'm not sure why.

Brooklyn carriage maker Joseph S.'s wife died in mid-May 1935, but he slept with her corpse every night for two weeks. The police dragged him screaming to the psychopathic ward on May 26.

But Joseph S. was a piker compared to another New Yorker, sixty-five-year-old Emily C. She refused to allow an agent from the Old Age Pension Bureau into her dwelling to see her husband, Frank. First Mrs. C. told the agent that Frank was sick. When the agent returned a second time, Mrs. C. said Frank was in a coma.

The agent returned a third time on September 8, 1937, with a patrolman. They found that Emily C. had shared the two-room apartment with the body of her husband wrapped in a blanket. A nearby death certificate stated that he'd left for the Land of the Gone Away on October 26, 1936. Mrs. C. explained: "I was waiting for him to get up. I was told that I could keep him for a year and it is not a year yet."

Neighbors said they had heard Emily speaking to an unusually taciturn Mr. C. She was taken to Bellevue for observation; for some reason, the police opined that she might not be entirely sane.

Once Again on Display

Two little boys, Rudy P. and Buddy G., were digging in a vacant lot two hundred feet from Main Street in Hempstead on December 28, 1934, when suddenly their activity turned into something out of a Charles Addams cartoon: they unearthed a rusted, humanoid-shaped iron cage with a skeleton inside it. Nobody in the village had any idea someone had been buried there and the skeleton's identity remained a mystery. However, the iron cage—with a hook on top—suggested that the individual inside once had been executed and then put on public display in a gibbet, not an uncommon decoration in New York's colonial days.

Simultaneous Departures: New York

On October 15, 1892, William and George W., two elderly brothers from Dexter, went camping. On October 24, William's body was found sitting in a boat on Perch River, with both hands on the oars. He appeared merely to be sound asleep. That was satisfactorily bizarre—and then investigators found, a short distance downstream, George dead in his own boat in the very same position. Their tents, food, and supplies were untouched.

At first it was thought that a storm had killed them; then it was theorized that they'd shared some kind of poisoned food or drink; others whispered that it could only have been murder. But the coroner's autopsies revealed that each man had a tumor in his heart. It was all a spectacular coincidence: both brothers died of heart disease within minutes of each other while sitting in separate boats just a short distance apart.

A similar case occurred on August 28, 1905, when June J. and her husband, Allan, died at almost the same time though they were a thousand miles apart. As would-be rescuers pulled June, a drowning victim, from the water at Coney Island, a telegram arrived bearing the sad news of her banker husband's unexpected death at their home in Little Rock, Arkansas. Both died around one p.m. June was a well-known magazine writer under the pseudonym Helen Dixie Johnson.

What a Trouper!

Armand Castelmary, famous for his "magnificent basso voice," was performing as Tristano in Flotow's opera *Martha* before New York's Metropolitan Opera House on February 10, 1897. He sank to the floor at the end of the second scene of act one, as the chorus sang and pranced around him, "almost in full view of one of the most brilliant audiences that has filled the theater this winter," as a contemporary account put it.

Castelmary managed to rise long enough to warble out a few more lines. Then he staggered off to the side of the stage. And there he bit the biscuit a few minutes later. Somehow the stage managers dropped the curtain and got Castelmary's body offstage so subtly that very few in the brilliant audience realized that a man had been fatally stricken onstage right before their eyes.

The Swan Knows When It Is Dying: New York

Rev. George S., pastor of Brooklyn's Wyckoff Street Methodist Episcopal Church, was suffering from pneumonia but did not seem to be in danger. Yet on January 31, 1899, he said to his wife: "My dear, I do not believe that I will live after midnight." He passed away that very night at the stroke of twelve.

Dr. Luke B. of the Astrological Society of America cast his own horoscope and predicted that he would expire on some September 22 in the future. He was off by only one day, dying in New York on September 23, 1899. Luke also accurately forecast the death dates of his son in 1885 and his wife in 1891.

⊱•⊰

On the morning of November 20, 1910, superstitious Mary B. of New York City said to her eight-year-old daughter: "Barbara, I want you to be a good girl today because I had a tooth drop out this morning and that's a sign somebody in the family is going to die."

"Why, that's me," said the girl. "I'm going to die."

Later that afternoon, while playing on a pier, Barbara drowned when she fell between a barge and a horizontal beam.

⊱•⊰

Henry P. was so convinced he would die at 8:45 a.m. on December 30, 1919, that he bought a coffin and dictated an advance obituary to a Hornell newspaper giving his time of death: "Henry P., at 8:45 Tuesday morning, December 30, aged 88 years." He died exactly when he said he would at his home at 75 Genesee Street.

⊱•⊰

Then there is the case of Mrs. N. of Jamestown, who predicted that she would die on a certain day in July 1908. When the day ended and she was still among the living, she saved face by taking strychnine.

At Least He Didn't Play an Accordion

They found Charles M. lying beside the New York Central Railroad tracks at Buffalo. He had a fractured skull and never regained consciousness, but he did whistle ceaselessly for ninety-five hours straight, until death ended his sufferings (and those of everyone else within earshot) on January 4, 1899.

Whippersnappers, Attempt This Not at Your Domicile

The "bullet catching" trick is one of the most famous in the annals of stage magic: a gun is fired at a magician who appears to catch the bullet, usually with his teeth. Of course it is only an illusion—but it can be a dangerous one. A few conjurers are known to have died while doing the trick. One of these unfortunates was Michael Hatal, who grudgingly made entertainment history during a performance on New York City's East Side on October 28, 1899.

Hatal loaded the antiquated musket himself. He intended to use fake bullets that would disintegrate when fired, but he mistakenly put two .38-caliber lead bullets in the weapon.

Onstage, the magician urged his assistant Frank B. to fire at his heart. Frank did as commanded—and the bullets passed cleanly through Hatal's body, one through the left lung and one barely missing the heart.

Hatal died in Bellevue Hospital the next day. A silly rumor held that he had switched the bullets intentionally so he could enjoy a showstopper of a suicide.

Final Stretch

Eighteen-year-old Harry D. of Tenth Street in New York City lay on his deathbed for two weeks in April 1900 before he won his share of peace. When the undertaker came to measure him for a coffin, Harry's family was astounded to discover that he was six feet tall—astounding because he had been five feet five inches tall before his final illness. Through some suspension of nature's usual laws, Harry grew seven inches within his last two weeks.

Back to the Old Drawing Board

Herman M. of Brooklyn spent twenty-five years and his life's savings perfecting his invention, an aerial toboggan slide (a sort of roller coaster). He tested it at Coney Island on June 13, 1902. The first car, without riders, went down the slide perfectly. So did other cars bearing passengers. Herman beamed with joy; it seemed his long years of work and sacrifice had paid off and he was about to become wealthy. Two passengers climbed into the last car for the final test ride; the proud inventor stood at the bottom of the incline watching them. Just as the car reached the top of the slide—some seventy feet—something broke and the car came down backward at lightning speed. It struck Herman before he could run away. The riders were uninjured but the inventor died two hours later.

Twenty-year-old Carl V. of Rochester built his very own electric chair. On May 14, 1917, Carl—who does not appear to have been overly freighted with common sense—decided that the needful thing was to try it out on himself. He sat down, chained his ankles, and put on handcuffs. These restraints only ensured that he could not easily get out of the chair if something went amiss. He turned the current on by tugging (with his teeth) a chain attached to an electric light.

Carl intended to turn the current on and off at will. Problem was, the chain broke after he turned on the voltage and he couldn't turn it off. The crown jewel of his many mistakes was that he performed his little science experiment while home alone. When he was discovered a couple of hours later, everyone solemnly agreed that the experiment had been a complete success—after a fashion.

Aiming for the Apple: New York

There is something primal about the legend of William Tell—the Swiss folk hero who shot an apple off his son's head with an arrow—that has inspired countless men and boys to shoot something off a willing dupe's head. Seldom does the stunt end well.

A sterling example took place onstage at Thespian Hall during a medicine show at Cold Spring Harbor on October 26, 1902. Salesman and magician Charles M. offered to shoot an apple off the head of anyone brave enough to volunteer. John V., a barber, offered to be that person.

One has to wonder about the common sense, even the sanity, of a person who would be a stooge in a William Tell act. In John's case, Fate gave him plenty of warning signs. Charles's aim was not good that night, and at the beginning of the act he missed a card target. The magician placed the apple atop the barber's dome, aimed, and fired—and missed both apple and John, not once but twice. The third shot entered the barber's forehead, and the next thing Charles knew he was being hauled off to the slammer on a charge of manslaughter.

When Modesty Is Not a Virtue

Eighteen-year-old Helen G. of 81 Horatio Street, New York City, wanted to share a chunk of chocolate with coworkers at the Kisch Manufacturing Company. The candy was too thick to break apart with her fingers, so she employed a pair of scissors—but she held the chocolate in her lap as she speared it. She used too much force and drove the scissors through both the candy and an artery in her left leg. (Pardon, her left "limb.")

Doctors said Helen's life could have been saved had a tourniquet been applied immediately, but she was so modest that she not only refused first aid, she wouldn't even let anyone see the wound. By the time she agreed to relinquish her modesty, it was too late. She died an hour later at Saint Vincent's Hospital on December 21, 1910.

Boys at Play: New York

Some Brooklyn lads playing cowboys and Indians in November 1913 thought hanging someone for real would add verisimilitude to their game; they seized first a rope, then playmate Frank K., and hanged him from a shop awning. They fled in panic. A passerby noticed Frank's plight and cut him down, and not a moment too soon.

Death's Little Ironies: New York

Garner R. of Niagara Falls died of blood poisoning on July 23, 1925, after a Safety First sign fell on him at the factory where he worked.

Home Remedy for Lightning Strike

Edward and Jennie S., young siblings, were killed instantly when a bolt of lightning hit them in the kitchen of their Little Neck, Long Island, home on July 22, 1920.

When the deputy medical examiner of Queens went to the family home to see the bodies, he found that their relatives had buried them up to their necks in the backyard in the belief that the children were merely stunned and if so buried, the earth would draw the electricity out of them and they would revive.

The doctor had his work cut out for him convincing the relatives that the children really were dead.

Dead Man's Hand

On October 10, 1921, Philip B. died instantly of apoplexy right in the middle of a poker game at his son-in-law's home in Far Rockaway, New York. The medical examiner was puzzled until he picked Philip's cards up off the floor. They were the ace, king, queen, jack, and ten—all of hearts. It was a royal flush! It appeared that Philip just couldn't take the excitement.

Final Communications: New York

Helen D., who conducted a school of instruction in embroidery and fine needlework, killed herself in a most unrefined manner on March 18, 1908, by shooting herself in a Brooklyn phone booth. Beforehand she called an acquaintance to tell him what she was about to do, and she left a note on a writing pad in the booth: "Somebody will come to identify me. Excuse me for making all this trouble."

⊷•○•⊶

B.G.P. of Flatbush, Brooklyn, whipped a five-dollar bill out of his wallet to pay for a shave in May 1912, when he noticed that some previous owner of the currency had used it for a suicide note. Written on the bill "in fine feminine hand" was the message: "This is my last five dollars in the world, and now I have no desire to live. Farewell, whoever finds this please say a prayer for a lost soul." Police were unable to determine if the pathetic message was real or—well, counterfeit.

⊷•○•⊶

David William D. shot himself in a New York hotel room on March 25, 1917. Near his body was a magazine article in which he underlined the phrase "Exit laughing."

⊷•○•⊶

A woman who killed herself in New York's Hermitage Hotel on July 28, 1929, left a note containing the peculiar declaration "By the time you get this I will be blooey blooey."

⊷•○•⊶

Star-crossed lovers Sophie B. and Edward S. decided to end it all in a Bronx apartment building on August 15, 1929. As the room filled with gas, they commenced penning their suicide notes—a task that saved their lives when a passing patrolman smelled the gas and investigated. The lovers made the nonfatal error of writing a time-consuming total of thirty-five farewell notes between them.

⊷•○•⊶

June 20, 1933: When custodian Herman M. entered the office of George B.—broker in an investment bond firm—he found the boss standing on an outside windowsill. Herman was deeply concerned, considering that the office was on the fortieth floor of New York's Cities Service Building.

"What are you doing there?" inquired Herman.

"You go out and you'll see," replied George.

By the time the custodian returned with help, the boss was gone. He left behind a note that lacked explanatory power: "I like to sit on the windowsill and look at the view. It is like an airplane."

⊱•⊰•〇•⊱•⊰

Alice D. gassed herself in her New York apartment on February 19, 1935. She left a note warning her husband Leslie not to enter the apartment by himself, "especially with a lit cigarette," and added: "I am an expensive luxury."

⊱•⊰•〇•⊱•⊰

Bridge expert Lewis O. turned on the gas in his New York apartment on February 22, 1939. He left a wax-sealed note to his wife, on which he wrote: "Police, do not open. If you do it will be in a civil action."

Crowd Dis-pleaser

The following attention-getting notice appeared in the *New York Herald*:

> Aug. 18, 1880. I beg your leave to inform the people of New York through your columns that on Thursday afternoon, at precisely 3 o'clock, I will take my own life in Central Park; in other words, I will commit suicide (August 19). I invite the public, one and all, to witness the performance. Admission free. No extra charge for reserved seats. The place of performance will be the rock near the summer-house. [This statement was followed by precise directions—very thoughtful of the writer!] . . . I will first shoot myself through the head and then dive into the water. Now, please do the best you can for me and give me a large notice. I have been striving after Fame all my life, but she has always eluded my grasp; and now, as I am sick and tired of this life, where when a man asks for bread you give him a stone, I at least would like to leave it with some little éclat. Hoping you will comply with this, almost my last request, I remain, yours respectfully, A MAN who has nothing left him but to leave a world that will not let him exist.
> P.S.—I forgot to add, it will be utterly useless to guard the rock or the path leading to it, for I will appear when you least expect me. No one will see me

until I am on the rock in full view from the terrace, so I hope no one will be ill-bred enough to try and stop the performance, or interfere in it in any manner whatever.

The aftermath was a depressing commentary on the human condition. On August 19, Central Park filled with sightseers, including small children and refined women of all ages, whose fondest hope was to see an attention-starved man blow out his brains, and who were willing to sit out in the broiling summer sun without benefit of shade to see the promised extravaganza of self-destruction. For hours they stared at the rock overhanging the lake, waiting for the man to turn up as advertised.

Meanwhile, the park police—many of whom openly resented the extra work involved—searched for the would-be suicide so they could convince him that the world was a grand place after all and should not be so rashly abandoned.

When three o'clock came, every eye in the park stared at the rock, but the showman never turned up. Had he changed his mind at the last minute? Or was the whole thing a tasteless prank? Nobody knew then and nobody knows now. As the crowd slowly departed, a reporter noticed that many countenances bore palpable disappointment.

Cats Are Not the Only Ones with Nine Lives

T. Julius J., a forty-year-old Methodist preacher and temperance lecturer in New York City, paradoxically saw nothing wrong with killing himself once life became burdensome. But for a man who was so bullish on suicide, he was uniquely bad at it. By his own reckoning he made eight unsuccessful attempts, including shooting himself on four occasions while formerly living in Pennsylvania; while in Boston he took laudanum twice and arsenic once. The reader with calculator in hand will notice that this list of failures adds up to seven. For some reason, Reverend J. did not provide details about his eighth venture.

On the morning of October 27, 1880, the reverend made his ninth, tenth, and eleventh attempts by shooting himself three times in the head with a small revolver at the home of his landlord, Edward N., at 816 West Thirty-Second Street. Edward investigated the peculiar noises in his tenant's chamber and found Julius conscious and perfectly lucid. Julius instructed the proprietor to call for an ambulance and a policeman, and spoke very elegantly for a man with three bullets in his brain: "I am perfectly well assured that I have again failed in my attempt to make away with myself, and I can recuperate much more rapidly in a hospital than here." He added, "The sooner I get well, the sooner I'll renew my efforts at self-destruction."

When the police arrived, Julius sprang from the floor, grabbed a knife from a table, and was prevented from stabbing himself only by the cops' vigorous efforts to rescue a man who had just vowed to murder himself as soon as he felt up to the job. The aborted self-stabbing made his twelfth suicide attempt, and his fourth in a single day.

A *New York Sun* reporter visited the reverend in his hospital room, and the wounded man unbosomed himself: "Well, I've failed again. It seems that fate has been against me from my birth. . . . In spite of the most determined efforts, I invariably fail." Then he complained bitterly about his strained relations with his family and the difficulty of making a living—also, his difficulty in making a dying.

But how does it feel to believe your existence so bleak and hopeless that the correct course of action is to shoot yourself in the head repeatedly? Julius covered that topic as well, in remarkably clinical and precise language:

When I awoke [on October 27], about 8 o'clock, I lay on my back in bed and mused upon my condition and prospects. I checked off the advantages of life and death, and found that a great preponderance was on the side of the latter. I saw that I would have to struggle on to make my living all the rest of my life. I knew that I would never marry. I was also convinced that I could never repair the rupture with my family. I decided on death. Then I arose and wrote the directions for the disposal of my remains and, dressing myself slowly, proceeded to a pawnbroker's shop and purchased a revolver and cartridges for $3.18. I returned to my room and hung up my outer garments to prevent them from getting bloody . . . I was afraid from long experience—it seems strange for a man to talk about long experience in suicide, doesn't it?—[that my blood] would fly around in, to say the least, an unpleasant manner. Then I carefully loaded the weapon and, placing the muzzle against my right temple, pulled the trigger. I admit that it required an effort to pull the trigger, and that I had a momentary chill as I did so. I felt the ball [bullet] crash against my skull, but knew it was not fatal. So I pulled the trigger again, but it missed fire, and I cocked it and tried again and again, but it would not go off. In the meantime the blood running from the first hole in my head had wet the revolver and I took it down from my head and examined it, brushing the blood from my eyes with the other hand. I raised the hammer and, looking closely at the chamber, saw that one of the cartridges was awry, and fixed it with my teeth. Then the pistol went off and sent a bullet through my hand. After this I became impatient and fired twice at my head, both balls taking effect. Then, hearing the proprietor coming, I became a little bewildered and, throwing the revolver onto the washbasin, I fell to the floor.

Perhaps the reverend should have considered the possibility that a Higher Power did not want him dead just yet. Julius died in Monroe County, New York, in 1894, but I could not discover whether the cause was natural or unnatural.

Corpse and Corset

Brooklyn society belle Lillian D. committed suicide in a bathroom at the Glen Haven Resort Hotel on July 30, 1889, using a method that modern feminists might deem highly symbolic: she hanged herself with her corset strings.

Foolproof

In the 1880s, it occurred to a German who lived on Grand Street, near New York's Bowery, that he ought to relieve his depression with some leaden solace. He loaded a rifle with slugs and powder and arranged it so the barrel stared him in the face. He tied one end of a string to the trigger and the other end to his foot so that jerking it would have the desired effect. Then he sat at a table and drank a final pitcher of beer.

Just to make the whole business foolproof, he put a loaded gun in each hand and placed the barrels on both sides of his head. He jerked his foot—and all three guns went off simultaneously!

But the rifle's charge went off over his head.

The bullet from the pistol in his left hand made a glancing scalp wound.

The bullet from the pistol in his right hand entered his head, but did not even knock him unconscious.

So the disgusted German went to a bureau, withdrew a razor and successfully (that is, fatally) cut his throat.

Sort of Like a Maypole, but Not Really

In contrast to the German in the last story, Mr. N. of East Eleventh Street, New York City, preferred simplicity. He killed himself in April 1890 by entering a woodshed, tying one end of a rope around a post and the other end around his neck, and then walking in circles around the post until he strangled.

Gag Me with a Spoon

Ernest B. of New York City unsuccessfully attempted to kill himself on November 10, 1891, by slashing his wrists. He continued his activity on November 11 by cramming a teaspoon down his throat—and it was one of his landlady's spoons, too. The *Philadelphia Inquirer*'s headline: "Tried Something Original." Ernest survived—and then was arrested for attempting suicide.

Suicide by Hair

Lillian N. was described as "one of the handsomest, most talented, and wealthy young women on Long Island." But there must have been a gap in her life that looks, talent, and riches could not fill. On May 31, 1892, her maid entered the bathroom and found Lillian's nude body in the tub. Lillian—perhaps having gotten the idea from Robert Browning's poem "Porphyria's Lover"—had strangled herself with her own flowing hair by wrapping it tightly three times around her throat.

Death Gets a Twofer

On June 13, 1894, Sarah D. of Manhattan heard weird sounds issuing from a room in her apartment. She found her maid, Mary T., in the throes of death after having drunk carbolic acid. Sarah was so shocked and horrified by the sight that she dropped dying to the floor.

Season's Greetings

Three days after Christmas 1897, John B. approached a policeman on New York City's Third Avenue and hailed him with these words: "Here, copper, take this corpse to the morgue." John produced a pistol, blew out his brains, and fell at the officer's feet. The suicide left a note reading: "Give my body to some college or hospital, so it will be of some use. It was not while I was alive. No work, all kinds of trouble and gout; that is too much."

A Musician to the End

William K. was once considered one of the best bass viol players in America. He hanged himself with the G string of his instrument in his apartment on East Third Street, New York City, on June 2, 1898.

Napoleon Leaves a Challenge

Napoleon F. Washington, budding author and bearer of an unlikely name, was determined to sleep under the dew after his manuscripts were returned to him. He hanged himself in his New York apartment on August 14, 1902, by attaching a cord to a hook on the transom over his door. In his nightgown pocket was a bottle of laudanum on which he had pasted a mysterious note: "Laudanum. Bought July 25, 1902. From whom? Find out."

Consideration for the Working Class

The manager of New York's Astor House Hotel received a letter written on that establishment's stationery and dated June 26, 1904, from Louis M. of Scranton, Pennsylvania—a current guest who was missing from the hotel. Louis related that he had committed suicide, but not in the Astor House out of sympathy for the maids:

> *Although I shall not occupy Room 316 tonight, taking my last long sleep in a softer, cooler bed, I beg to enclose $2 in settlement of my bill, which is $1.50. I shall not need the change. I think the meanest mean cuss is one who goes as a guest to a hotel to commit suicide, often messing up the room in a dreadful way and leaving an unpaid bill. The motto for all suicides should be that of the celebrated rat poison, Don't die in the house. My satchel and few effects kindly give to some of the help. I would willingly leave my watch, not having any further use for time, but—well, there is a dear woman's picture in it, and it will stay with me to the last, as she did, and go with me tonight out to sea with the tide.*

Was it just a sick practical joke? Probably not. The maids found a satchel in room 316, just as the letter claimed. The hotel manager made a phone call and found that a Louis M., dealer in investment securities, did indeed have an office in Scranton and was missing according to his stenographer.

Party Poopers: New York

Isidore S. was due to get married next week and so held a "farewell bachelor dinner" at his Buffalo apartment on January 12, 1906. After a merry dinner, the groom-to-be invited guests into another room. "I have a great joke in store for you," said he, as he gave each person an envelope. While they tried to figure out what the envelopes were all about, Isidore completed his "great joke" by downing a bottle of carbolic acid. His guests were left to wonder what was so great about that particular gag.

———•—○—◦—•———

Mrs. Helen Kim M.—Broadway actress, bride of a month, and only twenty-five—seemed to be planning a party to remember. Prominent New Yorkers received invitations via chain mail:

> You are cordially invited to a "mystery cocktail party" in honor of someone you know. It will be the most unusual and amusing one ever held in New York. Make two copies of this letter immediately and mail them to two friends. Be sure that your friends will not recognize your handwriting and that they are the type that will pass the letter on and thus keep the chain going . . . Above all, do not talk about sending or receiving this letter. In case you should be unable to attend, please do not end the chain.

On the appointed day, April 24, 1937, over 150 guests arrived at the lobby of her Park Avenue apartment—far more people than the apartment possibly could have held. They rang Helen's bell; she didn't respond. Where was their hostess? The superintendent unlocked her door.

They found her dead on the kitchen floor with a gas tube from the stove in her mouth.

Investigators found that she hadn't sent out the chain letter invitations to the cocktail party—in fact, she had known nothing about the party. The invitations were the brainchild of a practical joker, an anonymous "Broadway playboy" who said he just wanted "to see how many prominent persons could be fooled." It was a bizarre coincidence that Helen gassed herself just as would-be partygoers began flooding her apartment building.

Stranger yet, back in 1930 she had attended a cocktail party in Los Angeles, during which a poet named Robert Carroll Pew imbibed poison and died at her feet. After this unpleasant event, she spent three days in a hospital suffering from hysteria.

Better Late Than Never

"Domestic troubles" inspired Mollie D. of New York City to say farewell to the world in June 1906. She chose a fittingly "domestic" method: she swallowed 144 needles, ranging in size from tiny ones used in fine sewing all the way up to sizeable darning needles. Her attempt was followed by twenty-five operations during the course of which surgeons managed to remove all but twelve of the needles. Mollie's suicide attempt finally bore fruit on December 30, 1907, a year and a half after she launched it.

Photo Finish

Morris B., a Philadelphia dentist, shot himself in the abdomen in New York City's Central Park on August 8, 1908. Before he did, however, he had a series of photographs of himself taken, each bearing a different facial expression. Morris numbered the photos and wrote an explanation on each:

No. 1: Here I'm thinking of the best way.

No. 2: Here I am entirely lost and see I must do it.

No. 3: Here I am and know there is no other way.

No. 4: Here I am angry at the world, as I know I cannot change it.

The Turn of an Unfriendly Card

Michael C., a mechanic who lived on West Fifty-Sixth Street, New York City, played a game of solitaire on that night in March 1911. The stakes were high, as revealed by a letter he sent to his cousin:

> Dear Jim, I am going to kill myself, my wife and all the children. I have something pressing on my brain that makes me want to kill them. I must do it. I cannot help it. The only way I kept from doing it before is by playing solitaire. I've been playing it all the time at home so I won't kill them. Now, I am going to play just one more game tonight, and if I beat it I won't kill them, but if I don't make it, I will.

So six lives depended on the turn of a card. Michael's wife noticed that he seemed agitated as he played that night. "What are you doing, Michael?" she inquired.

"You will know soon enough," he muttered darkly.

After finishing his game, Michael disappeared into the night. The cards on the table revealed that he'd lost. But he welched on his bet with himself: instead of massacring his entire family, he killed only himself.

Courteous

Charles T., a wealthy retired Wall Street stockbroker, committed suicide in his New York City home on January 6, 1914, by asphyxiating himself in the bathroom. Before he turned on the gas, he wrote a warning message to his family on a large piece of cardboard: "Do not strike matches. Have Lawson open the bathroom door." Presumably, Lawson was a domestic who could refrain from smoking for a few minutes.

Who Could Have Seen That Coming?

Ethelbert C., to his physician: "Doctor, I always had a curiosity to know just where my heart is located."

The doctor: "Well, hold still and I'll draw a circle around it." And so he did.

As the doctor wrote out a prescription for his patient, Ethelbert stepped into the next room, produced a pistol, and shot himself in the center of the circle the doctor had drawn on his chest. This scene took place in Port Jervis on August 14, 1921.

"What Fools These Mortals Be"

An unidentified man hanged himself on the roof of New York City's Puck Building on October 25, 1922, beside a statue of the sprite from Shakespeare's *A Midsummer Night's Dream* after whom the structure was named.

An Unintended Consequence

Depressed by the upcoming holidays, Donald R. decided to snort gas in his New York apartment on December 21, 1922. He took notes as he expired. The first read, "I am leaving you now." The second, written ten minutes later: "I hear joy bells." The third, fifteen minutes after that: "I am going." Two further notations were indecipherable.

Donald successfully killed himself, but he also almost accidentally exterminated his upstairs neighbor, Rev. Anthony B., who was overcome by the gas fumes. The reverend was rescued in the nick of time by other tenants.

Advance Notice

On September 13, 1924, traveling salesman Louis W. sent a telegram to a friend back home in Steubenville, Ohio: "Louis W. was found dead here this morning; advise disposition of body." After sending the message, the salesman made his word good by drinking poison in his room at New York's Hotel McAlpin.

In the Days before Reality TV Shows Made *Everyone* Famous

Charlotte Carter Flather was born in Meriden, Connecticut, in 1896. She was beautiful, smart, talented, and absolutely certain that she would become a rich and famous actress if she moved to New York City.

She became a ballet dancer on Broadway at age eighteen, appeared onstage under the name Charlotte Carter, and earned the sobriquet "The Best Dressed Girl in New York," but got no further in her ultimate ambition than having a stormy love affair with the millionaire Reginald Vanderbilt. For a while she was Vanderbilt's kept woman, but when he married someone else, he refused to further support her lavish lifestyle. She made her first suicide attempt in 1921 by drinking Veronal.

When Flather's stage career petered out, she earned some success as a freelance writer of news stories for Features Syndicate. She befriended the famous mystery writer Mary Roberts Rinehart, who dedicated a novel to her.

Bitterly unsatisfied with life—because she never attained the fame she thought was due her, she was bankrupt with $25,000 in liabilities, and she couldn't find the love she wanted—Flather swallowed sodium cyanide in her apartment at 159 East Fifty-Sixth Street on March 13, 1925, after penning no fewer than eight suicide notes. She was only twenty-nine.

In spring 1927, the newspapers belatedly discovered that Flather had written an unpublished purple-prose autobiographical novel called *Down My Street*. Her fickle lover Vanderbilt, who also had died in 1925, turned up in the book as "Archie Pembroke." She called herself "Carlotta Leslie," and several figures in New York's theatrical and literary worlds turned up in the thinnest of disguises. The papers printed the more sensational parts of the manuscript, and for a day or two Charlotte Flather attained the celebrity she craved.

A Concerned Husband

January 16, 1928: As he looked into his shaving mirror, Dr. Shepherd P. of New York City saw a reflection of his wife about to shoot herself in the chest. Did he try to talk her out of it? Call the police? Strike the weapon from her hand? No, he demanded that she write a note first absolving him of blame in case the police thought he murdered her. Which she did: "I am tired of living this way. I cannot go on without my husband and I am afraid to go alone. My husband has enough money to take care of himself. I shot my—"

Suicide of a Cartoonist

Ralph Barton, cartoonist and confidante of Charlie Chaplin, was most famous for illustrating Anita Loos's 1925 novel *Gentlemen Prefer Blondes*.

His work also appeared in the *New Yorker, Life, Harper's Bazaar,* and *Vanity Fair.* On May 20, 1931, the four-times-married artist typed a satiric obituary and then shot himself in his Manhattan penthouse apartment at 419 East Fifty-Seventh Street. The maid found Barton's corpse with a pistol in one hand and a cigarette in the other. Nearby was a copy of *Gray's Anatomy,* opened to an illustration of the heart. It appeared that he had debated inwardly as to whether to aim for the heart or the head, and finally opted for the latter.

The humor in his self-written obituary, the *New York Times* noted, was as cynical as that in his cartoons. It read, in part: "Present my remains, with my compliments, to any medical school that fancies them—or soap can be made from them. If the gossips insist . . . upon a reason for my action, let it be my pending appointment with my dentist."

In a more serious vein, Barton stated that he regretted splitting with one of his wives, Carlotta Monterey, who afterward married playwright Eugene O'Neill. Barton explained: "[I] have run from house to house, from wife to wife and from country to country in a ridiculous attempt to escape from myself. . . . I am fed up with inventing devices for getting through twenty-four hours a day."

Seemed Like the Thing to Do

Edna G., an unemployed model, thought she swallowed cough medicine on that long-ago day, December 29, 1931. Instead, the bottle contained poison. Realizing too late her error, Edna pounded on the door of James D., a fellow tenant in her New York apartment building.

"I've burned my mouth!" she said. "Quick! Get me an antidote!"

"Never mind that," said James, taking the bottle from her and evidently thinking spontaneous suicide was a jim-dandy idea. "Give me the bottle. I'll finish it for you."

He drank the remainder of the bottle's contents and was dead by the time the doctor arrived. Edna survived her adventure.

A Real Stumper

Mrs. Winnie B., a reclusive rich widow, was found dead on her living room floor in Canisteo on December 7, 1934. Cause of death: sixty hatchet wounds to the head. A trail of blood began in the cellar and dripped through every downstairs room in the house. In light of these clues, the coroner arrived at the obvious verdict: a clear-cut case of suicide!

When Mrs. George P., another wealthy widow, was beaten to death on December 17 in her home at Bath, only a few miles from Canisteo, the coroner admitted that Mrs. B. might—just *might*—have been murdered after all.

Another First

Television was a strange and wonderful new technology in 1938. On June 23 of that year, an NBC experimental mobile transmitter was filming on the streets of New York when the crew unintentionally filmed stenographer Marian P.'s eleven-story leap from the Time and Life Building in Rockefeller Center. Luckily for sensitive viewers, the footage was not broadcast live but rather was being sent to the studio by cable.

Marian's death was very likely the first suicide to be filmed accidentally by a television camera. It would not be the last.

Politely Declined

A man bent on suicide jumped into the Harlem River on August 18, 1938. When would-be rescuers threw a rope to him, he shouted, "Sorry, I haven't changed my mind."

Pounded by a Poltergeist

Dr. Charles K. of Buffalo was tending to business one day in September 1884 when a man entered his office with a very unusual medical complaint: he claimed he had been roughed up by a ghost.

The skeptical physician examined his patient and "found a couple of severe bruises on his chest—one round, as if inflicted by a club, the other long and narrow like a knife cut." The man had a broken fourth rib and injuries to the right lung.

Dr. K. said, when recounting the strange episode a month later: "How the injuries could be inflicted I could not guess. The patient said he was asleep, felt himself suddenly seized by the throat, struggled to get away, but only succeeded in gaining enough liberty to scream. He was immediately struck in the chest, felt the bones crush and was stabbed. The blade entered his side several times. He was found lying on the floor senseless, with the moon shining upon him, the windows and doors all locked on the inside, and nothing disturbed."

The story has a sad ending, because if a ghost is determined to give you a royal beating, there isn't much you can do about it. Dr. K.'s patient recovered and returned to his home thirty miles away accompanied by the physician, who chose to spend the night there. The doctor was awakened in the night by a shriek and a loud crash. Investigating, the doctor found his patient unconscious on the floor, with a bloody mouth, a rebroken rib, and head-to-toe bruises. He briefly recovered his senses before he died, and claimed that an invisible enemy had lifted him bodily and thrown him against the wall and floor.

"I believe he could not have injured himself on either occasion," said Dr. K.

Haunted Honeymoon

Widower Samuel W. married Ida C. on September 7, 1923, after a three-month courtship. Samuel was the president of the Amherst Knitting Mills of New York, and therefore one might think him a practical businessman. But he said he was haunted nightly by his dead first wife and his equally dead former mother-in-law. He seemed particularly afraid of the latter.

The ghosts so disturbed Samuel that only two days into the marriage he told Ida he wanted out. "We packed up our things and returned to New York," complained Mrs. W. (the living one). "On the way back all he said to me was 'I'm sorry.'"

The couple were legally separated on December 22, after only seventy-four days of wedded nonbliss. If the ghosts were real, they cost Samuel W. dearly: the judge ruled that he had to pay his second wife fifty dollars a week in alimony.

The Haunted Women's Club

In the winter of 1928, there were rumors that a women's club in downtown New York City—which the papers declined to name—was regularly visited by a ghost. The member to whom the spirit appeared spoke anonymously to a reporter. This is the account as she told it:

> [It was] nothing to scare me. This is how I saw it first. I was reading in my room when suddenly the door swung open and in came a gentle, elderly man in somewhat old-fashioned clothes. I thought he was real, perhaps the father of some girl living in the house, who had by chance wandered upstairs from the reception room.

"Were you looking for something?" I asked.

He fixed a pair of dark, rather intense eyes on mine, nodded and beckoned. Thinking perhaps he was ill or for some reason couldn't speak, I walked across the room to him and to my surprise put my hand through his shoulder. The room was brightly lighted. Even as I stared at him, he vanished.

Well, of course, I supposed it must be merely my imagination. But the next night at the same hour the door opened and in he came. Again he beckoned. Again I walked over to him, put out my hand twice, and twice my hand went through his elbow, before he sort of swirled like a vapor and disappeared. In all, he has appeared five times since a week ago when we first met. At last I simply sat in my chair and he would come over to me, stand beside the chair with an earnest expression as if he wanted to tell me an important secret, then shake his head in despair and—not be there anymore.

Nobody ever thought I was psychic. I don't think so either. But last night an extraordinary thing occurred. The ghost didn't appear, perhaps because I went to bed early and I thought I slept soundly. But I had a dream so vivid that it seemed real. I dreamed that the old gentleman looked in at the door and beckoned; that I rose, threw on my dressing gown and, taking his hand, went with him up two flights of stairs to a storeroom.

The room had changed from what it really is; it had become an old, raftered, unfinished attic. In one corner against the wall was a shabby trunk. The old gentleman opened it and began to search desperately among dozens of packages of papers inside, documents of some kind, like property deeds or perhaps stocks. I knelt beside him and helped in the search. Whatever it was we didn't find it, for the old gentleman sort of shook apart into vapor and was gone. In my dream I walked down the two flights back to my room.

I've spent most of today looking up records and I find that on the site of the old clubhouse there used to be an old dwelling—attic and all—owned by a kindly but somewhat eccentric old man who was reputed to be wealthy. Strange how these ghosts are always hunting for lost treasure, isn't it?

That's all, except that when I woke up before daylight this morning I was standing in the middle of my room, in my dressing gown. There was dust on the front of my nightgown, as if I had knelt down, and dust on the soles of my feet. There were bare footprints, too, I discovered in the storeroom.

Head Injury Hijinks: New York

Edward S., a farmer who lived at Nichols, got conked on the noggin by a tree in spring 1904. Though the injury seemed harmless, Edward lost all memory of the previous forty years and imagined himself a boy again in 1864. According to one report, "He goes about the farm on which he lived when a boy and wants to play boyish games and pranks as of yore."

Oh, Rats!: New York

Hordes of hungry rats attacking humans is merely the stuff of Hollywood horror films like *Willard*, right? You wish! (Note: If you suffer from musophobia, you might skip the following vignette.)

Because of the unusually rainy weather in January 1889, rats in the vicinity of Ellenville sought dry places such as barns, outbuildings, and even people's homes. The rodents brought their famously ferocious appetites with them, as experienced by a family who lived north of town. First rats attacked the baby, and when the mother came to the rescue, they pounced on her. Her screams were heard by a passing mail carrier, Charles J., who ran into the dwelling with a whip. He slashed at the rats but the invading army did not retreat until he threw a dish of hot ashes and coals at them. "It was a bloodcurdling sight," said Charles, "and one which I shall never forget." Mother and child were bitten and bloody, but otherwise physically unharmed. Mental scars are another matter.

Phantom Limb: New York

One might think, logically speaking, that a person who loses, say, an arm or a leg could not feel pain in the missing area. After all, the nerves are gone along with the missing limb. But there is the well-known phenomenon of phantom limb—technically known as pseudesthesia, the pain one feels in an amputated limb or otherwise missing body part. The researcher who peruses old newspapers will be rewarded with bizarre accounts of phantom limb.

For example, in January 1886, a doctor amputated Mrs. William G.'s lower leg just below the knee at Byron, New York. The limb was buried in the cemetery with great dignity—it wore a stocking—but Mrs. G. continued to feel not only pain where the amputated leg used to be, but specifically in a corn on one toe. Three weeks later her husband disinterred the leg and found that the stocking had rolled down across her heel and instep, and that a bandage wound around her toes was constricting her corn. He removed the stocking and bandage and reburied the leg. After that the afflicted woman felt no more phantom pains.

Giving the Finger

How to make an ordinary summer's day much less ordinary: On August 11, 1883, a man strolled into New York City's Center Market, walked over to the butcher's stand, put his left hand on the chopping block, grabbed a cleaver, cut off his pinky finger, and then left the store without saying a word. Yes, he left the finger behind. The butcher was left alone to contemplate what a funny old world this is.

A Stripper Would Have Been Preferable

In July 1889, a celebration was held for over a hundred members of New York's Tammany Hall, the infamous Democratic Party political machine. One of the banquet's features was an enormous apple pie five feet in circumference, two feet deep, and topped with a crust two inches thick. But when the pie was cut open, out hopped a dozen rats, logy from eating apple filling but spry enough to send the Tammany members heading for the doors and chairs.

The disgusting mystery was soon solved. Before the banquet, the pie had been on proud display at Alderman George H.'s saloon, and there the rodents entered the savory morsel by eating a hole in its bottom. George had observed the hole but plugged it up on the *assumption* that there were no rats still in the pie. In other words, George H. was willing to feed his political cronies a pie that he knew had been invaded by rats.

When Diamond-Studded Watch Fobs Are No Longer Good Enough

A fad among New York doctors, circa 1889: owning wallets, purses, glasses cases, card cases, and other memorabilia made of tanned human skin, gleaned largely from the bodies of the hanged. Some even kept their surgical instruments in a human skin carrying case. Two coroners were known to carry such bags, and the fashionable wife of a surgeon had an epidermis purse.

One tanner reassured a reporter that the craze for products made of human skin would never become widespread because, unlike animal skin, it was too difficult to treat.

"The human skin when tanned and dressed can be put to but a small number of uses," proclaimed this expert. "It cannot be used as the skin of an animal can be. You see, the human skin is porous. It cannot be used where it will come into contact with water."

The tanner also observed that walrus skin bore the strongest resemblance to human skin, and his professional opinion must be respected.

George R. Returns

In 1886, George R., a young newspaperman, married a girl in Canandaigua. Not long afterward he decided that land speculation out west was the way to make his fortune, so he moved to Lakin, Kansas, leaving his new bride and his mother behind in Canandaigua.

His loved ones received letters from him brimming with optimism. He was buying land with two partners and his prospects seemed assured. He promised Mrs. R. that she would soon move to Lakin and dwell in a house he was building for her.

But on November 27, 1887, George was killed when he fell off the house he was constructing. Many residents of Lakin came to the funeral and saw him lying in his coffin. The tragic news was sent to Canandaigua but kept from the young widow, who had just given birth to George's son.

The dead man's mother sent word to Lakin that she wanted the remains shipped to Canandaigua. A reply came stating that he already had been buried.

The mother wired back insisting the coffin be exhumed and sent home. A second telegram came, stating that the grave had been robbed.

George's mother understandably thought the entire situation reeked of fish and she went to Lakin to investigate matters in person. She met her son's land speculation partners, who reassured her that he'd fallen off a house. They explained that he'd been buried in haste due to rapid decomposition and registered great shock that the poor fellow's body had been stolen.

George's mother returned to New York but she was not satisfied with the answers she'd gotten and hired a Pinkerton detective. He soon discovered that George's partners had insured his life for $5,000 and were attempting to collect. The Mutual Life Insurance Company's investigators agreed that things looked suspicious—but a number of witnesses in Lakin swore they'd seen George dead at his funeral.

The detective thought George was still alive and on a hunch sought him in western insane asylums. In November 1889, the detective found the missing man in an institution, alive and well but "mentally shattered."

George had not fallen off a house; rather, his business partners had drugged him so heavily that he'd appeared to be dead at his funeral—after which, they'd spirited him away. At least they'd had enough decency not to bury him alive. The drug that had produced the stupor also destroyed George's mind, and he ended up in the asylum with his memory erased.

George's partners made themselves scarce when it was evident that their plot was about to be revealed. But the "dead man" got a happy ending when he returned to his wife and a son he didn't know he had. His wife had worn widow's weeds the entire two years she thought her husband was dead.

I Prescribe a Honey Glaze at 350 Degrees

In 1890, the *New York Mercury* interviewed a wisely anonymous "celebrated physician" who advocated cannibalism—or at least pretended to. He felt that we are influenced by the *character* of the critters we eat. He provided the example of the pig, which is famously dumb and brutish; so eating pig meat will make the consumer dumb and brutish as well. Meanwhile, someone who ate an animal full of fine qualities, such as the horse or the dog, would gain those fine qualities. Therefore, it stands to reason—does it not?—that eating the noblest creature of all (he meant humans, but some might beg to differ) would be the most beneficial to the consumer.

The doctor believed in the utilitarian philosophy espoused by Jeremy Bentham—not to mention a number of *Star Trek* episodes much later—which held that an action producing the greatest good for the greatest number was ideal. He added that the progress of the human race should not be held back by mere sentimentality or selfishness. The doctor, clearly a dyed-in-the-wool Malthusian, also thought cannibalism would reduce overpopulation and as a bonus, "the status of the people will be considerably improved by the change in the character of its food." Fewer people, smarter people! What's not to like?

The skeptical interviewer asked why cannibal tribes were so degraded if eating other humans improved the character. The physician answered with breezy racism that these primitive tribes showed no improvement because they feasted on men who were of inferior quality to begin with. The doctor contemplated how much humans would improve if they dined on geniuses such as Gladstone, Bismarck, and Herbert Spencer. He didn't seem to wonder what these luminaries might think about being eaten.

The doctor admitted that it would be difficult to persuade selfish people to give themselves up to the chopping block, even for the public good. He thought the fairest way to go about it would be a daily lottery. He claimed that he actually had "tasted human flesh a number of times and that it is by no means a delicacy to be despised." So in addition to those other benefits, human meat tastes good.

The doctor often discussed his theories with colleagues, but they never could tell whether he was joking or serious.

Will Weirdness

Lizzie Perkins of Brooklyn passed away in Paris on September 23, 1891. One of the unexplained stipulations in her will was that all family portraits be burned. The strange order also turned up in the will of Susanna K. Pratt of Boston in May 1938.

Louise R. died in New York City on March 26, 1912, leaving an estate worth over $5,500. Touchingly, she did not forget her husband in her will: "I also give, devise and bequeath to my husband, Harold, $5 in installments of 5 cents a week."

Frederick C. of Syracuse received an extra $500 in his father's will in 1914. His father felt remorseful over giving Frederick an undeserved childhood spanking.

The 1922 will of Mary C., a sixty-four-year-old so-called spinster in New York City, directed that she be buried with an extra pillow. If any unknown relatives turned up for their perceived share of her swag, Mary ordered that they be given only a dollar apiece since "during life they had no affection for me."

Mrs. Clarence M. of 51 West Forty-Eighth Street, New York, left some eye-opening instructions in her will, which became public knowledge after her death at Cornish on July 5, 1922. She requested that two of her female friends move in with the widower. The lucky ladies were

Miss Emma A. of San Diego and Eleanor C. of Cornish, New Hampshire. However, Mr. M. was to pay all household expenses, including upkeep on a pet parrot and three dogs named Stevedore, Mrs. Grundy, and Duchy.

⊷⊶⊙⊷⊶

As some examples demonstrate, wills are often employed as a means to settle old scores. When William E. died in New York City in 1923, he left his widow $1,000—but only if his mother-in-law were not permitted to arrange his burial.

⊷⊶⊙⊷⊶

Kathrine Wilson, a one-time actress, adamantly refused throughout her adult life to admit that she was a wife and a mother. Even when she died in New York City at age eighty on January 23, 1933, she left her entire estate to her daughter but insisted on referring to her as "my friend, Mrs. Channing Pollock." The deceased's married name was Mrs. Edward Marble, but she signed the will "Kathrine Wilson."

⊷⊶⊙⊷⊶

A sour sentiment was expressed by Giuseppe G. of New York City, who died in 1936. The will, which was filed for probate on May 1, left $17,000 to a friend but only five cents to each of his five children "to purchase a piece of rope in the hope that each would strangle himself or herself with said rope." After a legal battle, the will was upheld on December 10, 1936, and each of Giuseppe's heirs was left with a shiny new nickel to do with as he or she pleased.

Women Have Their Terrifying Little Secrets

Twelve young women formed a secret society called the Lovely Dozen in Mount Vernon in 1898. Unlike most secret societies, however—which are exclusive by definition—the women allowed bachelor males to join. There was a caveat: new members were told a big, big secret that they were bound by oath not to divulge.

The secret died long ago with the original members of the Lovely Dozen, but whatever it was, it must have been fairly horrifying. When nine bachelors were initiated and the enigma revealed to them on January 14, 1898, witnesses noted that "they emerged white from top to toe."

Finger of Fate

In February 1934, Frank G., a Depression-era hobo in New York City, performed the good deed of returning a lost wallet containing $42,000 in bonds to its owner. He went insane after living it up on the reward money. "I am God!" he shouted. "I can look at a man and kill him with a look!"

He pointed and stared at passerby Michael G., who toppled over dead right on cue.

Frank was placed in a straitjacket and taken to the asylum. "I am a broker!" he cried, evidently not satisfied with believing himself the Deity. "See? Haven't I got a $15 hat?" he said by way of explanation.

Musical Saw

Fred L. made his living in vaudeville by having heavy electric currents and lit torches applied to his body. After twenty-five years of being professionally tortured, Fred broke his back in a car wreck in 1932 and was paralyzed from the waist down. Undaunted, he gave up his career in vaudeville and went on to a higher calling as a carnival freak-show manager.

His left leg had to be amputated a week before Thanksgiving 1937. Then the other one had to go.

As surgeons at Manhattan's French Hospital cut off Fred's right leg on December 4—without using an anesthetic—the patient played "Sweet Adeline" and other sprightly tunes on a harmonica. He told reporters brightly, "And I tried to keep the music in time with the doctor's saw!"

He added, "I can go on the stage as a midget."

Egregious Executions: New York

In the old days, the prevailing sense of justice demanded that convicted murderers pay for their crimes with their own lives, standing on a scaffold before throngs who took the spectacle as an object lesson. Hangmen were professionals who took pride in swinging their clients off to eternity with a minimum of discomfort, and the majority of executions went off perfectly. But not all did. Here are accounts of some that decidedly *did not*.

Alexander Jefferson, who went on a killing rampage in December 1882, was scheduled to be hanged in Brooklyn on August 1, 1883. According to capital punishment historian Daniel Allen Hearn, the sheriff lined his pockets by appointing five hundred men as special deputies in exchange for a fee so they could witness the hanging. These hard-drinking boors filled the jailhouse and behaved as if they were at a burlesque peep show. Jefferson's neck was not broken and he struggled at the end of the rope. The executioner did not tie his legs, so Jefferson kicked the air in his agony. He managed to tear off his hood with one hand. He lost control of his bowels, inspiring the audience to make colorful witticisms. After the condemned man strangled to death at last, the crowd was invited to come to the autopsy as a sort of encore. It came out later that the hangman had *intentionally* placed the rope incorrectly around Jefferson's neck to maximize his death agonies and give the audience a show worth writing home about.

※

The rationale for replacing the gallows with the electric chair in 1890 was that electrocution was a more humane and quicker way to dispatch the condemned—and so it was, usually. There were memorable occasions to the contrary. When William Taylor went to the chair at New York's Auburn Prison on July 27, 1893, the device shorted out in midshock, leaving Taylor burned but alive. He was taken from the chair and sedated while repairmen labored in vain. Daniel Allen Hearn describes their inspired solution: "Emergency cables were run from the electric chair to a telephone pole outside the window of the death chamber. When all was ready Taylor was put back in the chair and a lineman turned on the power." That did it! Ironically, Taylor had engineered his own horrible fate when he cut a fellow prisoner's throat, thinking that a death sentence was preferable to spending years in prison.

Those Final Moments: New York

Back when executions were not uncommon events, newspaper readers had an abiding interest in knowing how the condemned behaved in his last moments. Did he cry? Pray? Lecture the crowd? Crack jokes? Was he brave, indifferent, or cowardly? The range of human behavior displayed on the gallows was remarkable, as these examples illustrate:

For murdering his wife and later killing two of his fellow inmates, Angelo Cornetti was hanged at White Plains on May 11, 1883—but not before ten men had to force the hysterical Italian to the gallows.

William Henry Ostrander murdered his brother George on December 26, 1880. He was sentenced to be hanged at Utica on August 10, 1883. Instead of getting health-enhancing sleep the night before his hanging, Ostrander stayed up all night, singing, shouting, skylarking, and making noise. In the morning, peering through his cell window at the waiting scaffold and the gathering crowd, Ostrander exclaimed: "I'm going to be hung at 10 o'clock and the gallows is already in the yard. I'll walk out, by [expletive deleted], and tell them to cut the rope! I'll go plump to hell in a minute, and in a wheelbarrow too, and the man who cuts the rope will be in hell to meet me." (If the reader can decipher the meaning of that last sentence, please contact the author via the publisher.)

Earlier, Ostrander told the priest that he wanted to receive the sacraments and be baptized, but when the priest made arrangements, the condemned man changed his mind, saying: "I guess I'll worry along as I am." A reporter describes Ostrander's final unpleasant minutes: "He died with oaths on his lips, cursing his mother and sisters, whose testimony brought him to the scaffold, and protesting his innocence. He also cursed the court officers and even the friend who had shown him favors while he was in jail." Not only that, "the fall failed to dislocate Ostrander's neck and his struggles were horrible."

Clement Arthur Day was so jealous of his girlfriend Johana Rosana Cross that he would not even allow her to visit her dying mother. In a scene that sounds like it came straight from a folk song, he stabbed Cross eight times with a butcher knife on the bank of New York's Black River near Booneville on June 9, 1887. Day's father—who watched in terror as the scene unfolded, but was too elderly and far away to come to her rescue—turned him in and the killer was sentenced to death. While waiting for his appointment with the hangman at Utica, Day seemed determined to prove something to somebody. He never expressed regret for his crime. On the night before his hanging, he danced to a sprightly fiddle tune. On the walk to the gallows on February 9, 1888, Day laughed when the sheriff, the deputy, a reporter, and the minister slipped on the ice. He applauded when the death warrant was read, yawned ostentatiously on the scaffold when his legs were strapped, helped the deputy adjust the rope around his neck, and smiled as the cap was placed over his head. He was still grinning when his body was cut down.

—•—◦—•—

Gordon Fawcett Hamby was electrocuted on January 29, 1920, for killing a teller in the course of a Brooklyn bank robbery. He was notable for the many weird quips he uttered while standing in the Valley of the Shadow. Toward the end he refused to answer to the name Hamby but would respond if referred to by his alias, J. B. Allen. He wouldn't even sign his real name to get money from a fund set up for him, from which he could have purchased cigarettes and other comforts. He spent his time playing with a Ouija board right up to the last hour of his life. When a barber shaved his head in preparation for his electrocution, Hamby remarked, "I thought you were going to give me a pompadour." As he climbed into the chair he said, "Go ahead, boys." He said to Sing Sing's physician, "Smile, doc! I'd like to see someone looking cheerful today." Like Clement Day, Hamby died with a big smile on his face.

—•—◦—•—

"I deserve to die," said sailor Frank Henry Burness, "and the sooner they put an end to my troubles the better. I've got an uncontrollable temper and if released would only commit more violent crimes. I'd kill a man for five cents as quick as for anything else." In fact Burness, a native of Butler, Pennsylvania, was on Sing Sing's death row for killing Captain George Townsend over twenty dollars. Burness went to the electric chair on June 27, 1904, with a winning grin on his face. He helped guards adjust the straps. It required four jolts to kill him, which probably took some of the humor out of the situation.

—•—◦—•—

When George Appel went to the chair in New York on August 9, 1928, he allegedly said to the witnesses, "Well, folks, soon you'll see a baked Appel." Similarly, Frederick Charles Wood's final words before taking the seat of honor at Sing Sing on March 21, 1963, were: "Gentlemen, observe closely as you witness the effect of electricity on Wood."

The Lost Is Found

In February 1866, telegraph operator David S. vanished from the village of Ellenville. David's family thought his disappearance was due to some tragic love affair—after all, he was only twenty-two. Strange, though, that he should never have written!

The mystery unraveled in March 1879, when a long-abandoned lead mine was reopened and David's skeleton was found within. His mother, residing at Accord, positively identified him by the clothing; medical examiners found that the remains had a stiff hip joint, an ailment David was known to have had. Notably, the skeleton was lacking a wallet and gold watch, two items David carried on the day he entered oblivion. The presumption was that he had been robbed and murdered.

So who did it? Best guess was that Joseph F. was the murderer. He lived near the mine, had a notable cruel streak, and was abusive to his family. It was remembered that just before the disappearance, David and Joseph had had a quarrel at a dance. In 1876, Joseph started going insane. He often pointed at the sealed mine shaft and muttered, "There he goes, there he goes."

If Joseph was indeed guilty, he was forever beyond the reach of the law. His mental disturbance became so great that he was taken to the Willard Asylum for the Insane in Ovid, and there he died chattering like an ape.

Brutes of Husbands: New York

The neighbors often overheard Charles and Eva Herman quarreling vociferously in their cottage on Blossom Alley in Buffalo. They heard the familiar racket on Sunday, November 1, 1885, followed by an unfamiliar silence that lasted three days. Mr. Herman was observed entering and exiting the residence in that time, but no one saw a trace of his wife. The authorities investigated on November 4 and found the remains of Mrs. Herman lying in bed with a gashed throat and a plethora of defensive wounds. Charles Herman—who happened to be an unemployed butcher—confessed to murder and also to sleeping beside the corpse for three nights. He was hanged on February 12, 1886.

⊱•⊰

Adrian Braun was sentenced to two years in Sing Sing in September 1897 for wife-beating. He had battered her so badly that he nearly killed her. Mrs. Braun forgave this violence and visited the prison on March 5, 1898. She met him in the kitchen, where he had a job as a potato peeler. "When the two met they kissed each other and were very friendly," says a news account. They sat only a few feet away from the watchful eye of Detective Jackson. When the detective informed Braun that his time was up, the prisoner asked, "Can't we have a few minutes more?" Jackson agreed, and then wished he hadn't, because a moment later Mr. Braun cut his wife's throat with his potato-peeling knife, killing her nearly instantly. Before the detective and two other convicts seized Braun, he slashed the poor woman's head several additional times. Had Braun kept his murderous impulses in check, he would have been freed when his sentence expired; instead, he was executed for murder on May 29, 1899.

Conscience Makes Cowards of Us All

Edward Unger of New York City was sentenced to twenty years in Sing Sing in February 1887 for the January murder of his roommate August Bohle, who must have been very annoying indeed since Unger dismembered him, tossed his head in a river, packed the other pieces in a trunk, and shipped it to some person in Baltimore who undoubtedly would rather have gotten flowers.

Within a month of his imprisonment, Unger already was in the prison hospital suffering from a conscience-fueled hallucination so terrifying that officials seriously considered sending him to a lunatic asylum. On his first night in Sing Sing, Unger imagined he saw chunks of Bohle strewn about the room—all but the head. The fragments vibrated and then moved toward each other of their own volition; then the disarticulated pieces reassembled themselves into his murdered roommate. But the show wasn't complete until Bohle's sopping-wet head rolled into the room and fit itself on the dead man's shoulders. After that the ghost, whole again and sound as a dollar, smiled satanically at his killer.

Unger had this same vision every night for a week and could only be calmed with a heavy dose of narcotics. Earlier, during his trial, Unger was noted for his calmness and physical strength; once the vision commenced, he transformed without delay into a quivering physical wreck.

Old Habits Die Hard

While serving time in Joliet prison in Illinois, Carl Muller made three jailhouse buddies: Ludwig Brandt, a German immigrant named Baum, and Dr. Henry C. Meyer. The doctor was a talkative soul and confided to Muller that he had hit upon a brilliant plan to defraud insurance companies.

Dr. Meyer was paroled; perhaps Muller thought he had seen the last of his conniving companion. But when Muller was released on June 2, 1891, he went to Chicago and again met Dr. Meyer, who was practicing medicine there. Meyer reminded his fellow ex-convict about his insurance scheme and asked if he'd like to get in on the ground floor. Muller's reply was something along the lines of "No thanks, I've had enough prison life to suit me."

The disappointed doctor casually mentioned that he had recently gone to Joliet to visit their old pal Baum, and boy did he look sick and not long for this world! Evidently unable to take no for an answer, Dr. Meyer suggested that Muller impersonate Baum and get his life insured; then when the real Baum died, they could collect the money. Meyer was so confident the plan would work that he even took a trip to Germany to get background information on Baum's life to make the scam more convincing. Again, Muller refused to get involved.

It is wise to keep your diabolically clever plots to yourself, but Dr. Meyer was an incurable braggart. After a while, he told Muller that he'd given up on his plan to insure Baum. Instead, he'd insured their other old friend from Joliet, Ludwig Brandt—by now also out of prison—under the false name Joseph Baum. Mrs. Meyer married Brandt bigamously so she could pose as his wife and later as his widow. Brandt was in on the deception and understood that his role was to play sick and a person who'd died of natural causes would be used to masquerade as his corpse. Then when the insurance money came, he would get a cut.

The Meyers and Brandt traveled to New York City in early 1893 to pull off their con job—and brought along Muller, who really should have known better. They had the otherwise sporadically honest Muller rent an apartment and buy furniture under the name of Baum.

It didn't occur to poor Brandt that it would be an arduous, difficult chore for Meyer to locate a dead man who passably resembled him, and that the nefarious doctor would find it much simpler to make a genuine corpse out of Brandt himself. The doctor gave his trusting stooge doses of croton oil—to simulate dysentery, he said, but the net effect was to make Brandt deathly ill for real. Perhaps Dr. Meyer had no confidence in Brandt's acting skills.

A doctor was called in to see the patient—Dr. Winden, whom Meyer cynically chose because he thought Winden could easily be fooled. Dr. Winden left medicine for Brandt, which Meyer threw away at the first opportunity. To hurry matters along, he gave Brandt food sprinkled with antimony, which he later substituted with arsenic so his confederate wouldn't suffer so darn much. Ludwig Brandt, a.k.a. Joseph Baum, died miserably on March 30, 1893, possibly daydreaming about what he would do with his share of the insurance payment.

The guileless Dr. Winden was called in; he signed the death certificate, and Mrs. Meyer—posing as "Mrs. Baum"—got a $3,000 check from the Washington Life Insurance Company. Dr. Meyer paid off Carl Muller to the tune of $750 and urged him to go back to Chicago.

Dr. Meyer's "perfect crime" was anything but. The insurance company got suspicious and Meyer made tracks for Detroit and then Toledo, where he went under the name Hugo Mahler and schemed to insure and poison a young employee of his named Mary Neiss. He was foiled when Muller fell in love with the intended victim, alerted her that her boss wanted to murder her, and married her. It was a real fairy-tale ending.

The law caught up with Dr. Meyer and he went on trial for murder in New York on December 8, 1893. Muller testified against him under the promise that he would not be prosecuted for his minor role in the crime. A number of insurance experts and chemists also testified, as did the pharmacist who had sold Meyer the croton oil.

The trial was going along nicely—for the prosecution, that is, much less so for the defendant—when something strange occurred. On December 18 one of the jurors, Alexander B. Lowe, waggled his head from side to side; then he heaved his shoulders, shook violently, and went into convulsions. One lady in the courtroom peered through opera glasses to get a better view of the spectacle. A physician was called for—a physician other than Dr. Meyer, for some reason, even though he was conveniently present. Persons out in the corridors could hear Lowe ranting. He had been struck insane!

It was hoped Lowe's sanity would return so the trial could continue, but his case was hopeless and the judge had no choice but to dismiss the jury on December 21. Despite all the drama, Dr. Meyer was found guilty at his second trial and sent to Sing Sing.

Old habits die hard, and it appears that Dr. Meyer thought poison was the solution to all of life's problems. In October 1895, the warden confiscated letters the prisoner wrote in German to his wife, in which he urged her to poison some poor sap for insurance money, which she could then use to spring him out of prison. He even offered to send her a prescription for the poison.

The Martha Stewart of Murder

Ill-tempered Lafayette Taylor disappeared on January 25, 1903. The folks in Centerville Station assumed he had deserted his family, an action that would have been entirely in character.

On February 6, Mrs. Kate Taylor tried to sell one of her husband's horses to a local man, who refused to purchase it on the grounds that Taylor could return at any time and claim it. "Don't worry about that," said the none-too-crafty Mrs. Taylor. "I killed him and burned his body."

Naturally, this interesting story got around to the proper authorities, who asked the Taylors' fourteen-year-old daughter Ida May if it were true. She said it was, and Mrs. Taylor was duly arrested. She confessed on February 8, stating that her husband had come home on the night of January 25 drunk and abusive. She'd seized a revolver and tried to scare him with it. They'd grappled over the weapon. It'd gone off, and Lafayette Taylor died instantly from a bullet wound over his eye.

So there stood Mrs. Taylor on a cold winter's night with a murdered husband on the kitchen floor. What to do next? She was more than equal to the occasion; in fact, she became the Martha Stewart of murder. She burned the dead man's clothes in the kitchen stove. She transformed Mr. Taylor into smaller, more manageable pieces by beheading him and lopping off his right arm with an ax. She tossed the head and arm in the stove, after which she cut the rest of the body into four pieces, wrapped them in a sack, and placed them in the pantry. Over the next two days, she burned the remains in the stove a piece at a time. Then she ground up the charred bones and fed them to the family's chickens. She obliterated all bloodstains with a fresh coat of paint.

Kate Taylor prepared meals on the kitchen stove as usual, even while her husband's corpse was being cremated within. A jury found her guilty of first-degree murder on May 30 and sentenced her to be executed in the electric chair during the week of July 5. She was retried in May 1904; at that time, the daughter, Ida, testified that her uncle had helped cut up the body.

At the second trial, Mrs. Taylor's sentence was commuted to life in Auburn Prison. She was declared insane in July 1907 and died of consumption in the Matteawan State Hospital for the Criminally Insane on November 22, 1907.

Schmidt Out of Luck

Mary Bann was eighteen years old; her brother Albert, eleven. Their tar-paper shack was not an imposing home, but at least it was riverfront property, located across the Hudson from Woodcliff, New Jersey. On the morning of September 5, 1913, the siblings watched a brown paper parcel wrapped in twine lazily float by in the current. After some speculation as to what it might be, they lost interest and turned their attention to more pressing matters. They had no idea they had just played a part in the solution of a grotesque murder.

Around noon, Albert Bann saw the package again, this time snagged on driftwood at a dock in front of the family residence. Curious, the boy retrieved the wrapped object, no doubt hoping that it contained toys or candy apples. As a general rule, however, packages floating in rivers seldom contain pleasant things. After much wheedling Bann got his mother's permission to open his prize. When he removed the outer layer of brown wrapping paper, he saw a pillow with a floral design and red and blue stripes. Nestled among feathers inside it was the headless and armless upper torso of a woman, bisected at the waist and wrapped in an undergarment. The torso became an object of contemplation at a morgue in Hoboken, and Albert Bann was left shaking from a sight that haunted him the rest of his life.

County Physician George King opined that the woman's body had been dismembered with surgical skill. He estimated the woman had been about five feet four, weighed 120 pounds, and was between twenty and thirty years old. She had distinctive birthmarks on her right shoulder. She had probably been dead three or four days, and Dr. King thought that the remains had been in the Hudson a couple of days.

Though the detectives of 1913 did not have access to computer databases and DNA testing, they were far from helpless. The case of the "River Victim," as the *New York Times* called her, provides a striking example of how much could be accomplished in those days with old-fashioned detective work. It helped that the slayer seemed determined to provide the authorities with a cornucopia of clues. Detectives attempted to identify the undergarment found with the body but learned that it was impossible to trace, as similar garments had been made by a number of manufacturers of women's clothing. The law had better luck when Detective William Charlock inspected the pillow and found a label indicating that it was manufactured by the Robinson-Roders Company of Newark. Officials at the company claimed that that particular brand and size of pillow had sold poorly and was discontinued. The only order for it had been received from George Sachs, a secondhand furniture dealer located at 2762 Eighth Avenue, New York City, who had ordered merely a dozen of the pillows. Of these twelve, two had been sold to the public. Frustratingly, when the police visited the shop of the dealer, they found a sales receipt for only one of the pillows, and even that was incompletely filled out. Undaunted, detectives cased the neighborhood and found that the brown paper used to wrap the body parts had been bought at a drugstore across the street from Sachs's shop. The proprietor, S. H. Hurwitz, remembered the purchaser as the man seemed to be in a terrible hurry. He was about five feet seven and had a dark complexion and a closely cropped brown moustache. That the pillow and the wrapping paper were bought in the same neighborhood suggested that the crime had been committed nearby, perhaps within a few blocks.

The lower half of the dead woman's torso surfaced on September 7 at Weehawken, three miles downriver from Woodcliff, again wrapped in heavy brown paper and a newspaper dated August 31 and a pillowcase bearing the letter *A*, embroidered by an amateur rather than a professional, and therefore probably the initial of either the victim or the killer. Included with the lower torso was a nine-pound rock intended to keep the package from surfacing. Detectives determined that it was greenish-gray New York schist, common to Manhattan but not New Jersey. Thus they determined that the woman likely had been murdered in New York City. Dr. King noted that the two halves of the torso fit together like pieces of a jigsaw puzzle. Because the body appeared to have been dissected with a surgeon's saw, he believed at first that the young woman died "undergoing an operation," a euphemism for abortion. Closer inspection showed that the woman was pregnant at the time of death but had received no "surgery," unless one counts her slashed throat.

Most disturbing was the nearly total absence of blood in the woman's heart and arteries. Dr. King thought the poor woman might have been conscious as the killer amputated her limbs, and an examination of the lungs revealed that neither chloroform nor any other anesthetic had made her ordeal easier. Hemorrhage was the cause of death, but no one could say whether it had resulted from the cutting of the carotid artery in the neck during decapitation, the cutting of the brachial arteries when the arms were removed, the cutting of the femoral arteries when the legs were removed, the cutting of the abdominal aorta in the trunk when the body was bisected, or some combination of these ghastly injuries. Dr. King noted: "The blood flowed freely from each cut, and it is impossible to tell which came first. Any one would have caused death. The clean-cut character of the work and the speed with which it was done makes it certain that the murderer was trained to use a surgeon's knife and saw."

On September 10, another piece of the River Victim washed ashore at Keansburg, New Jersey, about twenty miles from Woodcliff: a fourteen-inch piece of leg, the bone neatly sawed through. The crime may have seemed insoluble, but five days later the mystery was no more.

It was the pillowcase that tripped up the killer. A more thorough examination of George Sachs's record books revealed the sale of two pillows and other furniture on August 25—only a few days before the estimated date of the murder—to an individual who lived in an apartment at 68 Bradhurst Avenue, New York. On September 8 detectives sought out the landlord, who told them that the man who rented and furnished the apartment had claimed that he was setting it up for a female relative who was about to be married. Police kept the apartment under constant surveillance for several days and grew weary when no one entered or exited. At last, on September 13, the authorities procured the key.

Few more suspicious-looking dwellings have been entered in the annals of American crime. The place was nearly bare of furniture and contained only a bed, a chair, a refrigerator, a stove, and a couple of trunks.

The bed's springs were present, but the mattress, pillow, and bedding were missing. Dark stains were on the green wallpaper of the bedroom and on the floor between the bedroom and the bathroom. Someone had industriously but ineffectually scrubbed the floor stain, as evidenced by a brush in the kitchen sink and six cakes of soap on the drain board. One of the trunks contained more than fifty letters and postcards written in German and addressed to a woman named Anna Aumuller. The other trunk held women's clothes, a fifteen-inch butcher knife, and a recently sharpened and cleaned steel handsaw. Several handkerchiefs were embroidered with the letter *A*, very similar in appearance to the monogram on the pillowcase that enclosed the River Victim's lower torso.

It was high time to find the man who rented the apartment. He'd given his name to the landlord as Rev. Hans Schmidt. A few hours after the search of the apartment, Inspector Joseph Faurot and Detective Frank Cassassa found him at Saint Joseph's Church at 405 West 125th Street, where he served as assistant pastor. (Church officials were understandably reluctant to admit that Schmidt was an ordained member of the clergy. Monsignor Lavelle, vicar general of the Archdiocese of New York, expressed the hope that Schmidt was an impostor. Later research proved that Schmidt had once been an authentic priest in Germany but had come to Saint Joseph's with forged ordination papers.)

Schmidt confessed immediately after being confronted by the detectives. They did not even need to take him to the police station; he broke down and admitted his guilt in the church rectory. The River Victim was indeed Anna Aumuller. As Schmidt spoke with the detectives, he revealed bits of his own life story. The remarkable villain had been born into a respected middle-class family in Aschaffenburg, Germany, in 1881. He'd shown a youthful interest in joining the priesthood and when he'd turned eighteen, he went to Saint Augustine's Seminary in Mainz, where he was given the nickname "the Mad Doctor." Some former acquaintances claimed his heart was not truly in a religious vocation and he pursued the priesthood only to please his mother, resulting in his living "a notoriously dissolute life" while there. His misdeeds included forging documents for his fellow seminary students and manufacturing bogus medical school diplomas.

Schmidt managed to hide his iniquity from the church authorities and he was ordained a priest by the bishop of Mainz in 1904. Schmidt sometimes claimed that the ceremony had been performed by Saint Elizabeth, patron saint of Hungary, notwithstanding the fact that she'd died in the year 1231. He had served at churches in Darmstadt and Burgel, but ran afoul of the law several times for fraud. He'd narrowly missed serving a jail term in Burgel; the courts acquitted him on grounds of insanity on January 29, 1909. Later that year, his earlier sins caught up with him and he was suspended from the priesthood for fraudulently obtaining a chaplaincy. (Though he was no longer a priest, once he became notorious the press insisted on referring to him as Reverend Schmidt anyway. The confusion may have been unavoidable since he continued to pass himself off as a priest.)

Humiliated, he immigrated to America by steamer. He lived in New York City briefly and then moved to Louisville, Kentucky, where he remained from August 1909 until March 1910. In December 1909, the dismembered remains of eight-year-old Alma Kellner were found in the basement of Saint John's Catholic Church. The finger of suspicion fell on Schmidt after he confessed to Aumuller's murder, but he had not worked at Saint John's and it was never proved that he had committed the earlier homicide.

After moving from Louisville to Trenton, New Jersey, Schmidt worked at Saint Francis's Church. In December 1910, he performed a wedding ceremony without seeking the authority of the diocese. He was fired by Bishop McFaul, whose letter of termination read: "You are hereby notified to leave the diocese immediately. It is evident that you are wanting in common sense and, therefore, I do not desire to have anything more to do with you." Schmidt moved back to New York. Beginning in December 1910, he was assistant to Rev. J. S. Braun, rector of Saint Boniface's Church at Forty-Seventh and Second Avenue. There he met Aumuller, who had moved to America in 1908. She had been employed as a maid at Saint Boniface's from December 1912 to August 1913, but Rev. Braun discharged her "because he was not satisfied with her way of life," implying some sort of moral turpitude. Schmidt, however, was taken with the attractive twenty-one-year-old and became her clandestine lover. In November 1912, he left Saint Boniface's for Saint Joseph's, where he continued to work until his arrest on the morning of September 14.

After she met Schmidt, Anna Aumuller lived a shadowy life. He secretly married her on February 26, 1913, in a ceremony officiated by himself out of fear he would be expelled from the church if it were known that he was married. In order to prevent anyone from finding out, he kept his bride hidden away in the squalid Bradhurst Avenue apartment. The marriage was as unhappy as it was brief, and just before midnight on September 2, Schmidt murdered the sleeping Anna by cutting her throat. "She never knew what happened," he insisted, swearing that her death had been nearly instantaneous and not the prolonged torture investigators suspected. Then he cut the body in seven pieces in the bathtub, wrapped the portions in blankets, and added schist rocks to weigh the bundles down. On four successive nights, he dropped them into the river from the side of the Fort Lee ferry.

Displaying the bewildering mixture of cleverness and foolishness that marked most of his actions, he put himself in peril when he dragged the bloodstained mattress out of the apartment one dark night and tried to set fire to it in what he thought was a vacant lot between 151st and 152nd Streets; several apartment dwellers came out to watch as the fire blazed up more brightly than Schmidt anticipated. While he disposed of the mattress, in another corner of the lot several hundred potential witnesses sat under a tent, listening to an evangelist. Schmidt could not exactly be dubbed a criminal genius. After hearing his confession, police went to the lot and found most of the mattress still there, as well as burned fragments of Aumuller's leg and bits of the telltale pillowcase.

Schmidt seemed pleased to discuss his dark deeds, readily telling the police precise details about how he killed Aumuller and disposed of her body. However, there was one matter he was reluctant to illuminate: his motive. When asked, he would say, "I loved her." Schmidt remarked to Father Luke Evers, the chaplain who visited his cell in the Tombs Prison: "I was in love with the girl and I wanted her to go to heaven. It was necessary to make a sacrifice, and the sacrifice had to be consummated in blood in the same manner as Abraham was going to sacrifice Isaac." When the chaplain—who must have been a detective at heart—asked why he thought it also necessary to dismember his beloved sacrifice and throw the carefully wrapped portions into the Hudson, Schmidt replied nonsensically about how the water was essential to make the sections of Anna go into "clouds of eternity." Despite the crazy talk, it was not difficult to guess his probable motive: Aumuller threatened to make their marriage public knowledge.

As if the evidence found in the apartment were not sufficient to hang the former reverend several times over, more incriminating items were found in his quarters at Saint Joseph's, including the keys to the apartment and two of Aumuller's rings, including her wedding band. Physicians who examined Aumuller's remains thought she was dissected by a professional surgeon; Schmidt claimed that he had studied surgery back in Germany. In the rectory, detectives found five hundred business cards reading: "Dr. Emil Moliere, formerly Assistant Surgeon of the Municipal Women's Hospital, Paris, France. Representative of the Chemical Hygienic Manufacturing Company."

Schmidt confessed that "Emil Moliere" was one of his many aliases and that the cards were for his personal use. Detectives found that he sold "preparations familiar in criminal medical practice" (i.e., abortions) and that his room contained bottles of illegally manufactured patent medicines. In other words, the reverend of dubious standing also posed as a doctor. To Father Evers he explained why he'd become a freelance abortionist: "My mission was to prevent children from being born into a life of misery." Inspector Faurot noticed that Schmidt was hesitant to talk about his fraudulent medical career and suspected that the reluctance was founded in numerous crimes as yet undetected.

Detectives received surprises on a daily basis as they investigated Schmidt. On September 15, they discovered that in addition to being a fake priest, a fake doctor, and a genuine murderer, Schmidt was a counterfeiter. In his room the authorities found a rental receipt for a second apartment, this one located on West 134th Street, and there they found a color-printing press, copper engraving plates, and some drying, incomplete ten-dollar bills. Obviously unaware of the economic truth that the more money there is in circulation, the less valuable it becomes, the former priest made the ingenious claim that he had wanted to print his own money and give it to the poor to relieve their financial distress. Schmidt might have counted himself as one of the needy, for there were accusations that he kept money donated as Easter offerings for his own use. Payments for wedding and baptismal ceremonies that he performed were supposed to go to the church, but instead went straight to Schmidt's bank account. Allegedly, he'd once picked a fellow clergyman's pocket to the tune of $400.

Another arrest was imminent: that of Dr. Ernest Arthur Muret, a disreputable dentist with an office at 301 Saint Nicholas Avenue. Muret had no license to practice dentistry but had studied the subject for a couple of years back in his native Germany, so he was just as qualified to call himself a dentist as Schmidt was to call himself a doctor. The top-hatted Muret was the picture of indignation when first arrested but became penitent when he realized the weight of the evidence against him. He confessed that he was Schmidt's partner and equal when it came to cheating the Treasury Department but denied having anything to do with the murder of Anna Aumuller, even though obstetrical instruments and books on gynecology found in his dentist's office suggested that he'd helped Schmidt perform "criminal operations." A day later Muret denied even being in on the counterfeiting, but detectives proved he had purchased the printing press under a pseudonym. He also found it a trifle difficult to explain a letter found in his pocket when he was arrested from a printing firm concerning the price of ink rollers. Muret countered that he had bought several items for Schmidt but had no idea what they were to be used for. Considering that the material Muret "innocently" purchased included a printing press, copper plates, bond paper, engraving tools, various inks, and a specially constructed camera popular among counterfeiters, we must conclude that either Muret was a manufacturer of currency or he was the dumbest man ever to wear a top hat and pretend to be a dentist. Schmidt assured authorities that Muret was innocent of murder. His word was hardly credible, since he also said that Muret was not a counterfeiter despite overwhelming evidence to the contrary.

It took detectives a few days to sort through the trunks and bureau drawers in Schmidt and Muret's apartment/counterfeiting headquarters, and while doing so they got another surprise. It was announced on September 18 that a *third* apartment rented by Schmidt had been located at 2562 Eighth Avenue. Schmidt hoped to confuse the police by smuggling murder evidence to this site but gave up his plan when the discovery of Anna Aumuller's body made the headlines. At the third apartment detectives found letters indicating that Schmidt's friend Muret had been wanted by Scotland Yard since 1911 on charges of fraud, white slavery, distributing pornography, and practicing medicine without a license. He had been living at various addresses under various names, much to the distress of his wife back in Europe. (He went by so many aliases that his real name remains a minor mystery; it may have been Arnold Held, Hermann Arthur Heibing, or Adolph Mueller.)

The former priest's trunk yielded yet another find for investigators: a number of blank board of health forms and four copies of a death certificate for sixty-nine-year-old Robert Smith, retired businessman, who'd died of heart failure at his home on April 29, 1913. The unfrocked, unqualified Schmidt had given Smith the last rites and officiated at his funeral. Somehow Schmidt had managed to obtain the death certificate. A professional photographer claimed that Schmidt, dressed in priest's vestments, had hired him to make four photographs of the certificate. Inspector Faurot, keeping in mind Schmidt's long history of forgery, suspected that he'd intended to make false death certificates. This prospect opened a new field of speculation: had Schmidt intended to create a death certificate for the missing Anna Aumuller? If so, did he plan to stop there or would he have created a cottage industry of murder, possibly with assistance from Muret? Detectives recalled the case of the notorious Chicago murderer H. H. Holmes, who twenty years before had done away with inconvenient though heavily insured persons and then enriched himself via forged death certificates. Holmes made a small fortune until the noose caught up with him in 1896.

On September 19, Schmidt admitted that "he had intended to use the blank death certificates in his room to make the official records show that a number of his parishioners and others, whom he meant to murder, had died of natural causes," as the *New York Times* summarized it without clarifying who the "others" were. Schmidt intended to turn in a spurious death certificate for Anna Aumuller but had not counted on her severed body parts coming back to haunt him. When his handiwork made the headlines, he thought it wise to keep a low profile. But to keep people from getting the wrong idea about him, Schmidt hastened to assure detectives that his intention was to painlessly murder "persons who would be better off in the other world." A true philanthropist, it seems, is willing to cut the throat of a sleeping woman and mutilate her corpse. He explained: "I meant to end the suffering of cripples, paralytics, persons suffering from incurable ailments, and others who were leading miserable lives and would be better off out of the world. Any man is foolish who wishes to live out his life on earth. I meant to benefit those I killed."

Schmidt unwittingly offered an insight into his shrewdness when he added that it would have been easy to lure victims into his apartments, since "no one would suspect harm from a priest." Whether he meant to seek permission from these wretched souls before doing them the favor of dispatching them, he did not say. Hans Schmidt's gusto for abortion and euthanasia made him a man well ahead of his time, but of course the great humanitarian had no objection to making a few quick bucks from his good deeds; otherwise, he would not have bothered with acquiring the blank death certificates and board of health forms. That greed was his chief motivator became evident on September 22, when a doctor told Inspector Faurot that Schmidt had tried to entice him into joining the plot. Schmidt had admitted to the physician that he was in it to collect insurance money.

Schmidt declared that Anna Aumuller was his sole victim, but the implication was clear: society had just been spared a murder spree. Detectives were not willing to take the prisoner's word for it that he'd killed only one woman, particularly since his correspondence revealed that he'd brought a second woman to America. Like Aumuller, she appeared to have been involved in a sham marriage with Schmidt. To this woman, he had posed not as a priest but as a professor of philosophy. She'd last written to him in 1911 and had not been seen since. The police found her impossible to track down since she'd signed her letters only with her first name, and her fate remains a mystery.

On September 23, Schmidt and Muret were indicted by the federal grand jury on a charge of counterfeiting. Schmidt never was tried for counterfeiting as he had to face the more serious charge of murder, for which he was indicted on September 27. As the date of the murder inquest drew near, the coroner Israel Feinberg expressed a determination to have the jury made up of powerful celebrities, such as J. P. Morgan and Cornelius Vanderbilt, because "matters of such weight would be involved at the inquest that it would take men of large affairs to figure them out properly." Why the coroner felt rich men were uniquely qualified to deliver a fair vote he left to the imaginations of *Times* readers. One suspects that he just wanted to meet celebrities. Feinberg went so far as to issue subpoenas for seventy-eight prominent New Yorkers to serve as a pool from which a jury could be selected. Some thought this absurd, considering that the duty of the inquest is simply to determine cause of death, and Feinberg was roundly jeered in Gotham's press. Morgan, Vanderbilt, and the richest man in the world, John D. Rockefeller, respectfully declined to fulfill their civic obligations, but enough celebrities answered the call to make Feinberg's stunt successful. When the coroner's inquest convened on October 3, the jury included financier Vincent Astor, railroad magnate Theodore P. Shonts, theater impresario Marcus Loew, and others whose fame has not stood the test of time. The audience in the courtroom could not resist gasping and snickering when Feinberg dropped a broad hint to the wealthy jury members that they should help pay the expenses of Anna Aumuller's burial.

Schmidt was present in the courtroom at Feinberg's insistence, even though Feinberg had been advised against it by both Schmidt's attorney and District Attorney Charles Whitman. When the prisoner heard the commotion in the courtroom, he leaped angrily to his feet and threw the contents of his pocket at the spectators: a handful of coins, rosary beads, and a dollar bill. A silver half-dollar hit one man in the temple with sufficient force to draw blood. After the spectators recovered from their astonishment, human nature took over and they dove to the floor and collected Schmidt's missiles to save as souvenirs. Court attendants ordered that the prisoner's property be restored to him, but a few people secretly pocketed their mementos. Perhaps some of Schmidt's coins and beads still exist as cherished family heirlooms.

Was Schmidt insane or was the coin throwing a ploy to fake insanity before the court? In either case, the illustrious jury determined that Anna Aumuller had been murdered and that Schmidt was the culprit. He would stand trial for murder in November unless it could be proved that he was insane at the time of the slaying.

Let us summarize the fate of Schmidt's partner, Dr. Muret, and then return to the chief villain of the piece. No direct evidence was found linking Muret to the murder of Aumuller, and when called to testify, Schmidt tried to exonerate the dentist from the counterfeiting charges. The jury would have none of it, and on October 28, Muret was sentenced to eight years in the federal prison at Atlanta for possession of counterfeiting equipment. He was lucky not to have faced more serious charges.

One of the great facets of American life is that even the lowest of low-lifes can win the free services of a first-rate defense attorney. True, the perpetrator of the run-of-the-mill homicide may have to take his chances with a court-appointed attorney, but if the crime is unusually heinous and generating sensational headlines, lawyers will line up for the honor of defending the murderer though they would move heaven and earth to avoid having him as a next-door neighbor.

Hans Schmidt attracted the notice of Alphonse Koelble, attorney and president of the German-American Citizens' League, who stood by his client at the coroner's inquest, at the grand jury trial held a few days later, and right on to the bitter end of the legal process. Koelble was convinced that Schmidt was insane, a reasonable belief. Less rational was Koelble's contention that the police could not prove that the body was Anna Aumuller's, despite the fact that she had disappeared from the face of the earth and her apartment had been decorated recently with a fresh coating of blood. After all, said Koelble, the corpse's head had not yet turned up. All the police had were a torso and a leg, and those were not enough to make a positive identification. Unfortunately for Koelble's case, a young woman came forth and advised the police to look for a brown mark on the torso. She was Anna Hirt, and she had been a servant at Saint Boniface's Church alongside Anna Aumuller. The authorities, who had overlooked the mole, checked the body and found it in the exact location described by Hirt. That pretty well clinched matters—that, and Schmidt's eager confession.

Observers were divided as to the prisoner's mental state. Koelble thought he was insane; so did Deputy Commissioner of Correction Wright and Warden John Fallon of the Tombs, who believed that Schmidt was the most dangerous lunatic he had ever seen. Another person convinced of Schmidt's insanity was his cellmate, Thomas Messmer, who also was being held for murdering and dismembering his wife. He got solitary confinement after convincing the jailhouse authorities that he had spent the most terrifying night of his life in the company of Schmidt. Messmer's breaking point came when he asked his cellmate why he had killed Anna Aumuller.

"I killed her because I loved her," Schmidt replied. Then he seized Messmer's hands and added: "I love you too."

Schmidt's relatives in Aschaffenburg claimed that insanity ran in his family. Several members had spent time in asylums and four had committed suicide since 1908; two others had tried and failed. Dr. Gustave Scholer, an alienist and neurologist at Washington Heights Hospital, examined Schmidt on September 21 and, after giving the case some thought, became convinced that the prisoner was insane. Before Scholer, Schmidt proudly defended his schemes to help the poor, the halt, and the world-weary through benevolent homicide. It was true, he said, that he had slept with women after becoming a priest, and he felt remorseful for those immoral acts. But the murder-and-counterfeiting plan could *not* be wrong, for it was divinely inspired! Schmidt became infuriated when Dr. Scholer questioned him, offended that anyone would dare suggest he was not in his right mind. He got so angry that several times guards had to keep him under control. However, note that Schmidt left out the part about personally profiting from his intended crimes.

Assistant District Attorney Deacon Murphy, Coroner Feinberg, and Inspector Faurot thought Schmidt was legally sane. Two physicians who met the defrocked priest in late September 1913 agreed that he was "shamming." District Attorney Whitman hired two respected alienists, Dr. William Mabon and Dr. Carlos MacDonald, whom we shall meet again in a later story. They, along with Drs. A. Ross Diefendorff and George Kirby, appraised the prisoner's mental state several times over the course of several weeks. The report was sealed by Whitman, but it was no secret that the four alienists had found Schmidt sane and fit to stand trial.

These conflicting opinions came pretrial; once Schmidt's life was actually on the line, the experts became more combative. Still, the weight of the evidence suggested that Schmidt, while not mentally normal, was sane. He suffered from delusions but could speak rationally when he felt like it. A postcard Schmidt recently had sent to his parents revealed that he had been planning to flee the country and move back home, implying that he knew his actions were wrong and he intended to avoid facing the consequences. He showed cunning by renting three apartments; Inspector Faurot found it significant that when confessing, Schmidt did not mention the third apartment, where he had intended to stash evidence, probably because "he realized that the caution and foresight shown in his attempt to hide incriminating evidence would be inconsistent with the irrational style of conversation which he has used since his arrest." Two policemen who questioned Schmidt, Capt. J. J. Henry and Chief William Flynn, noticed that he spoke clearly and rationally whenever they questioned him; he only blathered about blood sacrifices and the like whenever officials from the Tombs spoke with him. Flynn also pointed out that Schmidt's counterfeiting scheme was a pretty sophisticated undertaking for a crazy man. Long before his arrest, Schmidt gave speeches in churches and parish houses on subjects on which he was allegedly unbalanced, such as religion and social problems; listeners remembered his lectures as being quite rational. A lawyer working for the district attorney made a logical point: "If Schmidt were truly insane, his delusions would certainly have found their way into his sermons. He would have mentioned his belief that he was under the direction of Saint Elizabeth and his views on human sacrifice while he was a free man, instead of developing them immediately upon his arrest for murder."

Schmidt's attorney Koelble countered that if his client were such a clever archcriminal, why had he been an impoverished failure for most of his life? Why would he murder a poor girl like Anna Aumuller if money had been his object? But Koelble overlooked the fact that although Schmidt happened to be broke at the time of his arrest, he had been well-to-do in the past. After all, he had had sufficient capital to buy a printing press and other equipment necessary for counterfeiting, to give Muret a loan of $300, and to rent three apartments. In addition, Schmidt had stolen money intended for church use. As for Aumuller, it was possible that Schmidt had murdered her not for money but for a more obvious motive: she was pregnant and eager to tell the world about their secret marriage.

When the grand jury indicted Schmidt on October 10, the prisoner seemed delighted. Despite Koelble's best efforts to the contrary, Schmidt repeatedly expressed a hope that he would die in the electric chair at Sing Sing. "I know I am guilty and everybody else knows," he had said. "The District Attorney wants me to go to the electric chair and I want to go myself. Then why should there be any delay?" On another occasion he told his attorney Koelble that he would rather face a quick death in the chair than spend life in a prison or an asylum. When Schmidt was arraigned in the Court of General Sessions on October 20, he pled guilty. Koelble interrupted the proceedings by asking that the plea be changed to not guilty by reason of insanity, which Judge Warren Foster granted. He also allowed Koelble to form a commission to hear from Schmidt's relatives concerning his lack of sanity. To this end, Assistant DA Deacon Murphy set sail for Germany to gather testimony from various Schmidts and examine the police record the prisoner had amassed before moving to America.

It should be noted that the precise legal question at hand was not whether Schmidt was *presently* insane, but whether he had been insane at the moment when he'd murdered Anna Aumuller. Schmidt would never go to trial if the latter could be proved. The defense requested that a lunacy commission be appointed to examine Schmidt, but after reading testimony from alienists on both sides, Judge Foster denied the appeal. The murder trial began on December 8, largely attended by women, "most of whom were chewing gum," added the *New York Times*'s disgusted reporter, implying that the habit was a sure sign of moral bankruptcy. This time no celebrities served on the jury, though one almost did: the novelist George Barr McCutcheon, author of *Brewster's Millions*. The defense dismissed him with a peremptory challenge when he admitted that he believed Schmidt guilty and would be unable to set aside his opinion. When Schmidt was brought into the courtroom, he appeared to be mental illness personified. He'd let his hair and beard grow long during his months at the Tombs, and his head wobbled constantly back and forth. Some spectators were unkind enough to think that Schmidt was putting on a show to save his hide. Court officials, remembering how he had behaved at the coroner's inquest, stationed a beefy guard beside him.

The battle between the psychiatrists hired by the defense and the prosecution began anew. The defense offered professional testimony in the form of Drs. Smith E. Jelliffe and William A. White, who believed that Schmidt suffered from dementia praecox, the old-fashioned name for schizophrenia. For good measure, the defense added testimony from two of the ex-priest's family members, who traveled from Germany to state under oath that he had been crazy from childhood. On the opposing side, Drs. MacDonald, Mabon, Diefendorff, and Kirby represented the state in their adamant belief that the prisoner was "shamming."

Assistant District Attorney James Delehanty began the trial by calling Schmidt evil rather than crazy. His murder of Anna Aumuller had nothing to do with his religious beliefs and everything to do with her inconvenient pregnancy. Schmidt had impregnated Aumuller once before and sent her to Austria for an abortion; she'd returned to Schmidt and their "secret marriage," annoyed that she could not openly live with her husband and had to work as a servant. She became pregnant a second time and threatened to make their marriage public. This was too much for Schmidt, who turned to his butcher knife and handsaw. The accused was not insane at the time of the murder, thundered Delehanty, because he had displayed knowledge of his misdeeds and tried to avoid capture by dissecting her body and disposing of the evidence.

The defense countered with testimony from Joseph Eigler, Aumuller's cousin. Several months before Anna was murdered, Schmidt had told her that God had commanded him to sacrifice her. Eigler knew this because Aumuller herself had told him so. Another witness was Dr. Arnold Leo, who testified that Aumuller told him that Schmidt was "holy-crazy" and that she was afraid of him. The doctor had personally witnessed Schmidt's unconventional behavior: once when making a house call at the rectory, he saw the pseudopriest "for no apparent reason" jump up and grab a zither, which he played with passion. After a few minutes Schmidt sat down and spoke like a rational being. On another occasion Schmidt expressed a desire to go sea bathing in March, which his physician gravely advised was a foolish risk.

Schmidt's father and sister testified via an interpreter that as a child he'd seen visions, played at being a priest (complete with homemade costume), and "had a mania for cutting the heads from his mother's geese, drinking their blood and pretending to perform religious ceremonies with it." He enjoyed visiting slaughterhouses because he "liked to see blood." In addition, the defense read the depositions collected in Germany from Schmidt's friends and acquaintances, who thought he was eccentric at best and mentally irresponsible at worst. The point of the testimony was to show that Schmidt had been delusional long before his arrest.

On cross-examination, Schmidt's sister admitted that she had been reluctant to call him insane when the American investigator interviewed her. She also clarified that her family had not been alarmed at little Hans's displays of religious fervor; in fact, they had been rather proud of his precocity and enthusiasm. More testimony favorable to Schmidt came from Dr. Perry Lichtenstein, physician at the Tombs and an examiner in lunacy for the state of New York, who believed that Schmidt was insane based on conversations he had with the prisoner in which he claimed that God had commanded him to sacrifice his more-or-less legal wife. However, his testimony had less force than that of Joseph Eigler and Dr. Leo, who spoke with Anna Aumuller personally; Dr. Lichtenstein got all his information from Schmidt, who for all anyone knew was putting on an act.

At last came the testimony from the professional alienists. On December 22, Dr. Jelliffe told the court that in his opinion, Schmidt was insane. He described what the former priest told him of "the life he had led for years." The papers were not specific, but the details that leaked out from earlier court sessions ensured that only seven women attended court that day, chewing gum or not. Whatever Dr. Jelliffe revealed must have been bloodcurdling as one woman spectator fainted and had to be placed in the care of a physician. On a more wholesome note, Dr. Jelliffe mentioned Schmidt's habit of playing violin while in the bathtub. Schmidt had proudly told the doctor about his career as a counterfeiter and a forger, explaining that since he was divinely inspired he was above the law. The next day Dr. White of the United States Hospital for the Insane at Washington and Dr. Henry Cotton of the New Jersey State Hospital concurred that Schmidt was a paranoid schizophrenic. Attorney Koelble considered letting Schmidt take the stand, believing that if the jurors were given a chance to hear him expound upon his religious beliefs, they would agree that he was insane, but he changed his mind. Perhaps Schmidt refused to take the stand, as he resented being called insane. He protested vigorously when his other attorney, a former judge named W. M. K. Olcott, stated to the jury: "I will show that the defendant is now and always will be mentally unbalanced and legally insane." Was Schmidt genuinely crazy or was it a shrewd scheme by a sane man to convince the jury of his insanity by vehemently denying the one tactic that would save his life?

On December 24, the government got its chance to rebut. At the beginning of the trial, the prosecution contended that Schmidt had indeed considered Anna Aumuller a sacrificial animal of sorts—a cash cow. An insurance company physician testified that in April, five months before the murder, Schmidt had attempted to insure her life for $5,000. This revelation did not please the defense, as it enveloped his alleged insanity in an earthbound aura of greed. Dr. MacDonald took the stand and acknowledged that Schmidt had told him that he'd sacrificed Aumuller on orders from God. However, noted MacDonald, Schmidt had hesitated several weeks before committing the murder, which "indicated that he understood the nature of the deed he was contemplating" and therefore was not insane. He doubted that Schmidt suffered from schizophrenia as he did not have the classic symptoms of memory loss, inability to concentrate, and "a general weakening of the faculties." To the contrary, Dr. MacDonald believed that Schmidt came across as a man of superior intelligence. The famous alienist noticed also that Schmidt's visions increased whenever he realized he was being tested. The state's other three experts agreed; one, Dr. Kirby of the Manhattan State Hospital, testified that Schmidt's mind "worked rapidly and gave no indication of abnormality." The prosecution's alienists had grave doubts about Schmidt's inconsistency; he displayed the symptoms of so many different forms of insanity that the jury was obliged to believe either that he was acting or that he suffered from an unprecedented multitude of disorders at the same time.

The case went to the jury on December 29, 1913. It was not a question of innocence or guilt; the defense acknowledged that the accused had committed the murder. Rather, it was a question of his sanity at the time of the slaying. Judge Foster instructed the members that if, on the one hand, they had any doubt about Schmidt's mental state, it was their duty to acquit him due to insanity. On the other hand, "If the prisoner, at the time of committing the crime, knew the nature and quality of his act he must be held responsible. If the defendant knew that the act was wrong and that the law forbade it, the plea of insanity is no defense." While it is unwise to psychoanalyze Schmidt at a distance of over a century, it is evident that despite the disturbing eccentricities he had displayed since childhood, he was aware of the nature of his crime when he cut Anna Aumuller's throat. The murder was coolly premeditated, since he collected wrapping paper, twine, and cutting implements beforehand. It was committed not by a frenzied madman but by a man in control of his actions and aware of the possible consequences if he were caught. He took great care to rent a private location, made efforts to clean up afterward, dismembered and disposed of the body, and attempted to destroy other evidence, such as the bloody mattress. But the jury was confused by the judge's simple instructions, and it was reported twice that the members were hopelessly deadlocked. In the wee hours of the morning the stymied jury voted nine to three for conviction. A *New York Times* reporter observed that the alleged lunatic Schmidt, whose professed ambition was to go to the electric chair, "was visibly relieved at each announcement of a disagreement." After thirty-four hours of deliberation in a frigid jury room, the jury was still unable to get past a vote of ten to two for conviction. On December 30, Judge Foster discharged the jury with thanks and sent Schmidt back to the Tombs. He would have to be tried again.

The second trial began in the criminal term of the supreme court, with Justice Vernon M. Davis presiding, on January 21, 1914. Due to the graphic nature of the testimony, women were warned not to attend. The second trial was brisk since witnesses' statements were largely a repeat of the earlier hearing and both sides agreed to present only two alienists apiece. Again, the defense's strategy was to enter a plea of not guilty due to insanity. Drs. Smith Jelliffe and M. S. Gregory testified for the defense. The former made the not terribly brilliant point that "as a rule, Schmidt had been unable to answer correctly some very simple questions in arithmetic, history and geography which the alienists had put to him," as though it would be difficult for Schmidt to give intentionally wrong answers to simple questions. About a week into the trial Schmidt's new attorney, Terence J. McManus, presented to Dr. Jelliffe a hypothetical question 150 pages long. History does not record whether the doctor gave a 150-page reply, but it would have been a great moment in courtroom comedy if he answered with a simple yes or no.

Although it was a rehash, the second trial had dramatic moments. It was revealed that Dr. Lichtenstein, the Tombs physician and therefore an employee of the city, had given his notes on Schmidt to the defense but did not share them with the prosecution. A new witness with the cacophonous name Bertha Zech, former servant of the imprisoned Dr. Muret, testified that Schmidt persuaded her to impersonate Anna Aumuller when he made an unsuccessful attempt to buy life insurance for Aumuller in April 1913. Since Schmidt was to be the beneficiary, it cast doubt on the sincerity of his claim that he believed God had ordered him to commit a blood sacrifice.

The case went to the jury on February 5, and this time the verdict came quickly and forcefully: Schmidt was guilty of murder in the first degree. If he was disappointed, he covered it by laughing and telling his attorney Koelble that he would oppose any appeals since he wanted to die in the chair. Against the prisoner's wishes—or, at least, his *expressed* wishes—Koelble vowed that he would take his client's case to the New York Court of Appeals.

Justice Davis sentenced Schmidt to be executed during the week of March 23. As the prisoner was taken from the Tombs to Sing Sing, he left behind a verse from James Montgomery's "The Issues of Life and Death":

> *Beyond this vale of tears*
> *There is a life above,*
> *Unmeasured by the flight of years*
> *And all that life is love.*

Once on death row, Schmidt changed his tune. Despite his voluntary confession, the mountain of evidence against him and his repeatedly stated desire to take leave of this wicked world by way of the hot seat, in March 1914, he wrote a letter to District Attorney Whitman and Governor Glynn contradicting everything he had hitherto claimed. He now said he was not a murderer; Aumuller had died from a botched abortion, and he had only been trying to protect the guilty parties by disposing of the body and falsely taking credit for the crime. He named a doctor, a dentist, and a young woman as the real culprits. Schmidt even admitted faking insanity and asked the governor to spare his life by commuting his sentence to life in prison. Attorney Koelble's expression when he learned of this turn of events must have been worth walking ten miles to see.

The authorities spent two months investigating the prisoner's claim and proved that the three persons named by Schmidt in his letter were innocent. Koelble told the press that he would have Schmidt's claims presented in an affidavit and would use it as a basis for a new appeal. In other words, Koelble took a letter proven to be full of lies, turned it into a legal document, and used it as grounds to argue in favor of a reduced sentence for his client. A precarious maneuver, one might think, but as late as October Koelble was arguing on Schmidt's behalf in the court of appeals, whose judges unanimously upheld Schmidt's conviction and death sentence. Koelble made a motion to appeal anyway. The court refused to grant a new hearing, and the revised date of execution was set for January 1916.

Koelble was nothing if not determined, and somehow he managed to win a thirty-day reprieve for Schmidt during which he made an appeal although the motion had already been denied. This time he took his appeal to the Supreme Court of the United States, which refused to hear it. The only hope left was that the governor would grant executive clemency. The condemned man's lot seemed to improve when the governor promised to hear arguments from Schmidt's attorneys.

As is true of nearly every murderer, Schmidt had misguided sympathizers. "Killing Schmidt won't bring his victim back!" was their battle cry, as though a life sentence in prison would be any more effective at resurrecting Anna Aumuller. Some complained that poor Schmidt was being picked on by those bullies of the American legal system because he was an immigrant, and worse, he was a German at a time when the Great War was making Germans unpopular in the United States. Of course, it was difficult to claim with a straight face that prejudice against Germans was responsible for Schmidt's plight since he had been arrested in 1913, a year before the war started; his victim also was German; the courts had jumped through hoops to grant his defense every imaginable delay to provide sufficient time to present an effective case; and he had won a stay of execution. Rather than sensibly investing in munitions factories, Americans who were convinced of his insanity created a $15,000 fund for his defense during his first trial, and contributed another $10,000 during his second. Schmidt had supporters right to the end among those who argue with more passion than sense.

The former priest's attorneys pled their case before the governor in February. Despite their best efforts, he found no compelling reason to grant executive clemency and the jig was officially up for Hans Schmidt. At daybreak on February 18, 1916, he was led to the electric chair by guards, prison officials, and a priest—the state supplied a real one, let it be noted. After the requisite three jolts, Schmidt was declared dead. But he could not keep silent even in death. Through Koelble, the late Schmidt issued a statement to the press claiming again that he was guilty only of disposing of Anna Aumuller's body and went to his grave to protect her abortionist. He painted himself as a martyr and expressed distaste for his impending execution—a curious thing, given his former enthusiasm for the subject: "I happen to be the victim this time, and I hope and pray that time will prove every one of my contentions and that my judicial murder will help to abolish executions, for not one-third of the men who have been in the death chamber with me . . . were guilty of murder." Presumably Schmidt looked deep into the souls of his fellow convicts to declare their innocence with such sublime confidence. His prayer was not answered, for in the ensuing years no evidence ever turned up pointing to another suspect.

A footnote to the case: the Catholic church had a spiritual and legal problem to solve in the wake of Schmidt's arrest. Were the marriages, baptisms, and other rites performed by Schmidt while he'd masqueraded as a priest to be considered legitimate? It was decided that since the participants in the ceremonies had honestly thought Schmidt was a priest, the rites were valid. Likely some couples had the ceremony performed quietly a second time just to be on the safe side.

A Locked-Room Mystery

Writers of detective fiction consider the ultimate achievement a locked-room mystery with a logical, satisfying solution. In this sort of story, the murder victim is found in a sealed room to which, seemingly, no one could have had access. Classic examples include Edgar Allan Poe's "The Murders in the Rue Morgue," Sir Arthur Conan Doyle's Sherlock Holmes story "The Adventure of the Speckled Band," and Agatha Christie's novels *Hercule Poirot's Christmas* and *Murder on the Orient Express*.

One of New York City's most baffling murders was a real-life locked-room mystery. The humble Fifth Avenue Laundry was located in Harlem at 4 East 132nd Street. It was on the ground floor of a five-story tenement building occupied entirely by blacks, and the operator was a reclusive thirty-year-old Jew named Isidore Fink. One resident, Mrs. Locklan

Smith, lived in an apartment directly behind the shop. Around ten thirty p.m. on March 9, 1929, Mrs. Smith heard screams and the sound of blows issuing from the laundry. She found Patrolman Albert Kattenborn and returned to the scene with him.

As befits a locked-room mystery, when Kattenborn inspected the location he found that the door and all windows were locked tight, as was Fink's habit when he worked late, according to shoemaker Max Schwartz, with whom Fink shared quarters at 52 East 126th Street. Fink was terrified of robbers. The laundry's rear window was covered by iron bars so close together that "even a child couldn't squeeze through," as a reporter wrote. The only entrance was through the open transom over the front door, and Kattenborn could not fit through it. He had to lower a boy through the transom. Once inside, the boy pulled the door's heavy sliding iron bolt and let the police inside.

A hot iron sat on a lit gas stove, indicating that Isidore Fink had been hard at work when he'd met his killer. Fink lay dead on the floor in the back room of the two-room laundry with two bullets in the left side of his chest and one in his left thumb. The scene abounded in mysteries: Fink had not committed suicide, because no gun was found in the store, and what suicide shoots himself in the hand? There was no evident motive for the murder. Fink had no enemies, according to his roommate, Schwartz, and secondhand furniture dealer Morris Steinberg, one of his few friends. No money was missing from the cash register or the dead man's pockets. Even if robbery were the killer's motive, the pickings would have been pathetically slim, since the cash register contained only $4.75 and Fink had two dollars on his person.

On Saturdays Fink kept his shop open until midnight, but as he feared being robbed he opened his doors only for customers that he recognized. This indicates that Fink was murdered by a regular customer, someone he'd allowed into the laundry. Perhaps the killer had simply walked out the door, locking it behind him? It's an attractively simple theory, but there is a problem: the front door was the laundry's only door, and it was locked from the inside with a sliding bolt seven inches long and an inch thick rather than with a key. A killer could easily steal a key and lock the door from the outside, but sliding a bolt from *outside* would require reaching through the transom with arms ten feet long or having the magical ability to reach through wood or painstakingly lowering a long hook through the transom—while in view of passersby on the street.

Perhaps the killer had stood on a ladder and shot Fink through the open transom over the door? But Fink had powder burns on his left wrist, indicating that his killer had stood close when firing the shots. In addition, an empty cartridge was found near the body; therefore, the killer must have been in the shop close to his victim. (Adding to the confusion, the *New York Sun*, contrary to other papers, claimed no cartridge was in the room.)

Perhaps the killer had actually climbed *through* the transom? One of its hinges was broken. But to get through the transom unaided, the killer must have been an acrobat. Perhaps he'd used a ladder? But the shop's sole door faced the street. New Yorkers hardly consider ten thirty p.m. on a Saturday a late hour; if a killer squeezed through the transom, with or without a ladder, should not someone on the sidewalk have seen him? Even if a determined and very small murderer entered through the transom, why should he leave in the same overly complicated way when he simply could have unbolted the door and run out? In any case, the transom was open only two inches. Patrolman Kattenborn had to lower a child through it to get the door unlocked.

Another theory: Fink was shot in the hallway, ran into his shop, bolted the door, and then retreated to the back room where he died of his wounds. If there were bloodstains on the door or trailing into the back room, the theory would be strengthened. But as contemporary newspaper accounts do not mention bloodstains in those obvious locations, one may assume they were not there. (Chest wounds are notoriously messy.) In fact, the *New York Sun*'s account suggests that the crime scene was bloodless: upon opening the door, the reporter stated, Patrolman Kattenborn saw "the laundryman's corpse, but no blood." In addition, to advocate this solution we must overlook the empty cartridge found in the shop according to most accounts and Mrs. Locklan Smith's testimony that she'd heard Fink fighting his attacker inside the shop.

There were virtually no suspects. Rumor held that two well-dressed women had been seen in the hallway shortly before the murder, but Schwartz declared that Fink had had no lady friends. (Fink was married, but his family lived in Europe.) Morris Steinberg told police that a half hour before Mrs. Smith heard the cries of distress, he'd dropped by the laundry for a visit. Fink often sold unclaimed clothing, and when Steinberg entered the store, he saw a black man and woman asking the proprietor if he had any unclaimed underwear to sell. Seeing that his friend was busy, Steinberg left. Perhaps significantly—but perhaps not—an unclaimed bundle of laundry was found beside Fink's corpse. The police attempted to locate the couple who asked Fink about buying clothes, but never found them. Even if the couple were guilty, it remains to be explained how they'd managed to bolt the door behind them as they fled.

Detectives searched the store in vain for secret entrances. They dusted for fingerprints and found only the proprietor's. The Fink murder became a cold case that remains an "insoluble mystery," as New York Police Commissioner Mulrooney stated in a radio interview around 1931. A detective had a saltier comment: "That damn two-for-a-cent mystery gives me the creeps!"

The story took on a life of its own. Director Alfred Hitchcock found Fink's demise a fascinating mystery and allegedly planned to base a film on it, but he could not think of a logical way to end the story. Ben Hecht wrote a short story based on the murder, "The Mystery of the Fabulous Laundryman." Charles Fort, the dean of paranormal investigators and curiosity collectors, mentioned the Fink case in his 1932 book *Wild Talents*. Fort seemed to imply that because Fink so greatly feared being murdered, his thoughts somehow became reality—"his physical body was seized upon by his own picturization of himself, as shot by an enemy"—which really isn't very helpful.

Death Row Dramas: New York

Edward McGrath of New York City went on trial in early February 1910 for murdering elderly Benjamin Rose. The jury found him guilty of second-degree murder with a sentence of life in prison.

McGrath's attorney thought he could swing a better deal than that and demanded a new trial. His wish was granted.

On February 23, the second jury decided McGrath was guilty of first-degree murder, a verdict that carried the death penalty. As the *New York Times* said, "If [McGrath's] counsel had not made that perfunctory motion for a new trial . . . McGrath would have escaped with a sentence [of] life imprisonment, but now he faces the electric chair."

Somehow McGrath managed to escape his fate, and in 1935 he published a book called *I Was Condemned to the Chair*, demonstrating that being executed was the most interesting event that never happened to him.

Stanley Millstein and Charles Kumrow—age eighteen and nineteen, respectively—were on Sing Sing's death row, and both were scheduled to be executed on December 22, 1916. They volunteered to be electrocuted three days early "so that the grief of their relatives may be dulled as much as possible for Christmas." The teenaged killers went to the electric chair on December 19.

In July 1920 an artist asked permission from Lewis Lawes, warden of Sing Sing, to paint a picture of the electric chair. Warden Lawes denied the request.

"But I must have the picture to hang in an exhibit!" cried the artist.

"Hanging would be too good for it," replied the witty warden.

Thomas "Red" Moran, a young Brooklyn gangster, killed two cops in a shootout on November 21, 1926; was convicted and sentenced to death in January 1927; and went to the electric chair on December 14, 1928. The execution was held up several hours because it was on the same day as the annual prison play, but Moran didn't seem to resent the delay.

George's Attention to Grammar

George S. Jr. was totally nuts. On May 19, 1908, he dropped by his elderly millionaire father's office at a drug exporting firm at 79 Pine Street in New York City. There George fatally shot his father and committed suicide.

George Jr.'s motive was that his widowed father intended to marry—over his four sons' hearty objections—the much younger Miss Rachael B., a schoolteacher in East Orange, New Jersey. The wedding was scheduled for June 3; a newspaper announcement had already been written.

The killer left behind a remarkable note of explanation, which he wrote an hour before the murder-suicide. It displayed an odd sense of humor, high craziness, and admirable concern for correct grammar:

> Manhattan Square Hotel, May 19, 1908.—To whom it may concern, the coroner first, I presume: I took a solemn oath (to myself) that my father would never disgrace the memory of my sainted mother. There is not a bit of selfishness in me. Had my father engaged himself to a lady of mature age I would most certainly bid him good luck and trust he would live forever. . . .

There is a point which strikes me as particularly interesting. While riding down on the Ninth Avenue elevated I cast casual glances on those around me, as they doubtless did me. The thought which I desire to convey is this: How many thousands would have started from me had they known the prominent captions [headlines, that is] my double crime would warrant tomorrow?

There is a comical and laughable end to this. I would willingly give $500 to Rachael B. to hear the beautiful and touching prayer for the salvation of my soul she will offer up. Of course, I am under a violent strain and many of my sentences may not be grammatical and many sentences may be crude. . . .

Another point I desire to mention. Two seconds after my father starts I will follow, as the poor old man needs a guide and a guardian. Should we run across some of the bunch from East Orange [presumably referring to Miss B.'s family], we will glide up a side street.

Father and son were buried together. Thereafter came the inevitable fight over the terms of the elder man's will.

Helen Helps Harry Conquer His Phobia

Harry G., age twenty-seven, wasn't really the husband of Helen B.; they were each married to someone else, and she and Harry lived in the same apartment building at 135 West 104th Street, New York. They had been just crazy about each other since they met at the World Series in Pittsburgh in 1925.

Harry was crazy in another way: he had a pathological fear of knives, even though he worked as a butcher. Now, I'm no expert, but it seems to me that a phobia over sharp objects would be an insurmountable problem for someone in Harry's trade. Helen thought so too, and she constantly teased and mocked her boyfriend. She found that she could win any domestic spat simply by brandishing some cutlery.

But she went too far on October 15, 1927. On that morning, she refused to wake Harry up in time for work, cook breakfast, or iron his shirt. They got into a fight, during the course of which she pulled her old trick of waving a knife in his face. But this time Harry, in a blind fury, overcame his phobia and strangled Helen with his bare hands.

A Disgruntled Employee

Who was promiscuously scattering body parts around New York City? That was the question of the hour on July 9, 1927, when a curious citizen opened an abandoned bundle dropped near a subway kiosk in Battery Park and beheld segments of a woman's legs wrapped in a red tablecloth, a towel, and a pair of khaki pants. The legs appeared to have been removed with an ax three or four days previously.

Meanwhile, an employee of the Brooklyn-Manhattan Transit Company looked in a black bag left in the rail yard and found a woman's head looking back at him. A witness later reported seeing a man toss the bag down and hurry away.

A thigh was found in Grand Army Plaza.

On July 10, three more bundles containing feminine body parts turned up in Brooklyn: in Prospect Park, behind a theater, and near a church. It was clear from the accumulating number of severed arms and legs that there were at least two victims.

On the same day, a policeman was called to investigate a water leak in the cellar of Sarah Brownell's boardinghouse at 28 Prospect Place, Brooklyn. He found sections of two bodies in an ash barrel, two saws, two hammers, a bloody ax, and human internal organs floating aimlessly in the flooded basement.

The culprit responsible for this somewhat damning crime scene was an alcoholic Norwegian immigrant, Ludwig Halverson Lee, the boardinghouse's custodian. He loathed his job on the grounds that he got no wages for his labors, only room and board. It had dawned on Lee that he could murder his landlady, steal her money, and go back to Norway.

He bided his time until July 5, rent day. After Mrs. Brownell collected her tenants' money, Lee battered her with an ax and dragged her body to the cellar, where he cut her into pieces like cordwood.

The other female corpse was Selma Larsen Bennett, former owner of the building, who had the grievous misfortune to drop by for a visit while Lee was dismembering Mrs. Brownell. The gory sight was the last thing she ever saw. Lee couldn't allow a witness to escape, so he killed Mrs. Bennett with the ax and cut her up too. Then he had quite a time wrapping up the sections and foolishly depositing them in public places where they were certain to be quickly found—and all relatively close to the murder scene.

Ludwig H. Lee, who was clearly not the best planner, went to the chair on August 2, 1928.

Homework and Hatchets

It was just an ordinary grammar school assignment: "Write Your Autobiography." But what nine-year-old Martin D. wrote in his theme really got the teacher's attention:

"One day I heard my father and mother quarreling. Afterwards, I asked my mother what they were fighting about, and she told me I must never mention anything about it."

The police too found Martin's paper of interest, considering that soon after he wrote it the boy's father, wealthy druggist Herman D., was struck nine times in the head with a hatchet in their home at 580 Empire Boulevard, Brooklyn, on March 16, 1931. They arrested the widow, Mamie D., on March 17. The grand jury was not impressed with the evidence, and the widow was freed on March 25. The druggist's murder remains unsolved.

3-X: A Madman ahead of His Time

From 1968 to 1970, California was terrorized by a serial killer who attacked at least seven people, killing five; except for his last documented murder, that of a taxi driver, he specialized in attacking couples. Using the name Zodiac, he wrote taunting letters to the police and occasionally sent ciphers for newspaper readers to solve. He claimed that if the codes were broken, his identity would be revealed. But despite an investigation that lasted decades, Zodiac was never officially identified or caught.

In 1976 and 1977, New York City was likewise terrorized by Son of Sam, whose chief interest lay in shooting couples, mostly in the borough of Queens. Like Zodiac, he derived gratification from his notoriety and sent teasing letters to the authorities and newspaper columnist Jimmy Breslin. The killer, eventually identified as David Berkowitz, was sentenced to six consecutive life sentences.

These gentlemen were probably unaware of it, but a little-known serial killer preceded their actions by more than a generation. Like Son of Sam, his hunting grounds were the streets of New York; like Zodiac, he mailed coded letters to the newspapers and was never captured; like both, he stalked couples and sent pseudonymous jeering letters to the police.

On the night of June 11, 1930, a nineteen-year-old College Point girl, Catherine May, and grocer Joseph Mozynski (a.k.a. Moyzynski) were sitting in the latter's car in Whitestone, Queens. A stranger walked up to them and shot Mozynski through the open window. Then he pulled Miss May out of the car and escorted her, unharmed, to a bus so she could go home. He handed her a sheet of paper with a warning not to look at it until the next day.

When she did, she found that the killer had used a rubber stamp to imprint the name "Joseph Mozynski" in red ink on the margin. On the lower left side of the page he stamped "3X" and on the lower right side, "3-X-097." The rest of the paper was blank. Since the murderer had stamped Mozynski's name on the sheet before committing the crime, the victim had been chosen deliberately, not randomly. Detectives attempted to trace the sheet through its watermark without success.

Police were baffled. Catherine May claimed at first that a gangster named Albert Lombardo had killed Mozynski but soon admitted her identification was false. Assistant District Attorney Stephen Frontera said that he didn't think Albert Lombardo even existed.

After the killing, the *New York Evening Journal* started getting strange pseudonymous notes that seemed composed of phrases lifted from a bad spy novel. The writer stated that his victims carried "international papers" and added: "I am the agent of a secret international order and when I met Mozynski that night it was to get from him certain documents, but unfortunately they were not in his possession at the time." In another letter he said, "We always get them through their women."

The author of these letters signed his name "3-X." He warned that another body would be found soon in Queens and that his avowed goal was to murder thirteen men and one woman.

On June 17, twenty-six-year-old radio salesman Noel Sowley of Bergen Beach, Brooklyn, and twenty-year-old Elizabeth Ring of Hollis—a policeman's daughter—were sitting in his coupe in an isolated lane at 83rd Avenue and 246th Street in Creedmoor, Queens. A man walked to the car, pointed a gun at Sowley's head, and demanded to see his driver's license. After peering at it, the man handed it back and said, "You're going to get what Joe got." Then he fired two shots in Sowley's temple, killing him.

The killer seemed strangely uninterested in Elizabeth Ring. He muttered that he was going to go on a killing spree. He rifled through the dead man's coat—perhaps searching for "international papers"?—but rather than taking anything, he left something behind in Sowley's pocket: a newspaper clipping about the previous week's Mozynski murder, on which was written in pencil: "Here's how."

As in the Mozynski killing, the murderer escorted Ring to a bus and handed her a sheet of paper with orders not to look at it until later. She turned it over to the police, who found that it was stamped like the sheet he'd given Catherine May.

Ballistics tests proved that Mozynski and Sowley were killed with the same gun. Ring described her boyfriend's attacker as five feet six inches tall and looking like a foreigner. Both she and May said he had a foreign accent; Ring thought he sounded German. The man who called himself 3-X seemed to be between thirty and forty years old, lanky, small-eyed, thick-lipped, with a thin face and "peculiar teeth."

The assassin sent a letter to the *Evening Journal* stating that on June 18 he would murder a man in College Point, Queens, whom he referred to as "W.R.V.-8." What the *New York Times* called "the widest manhunt in the history of the New York Police Department" occurred that night. A total of 425 plainclothes detectives, two thousand patrolmen, and motorcycle, automobile, and gun squads converged upon the streets of Queens, including policemen from other boroughs. "Queens began to take on the appearance of an armed camp," said the *Times*. "Automobiles armed with machine guns were manned by two policemen each and sent to points known to be used for automobile rendezvous." The heavy police presence probably spooked the killer, who did not appear that night. The police concluded that he must be insane and strongly advised young lovers in Queens to refrain from holding "petting parties" in automobiles parked on dark streets and lonely lanes. Few needed to be told twice.

On June 18, Inspector John Gallagher, head of detectives in Queens, received a letter from a man claiming to be 3-X. It was mailed from the Hudson Terminal station and was written in blue ink on cheap note paper in penmanship similar to that on the letters sent to the *Evening Journal*. The envelope included a couple of empty .32-caliber shells. For reasons that made sense only to himself, the sender clipped off the envelope's corners. The full contents were not revealed, but the letter read in part:

> *For your information, one more of J. Mozynski's friends was sent to meet him—.*
>
> *V-5 Solwey [sic] was shot near Floral Park and not very far away from police signal station.*
>
> *I enclose the two empty shells—some of our money was found on his person and the N.Y. document.*

> The girl was, as in the case of Miss May, put aboard a bus and sent home—but no clues were left for you this time. Thirteen more men and one woman will go if they do not make peace with us and stop bleeding us to death.
>
> P.S. These facts have been disclosed to the New York Evening Journal.

Apparently, in the unpublished portion 3-X upbraided the police for their inability to capture him. The *Evening Journal* had indeed received a letter in identical handwriting—and the twisted author sent similar letters to the witness Caroline May and her mother. The letter to the *Evening Journal* read:

> Gentlemen: The young lady involved in this case is a victim of unfortunate circumstances. Her story is clean. I happen to know something of what happened Wednesday night.
>
> Mozynsky [sic] was a rascal. He had important papers belonging to us. We felt sorry for his wife and children, but is for the best that they shall not know what he was. This paper will certify the writer.

The police received a lengthy letter from 3-X on June 19 with cheering news: he now intended to murder only seven people rather than fourteen. This masterpiece of incoherence was addressed to the *New York Evening Journal*; as Zodiac would do many years later, 3-X demanded that the newspaper publish his letter and went out of his way to belittle the police trying to find him:

> N.Y.C. 6-17-30.
>
> Dear Sir: I beg to thank you for publishing the code message sent to you.
>
> W.R. V8 of C. P. has returned the Philadelphia XV346 to me tonight after reading your paper—also 37,000 of the blackmail money—thanks to God—if I may use his name.
>
> This means the following persons will be spared:
>
> W.R. V8 College Point.
> S 12 College Point.
> K 2 Brooklyn.
> Z 3 (the woman in question, the tall blond).
> M 6 N.Y.C.
> XX-V (NYC Police Department detective).
>
> The following document still is missing—NJ 4-3-44—and 39,000 dollars—for this document, the following people still are marked for death:
>
> X-14   X-7
> X-21   X1
> X-2   V-4

L-6

All initials withheld—too much of a clue for the super-detectives of Bayside.

   Mosinsky's number was R9.

   Sowley's number was X-4.

   Please print this final message to the seven men left on the death list.

   N.J.—CCk-2-33-Av. 3X-Rosmilt-R. P. 49-7.

   As in the Mosinski [sic] case, the girl with Sowley was sent home. She also proved to be an iron woman. I had to put the gun close to her breast to quiet her. She even tried to start the car. But when I told her I would fire she then to my surprise began to say her prayers and to prepare herself for death.

   This saved her, as God is the only one I fear, and I could not shoot a woman showing so much courage. . . .

   The shooting of Sowley should show it by now and also a second warning to the rest. I know who the other girl is and where she lives, and as she happens to be of good family she has nothing to fear. I never will reveal who she is. [Presumably he was referring to "Z 3," the tall blonde he had considered murdering, since Catherine May's name already had been released by the press.] As for the detectives and their commanding officer, to my estimate—well, what's the use?

   Sorry for them that's a black mark against them. But they never will find out who I am. One word from anyone means death or a long term in State or Federal penitentiary. Again thank you for your kindness.

   Please do not forget to publish the enclosed message, also the numbers of those who have been spared and those who are still marked for death. I will not shoot until they decide their fates themselves.

The letter was signed—as were all the others—with an inverted and underlined V followed by 3-X. The numbers and letters probably had no significance outside the mind of a killer, who appears to have been a paranoid schizophrenic, judging from the seemingly random proliferation of numbers and letters in his correspondence, his references to secret societies and mysterious papers, and his conviction that he was an international assassin. The *Louisville Courier-Journal* remarked that the "mumbo-jumbo of code . . . would be ludicrous were it not for the testimony of two bullet-pierced bodies."

At ten thirty p.m. on the night of June 19—as the more than four hundred detectives and two thousand patrolmen again scoured

Queens—Morris Horwitz, the fifty-year-old president of the Municipal Underwriters insurance firm, sat in his sedan in front of his house at 1287 Carroll Street, Brooklyn. He was speaking through the car window to his wife, Rose, who was sitting on the porch, when a short, blond, "wild-eyed, crazy-looking" man got into his car. He said, "Move over to the steering wheel and start the car and keep going. If you don't, I'll shoot you." Horwitz tried to follow orders, but the man shot him in the shoulder and fled on foot. The bullet traveled through the salesman's lung and abdomen, inflicting serious wounds. Horwitz survived and his wife was unharmed. Had they encountered the most wanted man in New York or was it a random, botched carjacking?

Another letter signed 3-X surfaced. It said, "Where is X8W-9? He is already dead. He is on the Boston Road. His name is Harold Bridenbach. Find the woman, old man, and you've got me." It certainly sounded like 3-X, but the penmanship differed from that in the authentic letters. The police found no dead persons on Boston Road in the Bronx and could locate no Harold Bridenbach whatsoever.

John Mozynski of Philadelphia, brother of the murder victim Joseph, got a 3-X letter on June 20, threatening him with death if he didn't return certain papers by the following day and deriding the efforts of New York Police Commissioner Edward Mulrooney and Philadelphia Director of Public Safety Lemuel Schofield. Detectives regarded the note as genuine because the handwriting matched the other letters and provided the plumber Mozynski with a round-the-clock guard. The letter said:

> I am here now in Philadelphia. You must have those papers, they're mine. Give them to me by putting them in a newspaper and leaving it [in the] back door entrance to men's room Broad Street station Sat. 21. If you don't have them, leave word who has. No foolin' and keep the gumshoe squad off.
>
> I won't be there, someone else will. Mulrooney, N.Y., didn't get me and Schofield won't. I either get those papers or somebody pays dear. C C Phila J M PDQ 3325 as Sat. 6 21 P.M. MNX.
>
> Your last Sat. night—Two more Phila after you if you fail. V 3-X.

"JM" probably meant "John Mozynski"; "3325" almost certainly referred to Mozynski's street address (3325 Almond Street, Port Richmond); and "PDQ" was a then-current slang acronym for "pretty damn quick." Naturally, Mr. Mozynski had no idea what "papers" the writer wanted and thus could not produce them. If 3-X was the actual author, he did not make good on his promise. Idle threats appeared to be all he had left: a letter in the familiar handwriting arrived at the *Evening Journal* on June 21 promising to shoot the actress Margalo Gillmore in her car. He never followed through on that either.

In fact, no more murders could definitely be attributed to the mysterious 3-X. He sent a letter to the papers on June 21 reassuring New Yorkers that his mission was completed and that he would not kill anyone else. Oh, and he added that he was a secret agent from Russia, sent by a worldwide secret cabal called the Red Diamond. Now that he had collected his documents, he was heading back to Russia. He ended, not with the usual insults lobbed at the police, but rather on a note of praise for their diligence and for the courage of American womanhood as exemplified by Elizabeth Ring.

The authorities, on the other hand, believed 3-X was in America and still dangerous. Even if the writer was true to his word that his murdering days were over, the police wanted to capture him. The investigation continued but it yielded nothing but one frustration and blind alley after another. A number of lunatics were brought in for questioning only to be released when none of the surviving witnesses could identify them. One, Joseph Ustica, murdered a Freeport contactor in 1928 and escaped from Long Island's Kings Park State Asylum a month before the slayings, but he was too old to be 3-X and bore no resemblance to the fugitive.

On June 22, a strange story came from Lancaster, Pennsylvania, where a former veteran and current drifter, Dewey Ede, claimed that he'd met a stranger in a restaurant fifteen miles east of Coatesville. The man kept papers written in code in his wallet, according to Ede, and said: "You don't know who I am, do you? Do I look like a maniac to you?" The stranger confessed that he'd killed two men in Queens (he even named them), attempted to murder a third (Morris Horwitz?), and had been on a mission to annihilate fourteen. He added, "They call me the 3-X slayer, but they made me do it. I was selected from the Red Diamond of Russia for a secret mission in America. Now that the papers have been returned, I can return to my country. I will head for Harrisburg and then to New Orleans and take a boat back to the old country." Despite the stranger's recital of his bloodthirsty deeds, Ede saw no problem with camping all night with him in a culvert near Coatesville. His description of the man tallied with eyewitness descriptions: forty years old, five feet six, 145 pounds, wrinkled face, foreign accent. Either Ede met the genuine (and very talkative) 3-X or he was an imaginative fellow who read the papers closely.

Rev. John V. Cooper saw 3-X's handwriting reproduced in the newspapers and thought it looked like the penmanship of a parishioner, a former

Secret Service man who'd gone insane. May and Ring looked at photos of the agent and denied that he was 3-X.

Joseph Oswald Clark was a madman of unusual interest because he had a mania for writing letters and had escaped from Creedmor Asylum in Queens in 1929—less than a mile from the Sowley murder site. He was found in Philadelphia on June 20, taken to New York, and displayed before the eyewitnesses, May and Ring, who agreed that he wasn't the man who'd shot their boyfriends. Clark was recommitted to the institution from which he'd escaped.

For a short time, Nicholas LaRoche, a Russian living in Mount Vernon, New York, was considered the best suspect because his handwriting on a forged prescription closely matched 3-X's. On June 24, Catherine May and Elizabeth Ring were called in yet again; they scrutinized LaRoche for a half hour before deciding he was not the man.

Twenty-one-year-old Clarence James Pratt of Chicago was arrested for vagrancy in Riverside Park on June 25. He had a notebook that included some code, the phrase "3-X," plus a drawing of a skull and crossbones. Pratt confessed that he'd written a message in code and sent it to a newspaper, but said that it was intended as a challenge for the real 3-X to decipher. Pratt further insisted that the code was one he had used since childhood. Pratt was deemed harmless and freed.

On August 16, Hudson Gallity was arrested in Elizabeth, New Jersey, for sending letters and telegrams and making phone calls in the guise of 3-X. He became violent when apprehended and was taken to a psychopathic ward. The two eyewitnesses visited, gazed at Gallity, and cleared him. He was guilty of nothing worse than being a crank and a pest, and his writing did not match 3-X's.

In November, a masked man held up Queens couples in parked cars on six occasions. He proved to be Clement Modzel, an ex-policeman. There was excited talk that he might also be 3-X, but he was cleared of the murders.

Police wearily investigated dozens of crank letters by citizens well-intentioned and otherwise, notes sent in by 3-X imitators, and a rumor that the killer had disguised himself as a woman and hid in the woods near Jamaica, Queens. Someone "with a foreign accent" who identified himself as 3-X twice called George U. Harvey, the Queens borough president. By June 24, not even two full weeks after the first murder, the NYPD had investigated and cleared fifty suspects. The investigation cost the city $10,000 Depression-era dollars per day. Even a $5,000 reward did not flush the killer out.

3-X promised in his eighth letter that he would behave, but police received a new threatening letter on June 23. The writer vowed to kill Meyer Newmark of 1115 East Thirteenth Street, Brooklyn, if Newmark did not hand over document "U.J. 4-3-44" by June 28. The writer did not sign with a "V" before the "3-X" as in the other letters, but the handwriting appeared to be the same. Newmark had no idea what his unwanted correspondent was talking about and no harm came to him.

The 3-X case stayed quiet—except for countless hoax letters and suspects who didn't pan out—until October 10, 1931, when police received a message on plain writing paper: "I am back. I will pay every cop a visit." At first the authorities dismissed it as yet another in a long line of fakes, but handwriting experts declared that it was written by *the* 3-X. The police theorized that he may have just been released from a private sanitarium. Two hundred plainclothes detectives explored the woods in Queens—but what they were searching for was not divulged to the press.

3-X hopped into the headlines for the last time on June 1, 1936, when Frank Engel of College Point—X's hunting grounds six long years before—was arrested in Elizabethtown, New York, for disorderly conduct in a garage and confessed to the murders during interrogation. To those with a discerning eye, Engle's confessions presented some problems. A strapping six-footer who was only twenty-nine years old, he was too young and powerfully built to match the medium-sized, wizened killer described by Catherine May and Elizabeth Ring. He also had no foreign accent. He was brought to Queens although District Attorney Charles Sullivan opined that the prisoner was "a mental case." As had happened so many times before, May and Ring observed Engel and declared that he wasn't 3-X—no way, no how. Engel was taken away for a professional evaluation of his mental state.

On that anticlimactic note, the mystery was closed forever. One of the most baffling things about 3-X—besides, of course, his true identity—was his seeming ability to abandon his life of crime and disappear. The passage of time has confirmed a boast he made in one of his letters: "They never will find out who I am."

2

NIGHTMARISH NEW JERSEY

Grave Robbers and Body Snatchers: New Jersey

ON THE NIGHT OF SEPTEMBER 23, 1921, LAWRENCE P., A MINER FOR THE New Jersey Zinc Company, heard a knock on the front door of his Ogdensburg home. Looking out a second-story window, he saw a man dressed in white and wearing a black mask scurry from the porch. Investigating, Lawrence found a box on his doorstep. It contained a woman's foot gaily wrapped in paper. The foot was embalmed and had been buried three or four years, so someone went through considerable trouble to procure it. Lawrence had no idea who would pull such a scurvy trick on him, or why. Your guess is as good as his!

Have a Heart

Mrs. Marion S., age fifty-four, was buried in Calvary Cemetery, Camden, on November 2, 1945. A couple of days later someone noticed that a fiend had exhumed the body and made off her with heart.

The coroner observed that several graves in the cemetery had been opened lately, but the perpetrator had always taken care to refill them: "This time the ghoulish lunatic apparently was frightened before he could refill the grave and he must have run away with the heart clutched in his hand."

The coroner also noted the great difficulty involved in violating a grave: "No one but a crazy man could have broken through the concrete and wooden caskets and then spent a lot of time fumbling around in the dark to cut through the flesh and ribs to reach the heart."

Who was this determined ghoul and what did he *want* with a human heart? We might be better off not knowing.

Premature Burial: New Jersey

In March 1900, a Mullica Hill undertaker exhumed the bodies of a family who had lived in the town circa the 1870s, so their bodies could be shipped to a burial ground in Philadelphia. One opened coffin revealed that its occupant—a boy—had died a death far worse than his relatives ever suspected. The skeleton's legs were drawn up and the arms were across the face. The inside of the coffin bore considerable wear and tear, and the window over the boy's face was broken.

※

William E. of Branchville had the bad luck to be bitten by a rattlesnake and the good luck not to be prematurely buried. He appeared to have died from the effects of the bite in August 1891 and was prepared for burial. Doctors decided it would be interesting to cut open a sore under his arm to see what would happen. The results were interesting, all right: the slicing revived William and he showed signs of life. The doctors—who were moments away from performing an autopsy—gave him some restoratives and he recovered.

※

Miss Edith C. posed as the Goddess of Liberty in the 1903 Washington's Birthday parade held at Red Bank. She caught a cold that turned into pneumonia. She died on February 27 and the family called the undertaker, who to Edith's good fortune noticed that her arm moved as he prepared a shroud.

Extraordinary Epitaphs: New Jersey

In Morristown: "Charles H. Salmon. 1858–1884. He met his death on the 12th of October, 1884, by the hand of a careless drug clerk and two excited doctors, at 12 o'clock at night in Kansas City."

When David Goodman Croly passed away in April 1889, the *New York Times* eulogized him as having been "one of the best known journalists in this country." Not only that, Croly's wife, Jennie Cunningham, was a famous writer under the pseudonym Jennie June. Yet either Croly or his widow must have considered his life a failure. His gravestone in Evergreen Cemetery in Lakewood reads: "He meant well, tried a little, failed much."

The Animal Kingdom Gets In On the Body-Snatching Act

The Methodist Episcopalian Church on Linden Avenue in Jersey City was overrun with stray cats during those summer days in 1879—"graveyard cats," they came to be called, and they seemed to nervous observers to be even more devious and worldly wise than the typical feral feline. "They are exceedingly fierce," remarked the *Jersey City Journal*, "and are so spry in their movements, and so watchful for the approach of danger, that all efforts to destroy them, even by the use of poison, have so far failed."

Worse, the cats seemed to have an unhealthy interest in grave robbing. A youth died in June and was buried in the churchyard. A half hour after the funeral the sexton happened to pass the grave and saw, "to his astonishment and horror, the earth flying out of a hole on the top of the grave, and on his approach a large cat sprang out and ran away." The cat had managed to excavate the grave to a depth of two feet before being so rudely interrupted. What on earth could its purpose have been?

Playing It Safe

Nineteen-year-old Minnie M. passed away in Millburn on February 9, 1881, in an attention-getting and unexpected fashion: while standing by her garden gate with friends, she groaned and dropped to earth. A doctor determined that heart disease was the cause of death. Minnie was duly laid out for burial, but suspicious friends noticed that her cheeks and lips were rosy rather than drawn and pale. Two physicians insisted she was dead, but her friends and relatives—no doubt having read horrifying accounts of premature burial in the papers—took no chances. Minnie's funeral was on February 11, but instead of burying her, loved ones took her body from the church to a cemetery vault, which they heated with a stove in case she revived. It was like a scene from that subconsciously disturbing fairy tale *Sleeping Beauty*. So many curiosity seekers dropped by the vault to see her that someone remarked that the local officers should have charged for admittance. Somehow the county physician convinced Minnie's relations to allow an autopsy, which proved that her heart's arteries were "completely ossified." Minnie's friends, satisfied, permitted a belated burial.

A Nasty Necropolis

Back in the days when even graveyards were racially segregated, Dempsey B.—described as "a magnate among the colored people"—owned a burial ground for blacks at the back of Evergreen Cemetery in Camden. Unfortunately, it was not well-kept; in fact, the condition of the place was so shocking that it attracted the attention of the board of health in March 1889. Their investigation determined that "state sanitary and burial laws had been grossly violated."

Specifically, this meant that investigators poked an iron rod in the soil at thirty-five locations in the cemetery to determine whether bodies had been buried at safe, legally required depths. Many coffins were buried a mere eighteen inches deep, and in some cases were just a foot beneath the sod. Few bodies were more than three feet down, and the graves were so shallow that the odor of decomposition was noticeable. The committee feared that when summer came, epidemics might spring from the bodies of persons who'd died of contagious disease and were buried too close to the surface.

In addition to doing soundings with a rod and performing the smell test, the board of health's members grabbed shovels. According to one account, "It was also said by the committee that when they dug up several graves, bones were turned up, and the feet of persons were plainly visible."

The committee found that no permits of burial had been granted to the cemetery for a month, yet illegal interments had occurred all the same.

Dempsey had some 'splaining to do to the press, and he was less than convincing: "I know nothing about ghastly rumors of dogs going into the graveyard and eating human bones. Dogs might have been seen there, but no complaint has been made to my knowledge. Bodies have been buried there without my knowledge and without permit, but what they were I cannot say."

Just Making Sure

S.J.F., a druggist of Hammonton, took ill in November 1890. He had a terror of being buried alive, and his last request was that someone would be so kind as to shove a dagger into his heart after he died as a precaution. When he passed away, however, his three sisters were reluctant to have his request fulfilled because he seemed so darn lifelike.

Thirteen days after the druggist's death, his sisters agreed that it might be time to apply the dagger test. They selected a physician to have the pleasure. No blood issued from the wound, proving that S.J.F. was dead for certain. Peculiarly, the family left the dagger in his heart, so the pearl handle protruded from his chest throughout the funeral service.

Bizarrely Buried: New Jersey

Martha W., the Voodoo Queen of Asbury Park, passed away like a flower of the field on December 15, 1893. In accordance with her wishes, she was buried facedown in Mount Prospect Cemetery at Neptune.

Skeletal Sailors

One might suppose one of the advantages of death is that the dead are no longer subject to the whims of nature. But this is not always the case! A heavy rain on August 10, 1902, inundated Hillside Cemetery in Madison, unearthing seventy-five coffins and sending many of them downstream. The next day, coffins were found "strewn about in all directions." But some, it was thought, had floated down the Passaic River like so many arks.

Keeping Them Around: New Jersey

Mrs. Mary B. and her daughter Martha shared a two-room apartment in Union Hill. Mary died at age ninety-two, probably in the last week of December 1925; but that didn't prevent Martha from wrapping the body in towels and blankets and treasuring it for seven weeks. The police gradually realized something was awry in the scheme of things and investigated on February 15, 1926. Because the body had been kept in an unheated room, it was in good condition.

Martha said she wanted to keep the body because she feared loneliness. The corpse was buried in Weehawken Cemetery on February 16, after which a warrant was issued for Martha "on suspicion of being mentally incompetent." The suspicions were well founded.

Mrs. B.'s Illness

A.H.B. was the postmaster of Ho-Ho-Kus in the late 1870s. This would be glory enough for most, but Mr. B. was ambitious and started a side career manufacturing decorative wax flowers. His wife was in charge of mixing the artificial coloring with the molten wax.

All was loveliness and fake flowers until 1877, when Mrs. B. developed unpleasant symptoms: severe pain in her wrists, numbness in her arms. Then discolored blotches appeared on her hands, feet, and face. The numbness in her wrists extended to her elbows. The blotches turned dark and scaly and then took on a "virulent appearance." The alarmed husband called in a doctor—or rather, three within a year, all of whom diagnosed his wife's ailment as rheumatism.

Mrs. B.'s case got worse. The numbness and pain spread to her hip joints, legs, knees, ankles, and feet. The trio of physicians was baffled; they continued to think rheumatism caused the aches in her bones, but they had no explanation for her skin blemishes. Finally Mrs. B. was paralyzed.

In desperation, Mr. B. sought a fourth opinion from Dr. P. of Ridgewood. His diagnosis was blood poisoning. But what was the specific contagion, and how had it entered her body? Through a process of trial and error, the physician determined that it was an unknown mineral poison.

The doctor's "Eureka!" moment came when he happened to glance at a basket of wax flowers colored by Mrs. B. He was struck by the artificial leaves' bright shade of green. He asked the suffering woman how she colored the wax, and she said that she sometimes touched up the colors with a paintbrush, and she had the habit of licking the brush to prepare it for fine detail work. In this fashion she had accidentally ingested deadly arsenite of copper.

It was brilliant deductive reasoning on Dr. P.'s part, but it came too late to do Mrs. B. much good. Under the doctor's treatment, the pain ceased and she regained some movement of her hands and feet. But she had absorbed too much of the paint's poison. She died at home in early November 1879 after an illness of two long years.

Illustrating the Point

On the night of December 7, 1890, a reverend preached to the congregation at East Millstone Reformed Church in New Brunswick. He said, "A man might fall as easily as a star from heaven." A moment later his face turned pale and he slumped to the floor. Church members carried him home, where he died the next morning.

The Swan Knows When It Is Dying: New Jersey

In 1896, James C. of Pleasantville dreamed that he would die on March 21, 1898. He was *convinced*—so certain, in fact, that he had a tombstone erected in the local cemetery reading: "James C., aged 62, died March 21, 1898." He also made out his will, purchased a coffin, paid the undertaker in advance, and had his grave dug. The hole in the ground gaped wide open for a couple of years, mute testimony to James's seemingly misguided eccentricity—until his coffin filled it after his death from natural causes on March 21, 1898.

‹—•—◦—◦—•—›

It was just an ordinary day at the machine belt factory in Paterson—September 15, 1922. Around eleven a.m. James S. turned to a fellow employee and said, "I feel as though someone is going to die. Death is near." James was so certain the Death Angel was afoot that he cautioned the coworker to be careful what he ate for lunch. A few minutes later, James expired from a heart attack.

‹—•—◦—◦—•—›

Fifty-six-year-old Giuseppe F. of Orange was confident that he would leave this world on April 17, 1937. He planned his own funeral a week in advance to spare his family the inconvenience; on the seventeenth he went to the cemetery to visit the graves of old friends. "This is my last walk," he announced when he arrived home. He died later that day, almost to the predicted hour, and was buried in a tuxedo as he requested.

Insane Clown without a Posse

J.F.W. once a famous circus clown, died in the insane asylum at Overbrook on June 17, 1901, where he had been confined for twenty-six years.

He had been driven mad by his own clown makeup, which contained bismuth and antimony, both potentially dangerous poisons.

Mabel's Dream

Mabel R. of Hoboken, age thirteen, had a disturbing dream on the night of October 20, 1904. She saw her mother sitting dead in a chair. She told the dream to Mrs. R. the next morning. Her mother reassured her, on what grounds I do not know, that dreams "went by contraries," and that a dream of death really portended a wedding.

Mabel had the same dream on the night of October 23. In the morning she found her mother sitting in a chair, head drooping on a shoulder, dead. The doctor said it was a case of heart disease.

Fatal Fear

Jersey City police arrested Frederick E., a young tradesman, on November 1, 1904, on charges of molesting girls. By day he spent his time protesting his innocence; by night he was subject to nightmares that made him wake up screaming. He told the jailers of "terrible dreams in which the faces of his accusers appeared."

Whether he submitted to a guilty conscience or to fear of being convicted—rightly or wrongly—Frederick was found stone-cold dead with a distorted face on the floor of his cell on November 11. Doctors opined that he'd died of fright.

Mesmerism or Manslaughter?

It started out as an ordinary stage hypnotist's show and rapidly went downhill from there.

Robert S. made a living as a subject for the hypnotist Arthur E., who'd recently changed careers after being a Newark piano salesman. On the night of November 8, 1909, performer and stooge were doing a turn at a five-and-ten-cent vaudeville house called the Somerville Theater in Somerville.

The afternoon performance went without a hitch. During the evening show, the hypnotist commanded Robert to become rigid as a board, which he did. Arthur placed his subject so that his head rested on one chair, his feet on another, and his body suspended in the air between them. Arthur climbed onto a table and stepped onto Robert's chest. Robert's body did not yield or bend. This feat wowed the audience.

When the hypnotist got down off his assistant, he told stagehands to put Robert back on his feet. But when they did, the man in the trance collapsed to the floor. The hypnotist, obviously surprised, unsuccessfully tried to revive Robert. The comatose man was dragged offstage. To put it simply, Arthur had put Robert into a trance—but Robert didn't come out of it.

Doctors happened to be in the house. They detected neither pulse nor heartbeat and immediately applied restoratives, including injections of strychnine and glycerin. When that failed, they tried artificial respiration and something called the "Laborde method," which, according to my medical dictionary, was a means—now extinct, thank God—of stimulating respiration via "rhythmic traction of the tongue" (by poking a needle through it, that is).

The doctors were pretty sure Robert was dead but they weren't positive, and he was rushed to Somerset County Hospital. Meanwhile, the cops arrested the panic-stricken hypnotist.

One of the strangest aspects of the story is the cavalier attitude the hospital staff had toward Robert, who, like Schrödinger's theoretical cat, was possibly dead, possibly alive. While doctors tried to figure out whether their patient was living, they kept him lying under a black oilcloth on a rough plank table in the tiny, unfurnished "dead room" (the morgue) in the hospital's basement—a room eerily lit only by a swinging electric light. It must have been a scene to behold.

Pending Robert's resuscitation—that is, *if* he could be resuscitated— hypnotist Arthur was taken to jail on a charge of homicide. He swore that his assistant was not dead but "in a cataleptic condition, in which the hypnotizer had placed him for exhibition purposes." Arthur begged the authorities to let his fellow hypnotist and mentor William D. make an attempt at reviving Robert.

The police shrugged and agreed that it was worth a shot, and on November 9 William arrived at the squalid hospital basement room accompanied by the county physician and three doctors on the hospital staff. The doctors thought Robert was dead, but had generously delayed the autopsy so William could have a crack at bringing him back to life.

Into the cramped morgue squeezed William, the four doctors, four nurses, the manager of Newark's Arcade Theater, hypnotist Arthur's distraught wife, two newspaper reporters—and of course Robert himself, lying very still on those planks and hidden by the oilcloth.

William pulled down the cloth and listened for a heartbeat. Nothing was detectable. Then he peered into the subject's dull eyes. He said "sharply and eagerly" in Robert's ear: "Bob! Bob, your heart!"

Silence.

"Bob, your heart is beating!"

Nothing!

"Bob, listen! Hear what I say! Your heart is beating! You hear me!"

No vital signs.

After a while William threw in the towel and put on his hat and coat. "I think he is dead," he said on his way out of the hospital. That was good enough for the doctors, who did an autopsy and found that Robert had died of a ruptured aorta.

Poor Arthur was charged with manslaughter. He threatened to argue that Robert had been alive when the autopsy was performed and thus was killed by the doctors. His point of view was supported by Dr. John Duncan Quackenboss of Columbia University, deemed "one of the leading authorities on hypnotism in the country," who opined that it was possible Robert had been in a state of suspended animation.

The eight physicians who performed the autopsy released a signed statement that Robert had died of natural causes—perhaps augmented by his known occasional overindulgence in alcohol—and that he had expired instantaneously as he was coming out of his onstage trance. His already weak heart may have been strained beyond endurance when the hypnotist stood on his chest. I have been unable to find out whether Arthur served time for manslaughter, but it seems unlikely.

Perhaps Arthur should have consulted the girls at Vassar. Only a few days after his embarrassing onstage faux pas, some students at the college succumbed to the temptation to hypnotize one of their number. After commanding her to sing songs and do the usual array of goofy, hee-larious stunts, they found to their horror that they could not get her to snap out of her trance. At last they succeeded via a desperate group effort woefully undescribed in press accounts, and the president of the college forbade any further experiments in such dark arts at Vassar. Maybe the prohibition stands.

Boys at Play: New Jersey

Charles S., William H., Caleb H., and Richard F. thought it would be a hoot to "play Indian" in Wall Township, near Belmar—though one might think they were too old for such juvenile pastimes, as all four were well into their teens. On August 26, 1923, Charles and William let their companions tie them to a tree and "burn them at the stake" by igniting wood shavings three feet away. But none of the boys noticed that the ground was saturated with waste oil from a nearby gas plant. You can guess what happened next. Caleb and Richard were tried for manslaughter and acquitted on December 31, 1923.

Death's Little Ironies: New Jersey

Richard F. of Paterson survived World War I despite receiving twenty-two wounds. On August 14, 1920, he was killed by a bolt of lightning.

⊱•⊰

John M. of Newark had been sickly all his life and required constant medical attention. On May 1, 1937, the doctor told him he was completely cured and would need no more treatments. Just an hour later, the fifteen-year-old was killed when he fell off a roof while retrieving lost baseballs.

Which Does Not Speak Well for His Musical Ability

When the liner *America* landed at Hoboken on December 9, 1922, two passengers had to be removed: Otto S., a coal stoker who'd died of heart trouble during the voyage, and an unnamed stowaway.

Otto's coworkers in the ship's hold insisted that he'd been frightened to death by creepy musical notes issuing from a coal bunker, which he deemed ghostly music. Upon inspection, the captain found the aforementioned stowaway hiding in the bowels of the ship. The man had been practicing playing a piccolo, as his major ambition in life was to join an orchestra.

Final Communications: New Jersey

Elderly unmarried sisters Frances and Isabel R. ended their lives in their Newark home on December 18, 1909. Their eccentric and spectacular method was discovered a day after the fact: Frances hanged herself and then Isabel did the same, thinking it a good idea. Strange, but it got stranger when the coroner disrobed the bodies for examination: both women had been pierced repeatedly with a four-inch hatpin. In fact, it was buried in Frances's chest, right up to the pinhead. Some investigators wondered if they'd fought before their deaths; others wondered if Frances had murdered Isabel by hatpinning and hanging and then strung up herself; still others thought perhaps they both were murdered. But murder wouldn't explain the note Isabel had scrawled on a box: "Frances hung herself at 2 1/2 Sat. Me too." Some thought the motive for suicide was that their dog had died recently.

Come, Sweets Death

Amelia S., a patient at the New Jersey State Lunatic Asylum at Morris Plains, escaped and went to Morristown with the intention of ending her existence. Her original plan was to hang herself but then she had a happier thought: the weather was hot—it was June 1903—so why not freeze herself to death by eating lots of ice cream? The attempt was unsuccessful, but by the time authorities found Amelia she had eaten more than a gallon and was in the act of packing away the contents of a two-gallon freezer.

None Other Would Do

William W. III desired to end his life—but it had to be accomplished in Fairview Cemetery in Westfield, a suburb of Elizabeth. No other cemetery would do! He made a cross-country trip to get there, which culminated in visitors to the graveyard finding him hanging from a tree limb by a length of picture wire on December 16, 1920. A note in his pocket was dated November 18: "Pardon me for coming 3,000 miles to use your cemetery. This is my reason for returning to my native country."

The Vengeful Pie Clerk Carries Out His Threat

Henry K., twenty-two-year-old Newark pie company clerk, was in a fury. He had been married to his wife, Florence, only four months—and already she wanted a divorce because she was romantically interested in his brother Edward!

"I'll do you more harm dead than alive," he threatened them. Henry thought they didn't seem very bothered.

So now it was late at night on April 26, 1930, and Henry was preparing to humiliate Edward and Florence by committing suicide. He went to his apartment room at 1149 Broad Street, taped a cone over his nose and mouth, and connected a tube from the cone to a gas jet. As he waited for the gates of heaven to creak open, Henry passed time by writing his dying impressions in increasingly illegible penmanship. The reader will note that the pie company clerk had pies on his mind right to the very end:

> It is now 11:15 p.m., and I have finished my letters, so will read for about an hour or so until everyone in the house has retired. This would be a real opportunity for an essay on "How It Feels to Sentence One-self to Die," but who cares if it wouldn't matter a bit a hundred years from now. And then, so many darned suicides have an idea that the rest of the world is going to be interested in their theories on the "use-lessness of living" or the "fascination of death"—horse feathers. They are interested in the Prohibition question or the price of eggs in pies.
>
> I'm fixing a little apparatus on the gas line—good idea. I'll get the full strength of the gas and prevent the odor of it from permeat-ing the house and bringing on discovery too soon. Incidentally, I was 22 years of age on Sep. 1, 1929. I've lived in those twenty-two years. The age on my Marine Corps discharge is three years over. I had to lie about my age in order to get by.
>
> There's two perfectly good pies here that someone might eat.
>
> It is now 1:20 a.m. All is quiet on the Western front. All the drunks and night owls are in, so I'm off—no reprieve.
>
> Took my "panacea" for all human ills. It won't be long now. I'll bet Florence and Ed are having uneasy dreams now. When the stuff starts to take effect, I'll plaster my little funnel to my face and turn on the gas.
>
> Ten minutes later: My head is hot. I'm perspiring and shaky, brain is still clear though. Wonder who will add up the pies tomorrow.
>
> Still the same. 1:45 a.m. Hope I pass out by 2 a.m.
>
> Gee, I love you so much, Florence. It's now 2:15 a.m. I feel very tired and a bit dizzy. I have the gas nozzle plastered on my face, but disconnected from the gas jet. It's quite uncomfortable, damn it. My brain is very clear. I can see that my hand is shaking—it is hard to die when one is young. Now I wish oblivion would hurry—

In addition to his dying thoughts, Henry left behind a couple of letters apologizing to his landlady for croaking himself on her respectable prem-ises and further excoriating his wife and brother. He wrote on one enve-lope: "From Ghost No. 12,785,496."

If Edward and Florence were mortified by the publicity generated by Henry's antics, they didn't feel the effects very long. They married on August 10, 1930. Obviously Henry never put stock in the antisuicide adage "They'll get over it but you won't."

Rachel Is Lonesome

Isaac and Sarah K., Jewish milliners who lived on Broad Street in Newark, were blessed with four daughters and five sons. Their youngest daughter, Rachel, died in 1873 and was buried in the Hebrew cemetery on South Orange Street.

Mrs. F., the eldest of the four daughters, reported that the ghost of her sister appeared silently to her in dreams several times over the years. In autumn 1881 the family had discussed buying a plot in a new cemetery and having Rachel's body exhumed and buried there. (None had visited Rachel's grave in several years.)

That night, Mrs. F. went to sleep and saw Rachel standing in her burial shroud, which bore visible needlework. The surviving sister asked, "What do you wish?" And the spirit replied:

"My bed over yonder [here she pointed out the window in the direction of the cemetery] is very lonely. There is room for one more there by my side. If Mama or any of our sisters should go 'across the river', tell them to come to me. On my right is room for Mama, but if there should not be room for her there, then give her my grave and let me rest in her arms."

The next day the curious family went to the gravesite and found that Rachel's tomb was crowded by other, newer graves—except a space beside her, just as the ghost had related. Mr. K., thoroughly spooked, purchased the plot and gave up the idea of having his family buried in a new cemetery.

Mrs. K. came down with dropsy and died on November 5, 1883. She was buried in the space beside her daughter. All family members vouched for the story and when it became widely known, Rachel K.'s grave became a minor tourist attraction. There was talk of erecting a monument on the site, to be inscribed with the strange story.

Spook on the Streets

Beginning in the summer of 1885, the residents of Moorestown were bothered by what they took to be a ghost. It became so feisty in the ten days preceding Christmas that, reportedly, citizens did their praying at home rather than risk walking to church; people strolled the streets only in groups; lovers did their courting strictly in the daytime; and merchants closed their shops at sundown, well knowing they would have no customers.

Abraham S. saw the ghost after he got off the train from Philadelphia late one night. As he walked away from the depot in the dark, he became aware that he was not alone. Looking to the side, he found that he had an uninvited companion who floated above the ground. His fellow traveler was six feet tall, garbed in black, and, bizarrely, wore what seemed to be an animal mask. The figure vanished before Abraham's terrified eyes. The same floating thing had been seen the night before by one Mrs. W. as she walked home from shopping. She had the impression that it was a man in dress, as if the animal mask weren't strange enough.

The evidence of the mask seems to point to a practical joker with a sick sense of humor, and some Moorestown residents thought it was a local constable, who happened to be a man of greater-than-average height. The constable countered that he was not the ghost and offered a reward to anyone who solved the mystery. He added that he had seen the ghost himself several times, but it always floated out of reach before he could act.

Organized mobs of would-be ghostbusters patrolled the streets at night looking for trouble. According to one contemporary report, they often got what they sought: "The ghost flitted in and out among them before they could recover their senses. In fact, the ghostly visitant has given several of the bullies such a fright and chase that it now prowls around unmolested."

The same report stated that the only two people who had confronted the ghost were women. When it approached Maggie R., she said defiantly, "You brute, you cannot scare me." The other woman, Mrs. M., said to the ghost (after it smiled at her, presumably with its mask off), "You had better go home, for I know you." Disappointingly, the article does not state what happened next.

Villagers noticed also that they had difficulty convincing their horses to pass certain points on the road, leading them to believe that their steeds could see things invisible to farmers, and frankly that was just fine with the farmers.

Will Weirdness: New Jersey

What is it about the dry, legalistic business of writing a will that brings out the poetic instinct in some people? When Newark insurance broker Frederick C. died in May 1922, his will consisted of a quatrain: "All my earthly goods I have in store, / To my dear wife I leave forevermore. / I freely give—no limit do I fix; / This is my will and she the executrix."

⊢•⊕•○•⊕•⊣

Likewise, Alfred H., an Atlantic City newspaperman and historian who died in 1937, left his estate to his daughter Jessie in a will as notable for its brevity as for its rhyming couplet: "All that's mine when I am dead / Goes to Jessie—enough said."

⊢•⊕•○•⊕•⊣

When Dr. Charles Freeman of Metuchen passed away in 1923, he left $100,000 to his chauffeur and one dollar to his widow, the novelist Mary Wilkins Freeman.

Superstitious, Eh?

The judge sentenced Thomas B. to thirteen years in prison for highway robbery and jail breaking on that cold day in Morristown in November 1905. The prisoner approached the bench and spoke (very finely for a highwayman, in my opinion):

"May I have the indulgence of the court in making a simple request? May it please the court, I would call your attention to the fact that thirteen is the hoodoo term. It gives me a feeling of vague uneasiness, close akin to terror. If you could make the sentence fourteen years I would not be under the sign of the cross or, rather, the double cross."

"Remove the prisoner," said the unimpressed judge. "The sentence stands."

Do Not Resuscitate—Please

Dr. Frank S., the county physician for Mercer County, was determined to do scientific experiments on the body of Giancento Ricci after the latter paid his debt to society in the electric chair. The doctor's pet theory was that the electric current did not kill condemned prisoners, but rather the autopsy afterward did them in. He wanted to see if he could bring Ricci back to life and urged that the prisoner's body be turned over to him as soon as possible. According to one account, he wanted possession of Ricci's carcass so badly that he "threatened" to resuscitate the body one way or another.

The doctor made such a pest of himself that the prison's head keeper consulted with the attorney general, who informed him that "the county physician had no rights or duties in the premises."

An unnamed high authority lowered the boom in his most intimidating legalese on December 8, 1908: "If the prison officials lend themselves to any experiment which seeks to revive a man executed in the electric chair under the law, they will be liable to indictment and impeachment for malfeasance in office." The official added that even if Dr. S. somehow managed to resurrect Ricci, the law required that the head keeper "take the revived man and put him back into the chair and have the current turned on again until life is extinct."

The keeper said: "The next electrocution will be in the evening, and [the doctor] will not be invited to be present. I will not turn the body over to him until the next morning, when there will be no possibility of his resuscitating [Ricci]."

Someone must have wised up Dr. S., because he was nowhere to be found when Ricci went to the chair on December 21. Considering that Ricci was executed for raping and murdering a three-year-old girl at Cliffwood, one has to wonder why the physician even wanted to restore him to the world of the living.

A Cheap Way to Remove a Tattoo

James S. of Shenandoah, Pennsylvania, got his right forearm tattooed when he was a boy and, like many a wearer of ink, he came to regret his decision.

On December 18, 1922, James happened to be walking on Alling Street in Newark when he noticed the train yard of the Pennsylvania Railroad. Suddenly he thought of a very efficient—and totally free!—method of tattoo removal.

He woke up the next morning in the Newark City Hospital in as good condition as could be expected, minus the tat and everything else from the elbow down.

Egregious Executions: New Jersey

For murdering his business partner to collect a life insurance payout, wealthy Benjamin Hunter was hanged in the Camden County jail yard on January 10, 1879. Rather than falling through the trap, Hunter was jerked upward on a newfangled "hoist gallows." The thing probably should have been tested further. Already weak from loss of blood due to a suicide attempt, Hunter had to be carried to the gallows—whereupon he fell unconscious on the platform. As noted by capital punishment historian Daniel Allen Hearn, because the rope was too long, the mechanism when triggered merely yanked him up on his feet. Deputies had to throw the slack rope over the gallows' crossbeam and then pull Hunter upward by the neck and let him dangle till he strangled. The audience pelted the deputies with cigar butts as a token of their affection.

───◦─◦───

When Joseph Hillman was hanged at the Gloucester County jail on November 13, 1889, for murdering a Jewish peddler, the execution did not go as well as it might have. The incompetent hangman fixed the noose poorly, and Hillman dangled with an unbroken neck, choking on blood. Two deputies had to hold the suspended man steady while the rope was adjusted. Hillman died at last and was cut down. But as he was lowered into his coffin the black cap was removed, and spectators got a good look at his contorted expression and bloody eyes, nose, and mouth.

───◦─◦───

Henry Schaub was executed in Newark on April 25, 1902. This is how the press described the formalities, according to historian Hearn: "Schaub's head was jerked off his shoulders and went spinning through the air while his quivering body dropped from the scaffold with such a concussion that it turned strong men sick. Undue anxiety on the part of the sheriff to have a successful execution was the cause." Perhaps we could charitably call the bungled execution a self-fulfilling prophecy on the sheriff's part.

───◦─◦───

Joseph Toth murdered his ex-girlfriend in January 1914; on November 2 of the same year the duly convicted man sat in the New Jersey State Prison electric chair. Some negligent bungler forgot to shave Toth's head and wet the electrodes beforehand. The results were like something out of *The Green Mile*: the prisoner's hair caught fire and his clothing smoked. The executioner adjusted the electrodes and the current was reapplied at maximum voltage. Toth's head and clothes caught fire; smoke and the smell of burned flesh filled the chamber. When it was over, witnesses left the room rather more quickly than they had entered.

⊱•◦❖◦•⊰

Hearn relates the mysterious case of a second deeply unlucky Toth from New Jersey—wife-murderer Julius Toth, who was electrocuted on January 3, 1911. Some horrible mishap occurred during the proceedings. Exactly what it was, we will never know because the prison authorities kept details from leaking out. Whatever happened, it took sixteen minutes to play out.

Those Final Moments: New Jersey

Orby Heathcoate passed away with a smirk on his face in the New Jersey electric chair on January 21, 1938—even though it required three jolts to do the job.

⊱•◦❖◦•⊰

Just before taking a seat in the New Jersey State Prison's electric chair on January 4, 1955, Frank Roscus threw a cigar he had been smoking at witnesses.

The Denmead Horror

New Brunswick, circa 1887, probably was not a place accustomed to sensations. Imagine, then, the excitement that was unleashed in mid-January when Mrs. Mary Ann Brundage of Piscataway came to town. She was intent on seeing her sister Cornelia, who had been the mate of Samuel Denmead for a number of years. But the Denmead family refused to let her in the house, and the increasingly angry and fearful Mrs. Brundage wanted to know why.

The Denmeads had local reputations for eccentricity. They had lived in New Brunswick for a little over forty years and had long forbidden any outsiders to enter their Commercial Avenue home, a board-covered house that fell under the architectural style known as "ramshackle." The dwelling—calling it a "house" actually affords it too much dignity—was an ugly one-room affair with only two windows (both covered). The building was enclosed in boards that slanted downward from the roof.

The family originally consisted of four brothers named Robert, John, Henry, and Samuel, and a sister who had the good sense to stay away from her siblings. The patriarch of the family had left a fortune of $400,000 to Samuel, but he proved an easy mark for swindlers and lost most of his inheritance. As a result, he developed a morbid fear of signing his name on any piece of paper. He had collected a mountain of checks over the years but was afraid to sign them.

Cornelia Denmead had had a melancholy personal history. Her mother came from a wealthy family, the Goodfellows of Piscataway. Around 1840, Cornelia married a shoemaker named William Ayres. She had a son by him, but in 1844 Mr. Ayres was led astray by a temptress from Perth Amboy and he abandoned Cornelia, taking with him a generous amount of her property. In the divorce settlement, Cornelia got custody of their son, but her former husband kidnapped him. She spent hundreds of dollars advertising in newspapers across the country for his return and fruitlessly searching orphanages. Her mind was never the same afterward, and for a time she was an inmate at Blackwell's Island Insane Asylum. After her release from the institution, she was much sought after by gentleman callers who were willing to overlook a touch of insanity owing to her great physical beauty. Eventually Sam Denmead came courting; he must have seemed a rock of stability in comparison with the fickle Mr. Ayres, although he was so startled when her sister—the aforementioned Mary Ann Brundage—entered the room as he was proposing that he jumped out the window. Her family strenuously objected to the courtship, so Sam and Cornelia ran off together in 1857, perhaps to elope—or perhaps not. Whether they were ever actually married is a dark mystery, but for the sake of convenience I will refer to her as Mrs. Denmead.

The couple moved into the later-to-become-notorious New Brunswick house that some papers uncharitably described as a "hut." There they joined Mr. Denmead's brothers Robert and John, and they all lived a hermitlike existence in the tiny shack for years. Then they were joined by two more people. Neighbors saw brother Henry and "a large, fat woman" entering the house in 1872; neither had been seen since around 1877, and it was thought that death had removed them from this domestic paradise. Despite Sam's financial incompetence, the Denmead brothers collectively were worth about $50,000. Their sister bought a nice home for them in 1885, but the residence stood empty as the brothers refused to abandon their squalid hovel. Sam owned one other house, described as "palatial," but would not live there. Among the more exploitive citizens of New Brunswick were hucksters who took advantage of Sam's financial naïveté and stolid refusal to come outside. One shameless person charged him several hundred dollars to paint an old buggy, and Sam paid it.

Of the house's inmates, only Sam and his wife, Cornelia, would go out in public, and even so Sam ventured outside only rarely. By contrast, Mrs. Denmead was a familiar spectacle on the streets of New Brunswick, gathering such refuse as empty bottles, cans, bits of wire, old clothing, and scraps of iron into a basket and carrying her treasures home. Despite her education and family connections, she made extra money working as a washerwoman. A news correspondent noted that she "played [music] and sung charmingly in the homes where she worked as a servant." She would return to the hovel every night after work, and nothing could induce her to come outside. Mrs. Brundage had not seen her sister since December 1886, hence the frantic visit to New Brunswick. Passersby had noticed sickening odors wafting from the Denmead residence, giving rise to unwholesome rumors. Was Mrs. Denmead sick? Had she died and been buried in the house? Had she been murdered? What was going on in that house, anyway!

When word got out that the Denmeads refused to allow Mrs. Brundage into the house, the hermits were beset by citizens determined to either torment the eccentric brothers or somehow make money off of them. In the former class were people who tried by any means to get a peek into the house. Sam Denmead sought to discourage their vandalism by standing guard at the door with a shotgun. In retaliation, the mob threw rocks at the house until the police broke up the festivities. The overseer of the county's poor—who also was refused admittance to the house—discovered that one of the policemen assigned to guard the house had been extorting large sums of money from Denmead. The overseer arranged to have a temporary dwelling constructed on the estate, but still the brothers declined to come out. A *New York Times* correspondent, showing the respect for privacy that makes journalists so beloved every-where, unsuccessfully attempted to enter the shack by crawling under the boards that covered it. Sam agreed to speak with the reporter, stating that his wife was alive but sick. The reporter shouted out Mrs. Denmead's name several times but received no reply from within the house.

After weeks of more or less gentle persuasion, Mrs. Brundage deter-mined to take legal action against those Denmeads. She announced that she would get a search warrant and the police would find out what had been going on the house whether the Denmeads liked it or not.

March 10 was the big day. An immense crowd gathered: no citizen of New Brunswick had ever seen the inside of the Denmead shanty and few could claim to have seen two of the brothers, Robert and John, neither of whom had ventured outside in decades. Ironically, once legal permission to enter the residence had been gained, the authorities seemed afraid to enter. Perhaps cowed by the satanic stink issuing from within, the police, the inspector from the board of health, and even Mrs. Denmead's relatives all had second thoughts. By late afternoon no one had proven brave enough to go inside. At last newspaper reporters took the initiative, as they always shall do if they think a good story is at stake, and shamed the authorities into performing their unenviable duty. It was decided to serve a warrant on Sam Denmead on a charge of criminal neglect for failing to provide medical attention for his wife, punishable as a felony under New Jersey law. The police chief, a detective, and a battery of lawyers and policemen walked to the door, knees trembling.

Their admission came in stages. First, polite knocking received no answer. Next came insistent pounding. Somebody realized that the door was barricaded. Out came the axes. After a few blows the men heard a sound that no one outside the house had heard in many, many years: the voice of ultrareclusive John Denmead, saying, "You can't get in here."

The police chief replied, "But I have a warrant for Sam, and I must get in."

"Sam isn't here."

"It makes no difference. I must get in anyway."

"This is no place to go into," John whined. But he did let them in, with plaintive cries of "Don't step on the dog." The door had been the one thin line of defense between the plaguey stench inside the house and the bright, pleasant world outside. When John opened the door, the odor of decomposition burst out, full-bodied and virile and looking for noses to assault. The investigators instinctively recoiled and one nearly fainted. The men regained their courage and stepped into the tiny, unlighted abode. When their eyes grew accustomed to the dark, they saw John Denmead, tall and elderly, with a long white beard and a cleanly shaven upper lip. He wore a filthy cap and had a nasty handkerchief tied around his neck. His clothes were so old and worn that they had faded into a uniformly dull gray. He was about sixty years old and had not been seen by anyone other than family members since 1845. John lit an oil lamp for the authorities, who then could see the source of the smell.

In a primitive bed made of two feather mattresses lying on boxes, and covered with rags and old discarded clothing, lay the eyeless, shriveled bodies of Cornelia and her brother-in-law Robert Denmead, dead several months at least. The papers described their remains in extravagant, almost loving detail. Mrs. Denmead's body was clad in a long, patched muslin gown and she wore a dirty macramé cap, its ribbons tied under her chin with tape. The exposed skin of her face, hands, and feet was hard and dried out, but the rest of the body was "soft and pliable." Her sister, Mrs. Brundage, insisted on seeing the remains and expressed her opinion that Cornelia never had been legally married to Sam Denmead. Worse, she thought Cornelia "was nothing but the mistress of the three men." As for her bedmate, his face had served as a snack for famished rats, but enough was left of his remains to make it evident that when alive Robert must have cut a frightening figure. His body from the ears down was covered with tough, long gray bristles. The hair on his head stood straight up, Stan Laurel style, and his shriveled hands were folded across his chest. He was dressed in a ragged suit. Adding to the sense of unease, investigators noticed that the bed in which the bodies lay was the only one in the house, leading them to conclude that Sam and John Denmead had been sleeping with the dearly departed every night. One witness, a lawyer, was so staggered by the sight that he had to be carried outside.

The decaying corpses were only part of the house's remarkable decor. There were only a few rough pieces of furniture, including a bureau, but plenty of rags, bones, and decaying vegetables strewn about, and even hanging from posts. Boxes contained old letters, coins, shin plasters, badly worn jewelry, hats and bonnets, shoes, staples, spikes, empty bottles, silver plates, rusty and broken hardware, swords, accordions. A barrel was filled with New Jersey newspapers dating from 1814 to 1840. The cramped house was so full of garbage and junk that explorers barely had room to turn around, and it was heated only by a stove so tiny that one investigator sat on it, thinking it a chair. The dog mentioned by John Denmead was lying on the floor, sick and barely able to move. (A saloonkeeper adopted the neglected bull terrier in an attempt to draw curious patrons to his establishment.) A box contained deeds to land in Philadelphia, New Brunswick, and Somerset County, New Jersey. A *New York Times* reporter commented, "Apparently Sammie had enough native shrewdness to turn his money into property, which would give him an income and could not be stolen." Despite the longstanding rumors that the brothers hoarded money in their hut, no great amount of cash was found. In an exquisitely dramatic moment, searchers found an old daguerreotype of Mrs. Cornelia Denmead, which proved that the stories of her beauty when a youth were not exaggerated. The house's occupants (living and deceased), their collection of junk, and all of their furniture had been packed into a single room measuring about *twelve feet by twelve feet*. A *Police Gazette* reporter commented that a jail cell was more spacious than the Denmead manor.

A curious throng of about five hundred waited outside, and so many people leaned on the house that its board covering broke. The rumor quickly spread that the two rotting Denmeads within had died of highly contagious smallpox, and formerly enthusiastic onlookers scattered like dandelion seeds before a tornado. The rumor was untrue, and some thought Sam Denmead himself had started it to make the crowd leave the premises. The folks watching the action at a distance had to be satisfied with seeing Sam and John arrested and taken to jail. John in particular was a figure of unusual interest as he blinked in the only bright sunlight he had seen, and breathed in the only clean air he had smelled, in four decades.

A reporter visited the brothers in their separate jail cells, which, being clean and spacious, lacked all the comforts of home the Denmeads were accustomed to, such as darkness, filth, sick dogs, and liquefying corpses. Sam commented, with great pathos, "I would rather be in the little hut." He made other statements varying from the suspicious to the deranged. He claimed that his wife, Cornelia, had been injured some months before when naughty lads scared her on the street and she accidentally ran into a post; if any bruises were found on her body, he said, they were due to the mishap. When the reporter asked him why he'd kept overripe corpses in his house, Sam said: "Are they dead? I hope not, I hope not. I kept them there because I wanted to look at them." Then he confirmed the police's theory concerning the household's sleeping arrangements: "We slept with their bodies."

The morning after the interview, the brothers were taken to the jail's washroom and instructed in the proper use of soap and water, but not without a struggle, for Sam "fought like a tiger" when the jailers tried to bathe him, at least according to one report. A conflicting report states that once he resigned himself to his fate, he submitted to his cleansing with a sense of stoicism much to be admired by our present generation. He and John were given new clothes by the jailer.

Thanks to the telegraph and wire services, within a day almost every reader of the nation's dailies had heard all about "the Denmead Horror," as the press called it. On March 11, New Brunswick schoolchildren and adult laborers skipped their lunch hour to gawk at the brothers' charnel house / living quarters. On the same day, the county physician released autopsy results. Robert Denmead had been dead so long, and his body so thoroughly decomposed, that it was impossible to determine the cause of death. (Robert had died a month or more before Cornelia, so the poor woman had been forced to share her deathbed with his decomposing body.) Cornelia's outer skin had rotted away, but the doctor was able to determine that she had suffered from both peritonitis and pleurisy. There were no marks of violence on her head, but her stomach was dilated and "did not contain enough food to fill a thimble." Her intestines, as well as Robert's, were completely empty. The doctor concluded that both had starved to death. When he announced his findings, public opinion about Sam Denmead, low to begin with, became positively subterranean. It was remembered that when Mrs. Denmead had taken ill, her former employers had offered Sam food to take home to her, and he'd refused. Based on the physical evidence and statements made by Sam Denmead, the experts guessed that Robert had died around Christmas 1886, and that Cornelia had died not long afterward.

The police theorized that Sam had neglected his wife and allowed her to starve after she'd gotten sick. It was a fact that he had made a recent attempt to hire a judge to draw up a will for her that was in his favor, though at the time Mrs. Denmead had been dead and decaying in bed. Citizens who were more kindly disposed toward Sam Denmead thought he had not intentionally murdered her or allowed her to die through neglect; they believed that after his wife had died a natural death, he had not alerted the authorities about her passing because he'd wished to forge her will. But the process had taken longer than he thought, and he'd been stuck with her body and had no easy way to dispose of it. This theory did not explain why he had kept the corpse of Robert around as well.

The police futilely searched for the bones of brother Henry Denmead and his female companion, whose remains were rumored to have been buried under the hut. New Brunswick must have been a thrilling place that week.

Sensations grew afresh when the Denmeads were taken to court on March 12. The brothers were cleaned up and in new clothes, and thus were unrecognizable, probably even to each other. John was particularly amazed by the courthouse. When he'd first gone into seclusion, construction of the building had just started; now, like Rip Van Winkle, he'd returned to the world of light decades later to find the courthouse completed and the village grown into a city. The brothers were formally charged with "keeping a nuisance"—quaint legalese for storing two rotten relatives in the house and not reporting their deaths. They were also charged with murder or manslaughter through criminal neglect. A Dr. B. aired a sinister theory: perhaps Mrs. Denmead had not taken sick at all. He noted that despite the deplorable condition of her outer body, her stomach and intestines had remained in mint condition, suggesting the presence of arsenic. Dr. B. had her body reopened—yet another indignity for the corpse, but she was used to it by then—and sent her stomach, liver, and other organs to chemists to search for traces of poison just in case Sam thought death by mere starvation was not fast enough to suit his purposes. After this, her remains were given a much deserved and long overdue decent burial at Saint James Cemetery in Piscataway. If it should happen that the chemists found poison in the corpse, Sam's attorney offered a novel alternative theory: maybe Mrs. Denmead, sick, neglected, starving, and stuck in a bed with the moldering Robert, became so disgruntled with her lot in life that she committed suicide. The attorney pleaded that the Denmeads be given bail. The request was denied, and the brothers were returned to jail.

Things looked pretty serious for the Denmeads, but then everything started going their way. On March 15, the coroner's jury deliberated for an hour and announced that both Robert and Cornelia had died of natural causes, "hastened probably by not having had the proper medical attendance during their sickness." Yet the authorities decided not to charge the brothers with criminal neglect. If we read between the lines of the press reports, it appears that the court concluded that the brothers were insane, and therefore were not to be tried or given any punishment. They were not even indicted for the one crime of which they were manifestly guilty, violating health ordinances by keeping the dead unburied.

Despite the perfunctory solution—or nonsolution, depending on your point of view—to the case, there are nagging loose ends. Were there traces of poison in the bodies of Robert and Cornelia? The possibility was raised and then abruptly dropped, and the press never reported the chemists' findings. What happened to Henry Denmead and his female companion, who'd entered the Denmead domicile in 1872 and had not been seen outside the house for the past decade? And what about Sam's attempt to have a will drawn up in his favor after Cornelia was already dead? It is difficult to think of an innocuous explanation for that action, but the police seemed content not to explore such questions too deeply.

One loose end, however, was resolved most unexpectedly. The reader will recall that Cornelia's first husband, William Ayres, had triggered her descent into insanity by kidnapping their son. After the Denmead Horror became front-page news coast to coast, the missing son turned up in the form of forty-seven-year-old Thomas Henry Ayres, a wealthy farmer of Sunnydale, Kansas, who revealed that his villainous father had died in Lacon, Illinois, in 1861. It turned out he had not been quite such a long-lost son after all. He had tracked down his mother's whereabouts in 1871 and had visited her in New Brunswick, begging her to abandon both Sam Denmead and her life of degradation, but she had refused. She must have been having just too much fun.

In short order, Mr. Ayres proved that he was the direct descendant of Cornelia Denmead and he left the city a wealthier man than he had been when he'd arrived. It was like a fairy tale, except for the bed full of rotting bodies. The Denmead Horror passed from memory; and New Brunswick would know no more such sensations until September 1922, when Rev. Mr. Hall and Mrs. Mills took an ill-fated stroll down a moonlit lovers' lane.

Brutes of Husbands: New Jersey

In January 1890, a man went on trial in Newark for beating his wife. The jury reached a singular verdict: "Not guilty, but we don't want him to do it again."

A New Jersey "Burker"

There have been body snatchers who, like the infamous Scots Burke and Hare, got too impatient for their own good when it came to supplying medical schools with cadavers. Sometimes Mother Nature required goosing to hurry her along.

In May 1892, Mr. Venn, a medical student at the University of Pennsylvania, got a letter from James Moulton, a black resident of 1142 South

Sixth Street, Camden, New Jersey, in which Moulton offered to sell "the body of a fat Negro woman seventy-three years old" whom he claimed was a mortally ill relative—dead *or* alive, he added. Nudge nudge, wink wink! Venn turned the disquieting letter over to the authorities.

Moulton made the same offer, perhaps worded a little more discreetly, to a Philadelphia medical college. The instructors were interested and invited him to their office to fill out the required forms. Of the pending merchandise, Moulton foolhardily told them: "The woman ain't dead yet but she's old and one stick under the ribs will kill her as she ain't got long to live anyway." After he left, the Philadelphians alerted the Camden police that they had a man in their midst who warranted close observation.

On May 6, two undercover Camden policemen went to the address on the letter, posing as medical students in need of a body to dissect. Moulton made them the same ghoulish "dead or alive" offer he made in the letter and even allowed them to peer through a peephole at the intended victim, his elderly housemate, Lydia Ann Wyatt.

But the police dropped the ball and did not follow up on Moulton until it was too late. On May 9, Moulton pushed Wyatt down the stairs and then brained her with either a hatchet or a cane (accounts differ). Moulton didn't think the medical schools would be suspicious in the least if he delivered a corpse with a pulverized head.

When arrested, Moulton was drunk, liberally coated with bloodstains, and in possession of a few hundred dollars of Mrs. Wyatt's money. A defense was impossible and he confessed. Moulton marched to the gallows on August 26, 1892.

The Legal Conundrum of Harrison Noel

Four children were playing on Joseph Bower's front lawn on the afternoon of Friday, September 4, 1925, in an upper-class neighborhood in Montclair. Two were Janet and Nancy Dix, daughters of a prominent New York businessman; the other two were the children of David S. Daly, president of the Washington Hardware Company in Manhattan: Mary, age six, and her brother David Jr., age four.

A black sedan taxicab pulled up near the children and stopped. The driver jumped out, and before several witnesses, he grabbed Mary, threw her in the auto, and fled. The Bowers's daughter Phyllis returned from a shopping trip just in time to see the crime in progress. She asked the family chauffeur, John Sandin, to follow the taxi while she called the police. Sandin stopped just long enough to pick up two friends he saw walking on the roadside in case their assistance was needed; then he chased the taxi for five miles. He almost succeeded in forcing it into the ditch when the driver stuck a gun out the window and fired a shot at the chauffeur's head. Sandin's friends, fearing for his life, drove him to the hospital only to find he'd received a superficial wound. When last seen, the kidnapper was driving in the direction of the Watchung Mountains.

A kidnapping brings out the best in citizens. As word got out that a little girl had been abducted by a dangerous felon, battalions of police, state troopers, and armed posses headed for the mountains. Radio broadcasts described both child and suspect to the public. Motorcycles and an airplane were employed; within hours a $3,000 reward was offered. At first, police thought the kidnapper might be Philip Knapp, a young, Cornell-educated thrill killer who was still on the loose after shooting a Long Island taxicab driver on July 7.

Little Janet Dix was observant, despite the terrifying scene that took place before her, and she gave the mystery car's license number to the police. They found that the taxi belonged to James Scanlon, operator of a Verona garage and taxicab service. The cops made haste to Scanlon's establishment, where the astonished businessman told them that a former employee, a black taxi driver from Newark named Raymond Pierce, had hired the car the day before. (Investigators later found that after he rented the taxi, Pierce received a call to pick up an unidentified passenger at the Montclair Athletic Club.) Both Pierce and the taxi had been missing for hours.

The Dalys were frantic with worry; the father was so distraught he could barely give the police a coherent description of his daughter. Adding to the parents' misery was the fact that the kidnapper had not contacted them with demands. The only ransom call was made not to the Dalys but to the Bowers. The caller demanded $4,000 but, suddenly flustered, hung up.

Several hours after Mary was taken, police received positive proof that the missing Raymond Pierce was not the kidnapper. In Little Falls, a man was standing on the bridge over Peckham Creek at Van Geisen's Gap, pointing out the beautiful scenery to visitors, when he noticed a pair of legs sticking out from under some bushes. The dead man was Pierce. An autopsy proved he had been shot hours before the kidnapping.

The forensic evidence suggested that he had parked the taxi on the side of the road, probably at the request of his passenger from the athletic club; then the rider fired at the back of his head. The killer hid Pierce's body in the bushes and stole the car. He abducted Mary Daly the next afternoon.

Within a few hours of the kidnapping, the woods were searched by police from a dozen New Jersey cities and as many citizens' posses, some including women, Boy Scouts, and bloodhounds. David Daly himself led one search, exclaiming that if his girl were harmed, he would kill the fiend himself.

Meanwhile, as all this activity took place in the wilderness, a strange scene was being enacted in the luxurious Montclair home of Dix Noel, located a block away from the Bower house, where the kidnapping had taken place. Noel was a wealthy New York City lawyer; his wife, Anne, a professional writer and frequent contributor to the *Atlantic Monthly*. Their eldest son was strikingly handsome and athletic, nineteen-year-old Harrison W. Noel. On Saturday, September 5, Harrison told his mother that Mary Daly was alive and he knew where to find her.

Noel's parents were accustomed to his making cryptic comments, for despite his normal, healthy outer appearance, he was not quite right in the head. In fact, he'd spent some time in an insane asylum and a sanitarium. Even as she pondered his statement, the police were heading for her door. Two residents had noticed a strange car, a distinctive red Oakland, hidden in a quarry at Little Falls. They'd reported the license number. The car was owned by Harrison Noel's mother. When the police arrived, they took the young man in for questioning. He told them he would reveal the whereabouts of Mary Daly, but only if he were paid $4,000 in cash. The police rewarded him only with a grilling that lasted for twenty-three hours. Noel remained unresponsive to pleas from Mr. Daly and his mother, but on Sunday evening he confessed.

The authorities took him to Montclair Hospital, where the chauffeur, John Sandin, positively identified him as the man he'd chased in a hopeless effort to save Mary. Harrison Noel was then taken to Preakness Mountain at Little Falls, where he led police to the girl's body, hidden in sumac bushes beside a mountain road. She'd been shot twice in the head but, as one newspaper put it, "she had not been otherwise maltreated." Noel admitted that he'd also murdered Raymond Pierce and allowed reporters to take his photograph.

Once the police had their suspect, enough evidence fell into place to drive a defense attorney to drink. The abandoned stolen taxicab was found with the suspect's fingerprints all over the inside. When the police searched the Noel residence, they found a .30-caliber revolver with steel-jacketed bullets, the weapon and ammunition used to kill Pierce and wound Sandin.

The police and the papers tried to make what they could of the unlikely killer. Reporters and friends of the family used overwhelmingly positive adjectives to describe him. He was "well dressed," "polite," "quiet," "likable," and "mild." At worst he seemed sullen, absent-minded, and indifferent. We often are admonished that poverty, lack of opportunity, and lack of education are sure breeders of crime, yet Harrison Noel came from the privileged class, had graduated with honors from Montclair High School, and had entered Harvard at age seventeen in fall 1922, though he left the university after one semester due to mental problems. Recently he had been the patrol leader of Montclair Boy Scout troop number 5 and won medals for doing good deeds.

Despite the all-American-boy exterior, Noel had a reputation for being deranged. His supporters claimed that studying too hard at college had destroyed his mind. Recently he'd been confined at the Essex County Hospital for the Insane, also known as Overbrook. When he'd improved, he was allowed to wander the grounds at will. He escaped on June 28. The next day, he was found in a coma at Ninth Avenue and Thirtieth Street in Manhattan. He was brought to the psychopathic ward at Bellevue and sent back to New Jersey a few days later. His stay at Overbrook was not happy, and later he claimed that he'd bought his revolver to shoot any officials who might try to take him back to the asylum. When the doctors at Overbrook tested Noel at the end of July, his father took custody of him.

Noel's motive for kidnapping Mary Daly was the ransom money. The reader will remember that three hours after Daly was kidnapped, her family's neighbor, Mrs. Joseph Bower, received a call demanding a $4,000 ransom—the same amount Noel asked of the police in exchange for revealing the location of the girl's body. Under questioning, Noel admitted that he was the caller. Some thought he intended to kidnap Dorothy Coates, a seven-year-old niece of the wealthy Bowers, but had mistakenly abducted the Daly child. Supporting this belief was the testimony of Mrs. Bower, who said the caller was self-possessed and cool at first, but seemed "taken aback" when he realized that she was not related to the missing girl. He began speaking incoherently and then ended the call.

The fact that Noel was greedy does not necessarily rule out insanity, since even crazy people need money. The press revealed that he wrote bizarre letters to Frank Gray, the scoutmaster of the Montclair Boy Scouts troop 5, demonstrating that he wanted money and was not particular about how he got it. One began with an admirably polite request: "Please die. I wish you had some money so you could leave it to me. But if you haven't, never mind. Die anyway. You see, I'm sure there's somebody somewhere in the world who wants to be preserved, protected and defended by me, so please die. P.S.—If this request meets with your approval, kindly O.K. and return."

In another letter to Gray, Noel wrote: "Please send me twenty-five dollars and have the rest of your estate put in my name. . . . If you do not wish to comply with my demands I shall consider you unfit to be shot and will spurn you utterly." When the press contacted Gray, he said that Noel would sometimes drop by his office and, after an initial greeting, would sit and stare silently and disquietingly at him for hours.

Once confined in the Essex County jail, Noel slipped into a state of total indifference, something he often did in the past; it was the reason his father had him committed to the asylum on February 23, 1925. It was thought that he suffered from catatonic dementia praecox. Naturally, the public demanded to know why Noel had been released from Overbrook, and the doctors in charge at that institution found themselves on the defensive. The assistant superintendent of the hospital, Dr. H. G. Smith, insisted that Noel seemed normal when discharged: "I think he was lying in his answers to me and others while he was here. . . . I think his chief motive was the desire to make some money through a kidnapping plot, rather than an insane prompting of a diseased mind." And why had Noel not been returned to the asylum after he was found wandering in Manhattan back in June? Dr. Smith explained: "When his father brought him out here about a month later we examined him again, and he seemed to be greatly improved. Patients are frequently released in this way when we satisfy ourselves that they may be safely sent back to their families, but we had the right to recall him at any time, and would have done so if our examinations from time to time had indicated that his condition had become worse."

The authorities were not satisfied with the doctor's explanation, and three investigations were made into the staff's tragic decision not to recommit Harrison Noel, including one headed by Senator William H. Bright. The Essex County Board of Freeholders demanded the immediate resignation of the asylum's senior resident physician, Dr. John M. Thompson. They complained that Thompson had meant well but overstepped his authority by granting "a virtual parole to Noel, without knowledge or consent of his superiors." When the board held an inquiry, they found that Mrs. Noel had tried to have her son reinstitutionalized five days after his escape in June, but Dr. Thompson had not been in at the time. The asylum had turned her down. Thereafter, Dr. Thompson requested that Harrison be returned, but felt he had no legal grounds to enforce it as the young lunatic had been voluntarily committed by his parents. The embattled physician considered himself a scapegoat; he dug in his heels and refused to resign, and threatened a lawsuit if he were fired. On September 17, the board adopted a resolution to discharge Dr. Thompson, but he refused to leave Overbrook unless he were forcibly removed.

The board took him at his word. On a fine Sunday morning in early October, the doctor, his wife, and five-year-old daughter went for a walk. When they returned to their apartment at Overbrook an hour later, they found the door padlocked. The same day, Dr. Thompson announced that he would sue the board members for financial loss and damage to his professional reputation caused by his dismissal. I do not know the outcome of the suit but assume it was settled to the satisfaction of absolutely no one.

Many felt the responsibility lay not with any of the asylum doctors but with Dix Noel, who'd allowed his son to roam the earth freely even though he had been committed to two institutions for the mentally defective. Dr. Thompson claimed that he'd advised Mr. Noel many times to bring his son back to the asylum and publicly called Noel a domineering know-it-all who thought he could diagnose Harrison's case better than the doctors. Mr. Noel countered that by allowing his son freedom he had been guilty only of believing the doctors who told him Harrison was well on the road to recovery. Ellis P. Earle, chairman of the board of freeholders, told the *New York Times* that he thought the Daly and Pierce families had grounds for a civil suit against the Noels: "I consider that the parents . . . are highly culpable for having him allowed to be at large. They permitted him to drive a New Jersey automobile without a license, they knew he had a gun in his home, they knew he had expressed a threat to kidnap some child and they were familiar with his previous murderous attacks on several people."

Indeed, there was evidence of Harrison Noel's potentially violent nature long before he abducted Mary Daly. He'd attacked his father with a Boy Scout hatchet while camping in July 1923. Immediately afterward, Harrison had seemed unaware that he'd struck his father and helped apply first aid. Harrison slept soundly that night, but the other family members thought it prudent to stay awake until dawn. Dix Noel emerged from the campout with a deep scalp wound and severed veins in his right hand. Soon afterward, Harrison was confined at the Craig House Sanitarium at Beacon, New York, where he clubbed an attendant with a chair arm. In 1924, Noel worked as a seaman on the steamer *George Washington*, and there he attempted to murder a cook.

Understandably, nobody wanted to claim responsibility for turning Harrison Noel loose, and his father and the asylum officials expended a substantial amount of newspaper ink blaming each other. Dix Noel hired lawyers on his son's behalf and vowed to reporters: "I shall perform my duties as a father toward my insane son."

As the squabbling between Dr. Thompson, Mr. Noel, and the board of freeholders continued, life went on for the families of Harrison Noel's victims. Mary Daly was laid to rest in a Catholic cemetery in Jersey City. Money was raised for the taxi driver Raymond Pierce's widow and four children. Harrison's mother sold her Oakland automobile, which her son had used in the commission of his crimes. She donated the $275 to the fund for the Pierce family, saying only, "I don't want ever to see that car again." By early December, the fund had grown to $5,247. The money was placed in a local bank, and Mrs. Pierce received $46 per month, as well as an additional $34 per month from the state's widows' pension.

Noel spent his days in jail steeped in apathy, one of the major symptoms of dementia praecox. He sat on the edge of his cot and stared at the wall. He spoke very little. On September 9, he was indicted by the Essex County grand jury on charges of kidnapping Mary Daly and murdering Raymond Pierce. (The charges of assault on the chauffeur Sandin and the murder of Daly were pending, as those acts had taken place in Passaic County.) Noel's mental state was the crux of the matter. If he were sane, he could be sentenced to life in prison, at best, or death in the electric chair. If experts judged him insane, he probably would not be tried and would live out the rest of his days at the New Jersey Asylum for the Criminal Insane at Trenton. The prisoner got the ball rolling in fine style by recanting his signed confession. He pled guilty to kidnapping but claimed, despite the overwhelming evidence, that he'd murdered no one.

The arraignment was held in September at the Essex County Court of Common Pleas in Newark. Noel's attorney Merritt Lane made a motion to defer the trial a few more days. He argued before Judge Edwin Caffrey that his client had been legally committed to an insane asylum and was never released as sane; therefore, he was to be considered insane and not responsible for his actions. Lane tiptoed around the fact that Noel had never been released from Overbrook as sane or otherwise because he'd escaped and was not recommitted, but such fine legal hairs are what lawyers are paid to split. Lane's "insane until proven otherwise" argument won the day, but Assistant Prosecuting Attorney J. Victor D'Aloia promised after the court session that the state would prove that Harrison Noel had been sane when he'd committed his evil acts.

The great battle over Harrison Noel's sanity began on September 21, when Judge Caffrey directed that a plea of not guilty be entered for Noel when the prisoner refused to plead one way or the other to the charges. Perhaps Noel was made nervous by David Daly, who sat glaring at him only eight feet away. The judge also ruled that there would be a hearing to determine whether Noel was sane enough to be tried for the murder of Raymond Pierce; his indictment for kidnapping and murdering Mary Daly would be heard at a later date. The question to be answered was the famous M'Naughten rule, the legal standard for determining insanity since 1843: did Noel know the difference between right and wrong? Under New Jersey law, even if alienists could prove Noel insane, he could still be held criminally responsible for his actions if he were able to distinguish between the two. Assistant Prosecutor D'Aloia pointed out to the press that for a crazy man, Harrison Noel was crafty. He'd purchased his gun in New York and mailed it to his home in New Jersey, switched cars during the kidnapping to avoid detection, and kidnapped a girl from a wealthy family. Newspaper reports describing Noel's gestures suggested that he'd felt guilty. He was unable to look Mr. Daly in the eye when they passed each other in a court house corridor; once, when riding in a police car past the Bower residence, Noel had averted his eyes from the scene of the kidnapping.

Six doctors, including three who were psychiatrists, interviewed Noel for Prosecutor D'Aloia. One problem faced by this battery was getting the silent, sullen Noel to talk. After several failed attempts, the doctors gathered in a corridor and one said, loudly enough for Noel to overhear, "I believe he has lost his voice. We must operate on his throat." The prisoner was plenty talkative afterward.

The defense hired its own alienists to speak to Noel, and their findings contradicted those of their rivals, giving Judge Caffrey a tough problem when the hearing on Noel's sanity began on September 24. Five physicians took the stand on behalf of the prosecution and gave their expert opinion that while Harrison Noel was mentally abnormal, he was sane enough to be put on trial. Despite withering cross-examination by Merritt Lane, they pointed out that "the youth appreciated the enormity of his offenses and was capable of consulting intelligently with his counsel."

The prosecution's doctors admitted that the files from the Overbrook asylum indicated that Noel was insane—or, at least, had been insane in the past. But he knew the criminal nature of his acts. To one witness, Dr. Ambrose Dowd, Noel said: "I knew it was wrong. I know the predicament I am in. I want my friends to help. It is wrong to kill any human being. It is wrong for you to kill me. I don't know right and wrong in the same way you do. I know it would be wrong to shoot anyone." To Dr. Christopher Beling, he said: "I killed the child because I didn't want to be seen with her. I would be caught." Noel told the doctor that his motive had been strictly pecuniary: he wanted the ransom money. He'd planned to send the girl's parents a postcard instructing them to throw the money out of a train window when they saw his signal, a red balloon he intended to tie beside the tracks. A deflated red balloon had been found in his coat pocket when he was arrested.

Defense attorney Lane spent four days rebutting the state's witnesses. His star psychiatrist was Dr. Carlos MacDonald, who had fifty years' experience as a specialist in mental diseases and who'd examined such celebrated madmen as presidential assassin Leon Czolgosz and Harry Thaw, whose tawdry murder of the architect Stanford White in Madison Square Garden had held the nation in thrall twenty years before. Mac-Donald and two other specialists contradicted the prosecution's alienists by stating that Harrison Noel was a hopeless victim of advanced dementia praecox and did not comprehend the enormity of his crimes. One doctor, William Pritchard, had asked Noel if he did wrong by killing Mary Daly. Noel had responded that he was justified in anything he did because he had been wrongfully shut away at Overbrook in a room with decor that troubled him, "green walls with dragons on them and two registers in the floor." Dr. Thompson, the recently fired head of Overbrook, testified that his former patient was crazy as a spider monkey (to put it in layman's terms). The defense also inserted into the record the letters Noel had written to his scoutmaster, Frank Gray, demanding that he die and leave Noel money. Nevertheless, under cross-examination by Assistant Prosecutor D'Aloia, the psychiatrists admitted "that the details of his crimes, covering a period of more than three days, were carefully carried out and rationally related," according to the *Times*.

Throughout the insanity hearing, Harrison Noel sat staring ahead, isolated and impassive. One attendee who did not remain so quiet was David Daly. During recess on October 1, he shouted at an Overbrook doctor who passed by outside the courthouse: "You're one of a pack of liars. You are one of a paid gang trying to save your reputations." Two days later, Assistant Prosecutor D'Aloia delivered his final address to the court. He raised the possibility that Noel was malingering, faking insanity because he knew his life could depend on it, and demanded that he be tried by jury and receive a fair shot at the death penalty. Defense attorney Lane claimed Noel was "hopelessly insane" and pleaded that he receive justice.

With these eloquent speeches, the sanity hearing was over. A total of eleven learned, experienced psychiatrists had testified, and their combined 150,000 words of expert testimony could be boiled down thus: some thought Noel sane, some thought him insane, and some thought him insane yet capable of telling right from wrong. It was up to Judge Caffrey to decide whether Harrison Noel was sane enough to go to trial. The judge was so troubled by the conflicting testimony that he took the unusual move of visiting Noel for more than an hour in his cell. On October 8, he announced his decision: because Noel had displayed enough rationality to help his counsel in preparing his defense, he was sane enough to face a jury on a charge of murdering Raymond Pierce.

When Harrison Noel went on trial for his life in November, he appeared as apathetic as ever. The same could not be said for his attorney William Wachenfeld, who worked feverishly to save him. Interestingly, Wachenfeld had been appointed by the court to represent Noel; despite Dix Noel's promise to "perform my duties as a father toward my insane son," he'd declined to provide an attorney this time around, and neither he nor Mrs. Noel attended the first day of their son's trial. Again the prisoner appeared before Judge Caffrey, and again he faced his nemesis in the form of Assistant Prosecutor D'Aloia, who demanded that Noel be found guilty and receive the death penalty for "deliberate, premeditated and malicious" murder in the first degree. Reporters noted during the first day of the trial that at no time did Wachenfeld and his client confer. Undoubtedly they feared that having a conference would make Noel seem concerned about his predicament and therefore aware of the nature of his actions.

D'Aloia wasted no time reviewing for the jury the activities of the defendant on September 3, 1925, when he'd murdered Raymond Pierce several hours before kidnapping and killing Mary Daly. Defense attorney Wachenfeld objected that the mention of the Daly crime was prejudicial and "irrelevant," claiming with dubious logic that "the murder of Pierce was not necessarily connected with the murder of the Daly child"—never mind that Daly had been abducted in a car that Pierce had been driving and was murdered for. Judge Caffrey overruled the objection and the reference to Mary Daly was allowed to stand. Noel's actions on that day, argued D'Aloia, "were all acts of one who was not only sure of what he was doing but equally sure that he was doing wrong"—for example, the call he made to the taxi driver Pierce as a subterfuge to ride with him into isolated country, the hiding of Pierce's corpse, the hiding of the taxi after he abducted Mary Daly. D'Aloia referred also to the evasive way Noel answered questions after he was arrested, making it seem that he was sane enough to know he should keep his mouth shut about certain matters.

Perhaps deciding to avoid the confusion wrought by the plethora of experts at the insanity hearing, D'Aloia called only one alienist to the stand, Dr. Walter Washington, who had interviewed Noel three times. The doctor testified that he believed Noel was sane when he committed his crimes, but on cross confessed that he had thought Noel insane two months before the murder. Score one for the defense, but then Noel's signed jailhouse confession was admitted as evidence, over Wachenfeld's hearty objections. For the first time since he went to trial, Noel showed interest in the proceedings.

The defense struck back. Wachenfeld said to the jury, "This boy is insane. There's not a doubt in the world of it." In order to prove it, over the course of two days he called to the stand six alienists, including the beleaguered and presumably still homeless Dr. Thompson, formerly of Overbrook. Nurses and other attendants from the asylum described Noel's "abnormal conduct." Dr. Menas Gregory of Bellevue testified about the time when Noel had been briefly committed there after being found unconscious in New York. The cumulative opinion of the witnesses was that Harrison Noel was insane and had been so back in September when he'd committed the two murders.

The most important defense witness, at least in terms of winning jury sympathy, was Mrs. Noel—still no trace of the father—who testified in detail about her son's mental decline, which had been especially marked over the past three years. He'd failed every one of his final examinations his junior year of high school, she said, but in the fall he'd retaken the exams and passed them all. He had been erratic when deciding where to go to college, had remained at Harvard only one semester, had held down odd jobs after failing school, and had become increasingly secluded. He'd complained that there was too much light in his room. On several occasions he'd left home to go traveling on a whim. At one point he was determined to live on a diet of bran. Then there was that time he went after his father with a hatchet, after which he spent time in the Craig House Sanitarium and Overbrook.

Attorney Wachenfeld elicited from a tearful Mrs. Noel the information that her insane sister had committed suicide at age nineteen after six unsuccessful attempts. In 1925 the idea of heredity as a factor in criminal behavior was very much in flower, and crafty defense lawyers realized that if they could find even one black sheep in a defendant's family tree—not a difficult prospect—they could try to get their client free based on the idea that since people have no control over their ancestry, no one can be held accountable for anything. I exaggerate, but not much, and the idea still finds its way into the courtroom from time to time.

Under cross-examination, D'Aloia got Mrs. Noel to admit that she'd allowed her son to drive her car even though he had no driver's license, the implication being that if she'd truly thought her son was insane, she would not have let him drive under any circumstances. The next day D'Aloia called to the stand two alienists, Drs. Dowd and Beling, who testified that while they believed Noel suffered from dementia praecox, he still knew that murder was wrong.

The case went to the jury on November 16. After an hour and ten minutes of deliberation, the members returned to the courtroom with their decision: Harrison Noel was sane enough to tell right from wrong when he killed Pierce, and therefore was guilty of murder in the first degree. Their recommended penalty was death in the electric chair. Noel lost his apathy just long enough to call the jury's verdict "rotten" and then went back to his favorite jailhouse occupations: reading magazines and staring blankly at the wall.

Passaic County had two indictments against Noel for the kidnapping and murder of Mary Daly, but it looked as though he would never be tried for those crimes since he was sentenced to go to the chair sometime during the week beginning January 10, 1926. Regardless, David Daly said he was satisfied with the verdict. Attorney Wachenfeld moved to have his client's case appealed, calling the jury's decision "the greatest blot ever made upon Jersey justice." He added, "It was not for the killing of the colored man that Noel was convicted. He was found guilty through prejudice against the slayer of the little girl. It is the first case in New Jersey where an admitted mental deficient has been found guilty of first degree murder."

As Noel was moved from the Essex County jail to his death row cell at the state penitentiary at Trenton, his attorney pleaded for clemency at the Court of Pardons at the state capitol. On December 1, the court refused Wachenfeld's request on the grounds that it was a court of mercy and he should come there only if his appeal for a new trial were denied. Within a week, Wachenfeld's second appeal had been denied by the New Jersey Supreme Court. The attorney then appealed to the Court of Errors, the highest tribunal in the state. One effect of the legal battle was that the appeals automatically gave Noel a stay of execution, so he did not go to the chair in January as scheduled.

In late February 1926, the Court of Errors heard Noel's case. Wachenfeld submitted a brief in which he claimed that the lower court had committed errors prejudicial to his client, and therefore the verdict of first-degree murder should be reversed. Specifically, Wachenfeld declared that Noel's confession had been "improperly admitted in evidence because testimony tended to show that Noel was insane and because the youth was said to have received a promise of immunity if he confessed." He also claimed that Prosecutor D'Aloia and Judge Caffrey had made prejudicial statements to the jury, contentions that were disputed by Essex County prosecutor John Bigelow.

With time, the Harrison Noel case faded from public view. A compromise of sorts was reached: his sentence was commuted and he ended up not exactly in prison, but in the prison ward of a Trenton mental hospital. Given Noel's professed fear of asylums, sending him there may have been far crueler in the long run than a few exciting seconds in the electric chair ever could have been. Passaic County never had the chance to try Noel for kidnapping and murder but never dropped its indictments against him. In May 1973, Superior Court Judge John F. Crane finally dismissed the nearly fifty-year-old charges against Noel. Nobody much cared by then; his victims, their families, his parents, and anyone else he had wronged were long dead. Harrison Noel was transferred to a private mental hospital where he died in June 1977.

Dead Man Waiting

Reverend P. was not only a Methodist minister; he was also village recorder of Metuchen. It was in the latter capacity that he sentenced Archibald H. to ten days in jail in 1906 on a charge of disorderly conduct.

Archibald spent his required ten days fuming and then plotted revenge for the next two years. His opportunity came on July 15, 1908, when he shot his old enemy to death on the streets of Metuchen. He was sentenced to death in the electric chair.

Then a legal problem arose. Year after year, revised dates for the execution came and went because Archibald's attorney contended that "if [he] was not insane at the time of the crime he became insane immediately afterward and the state could not execute an insane man."

Finally, an absolute date for Archibald's death was set—and passed, with no execution. The condemned man's attorney then argued with dubious logic that the still-thriving Archibald was "legally dead" and could not be sent to the chair. On March 10, 1922, the New Jersey legislature passed a bill that would declare Archibald officially once again alive and ripe for taking his long-delayed punishment. His name does not turn up in Daniel Allen Hearn's authoritative book *Legal Executions in New Jersey*, so it can be assumed the situation was resolved to the satisfaction of absolutely no one except Archibald and his attorney.

3

VERMONT VAGARIES

See-Through Tomb

ONE NEW ENGLAND GRAVE IS A STRIKING MONUMENT NOT ONLY TO ITS occupant, but also to the lengths people would go to avoid being buried alive.

Dr. Timothy Clark Smith of Monkton, Vermont, served as American consul to Odessa, Russia, in 1861 and to Galatz, Romania, in 1878. The surgeon had a fear of premature burial that bordered on the pathological. He died in an inn in Middlebury on Halloween 1893. His family, who seem to have shared his phobia, kept his body in the rented room until the health authorities ordered them to remove it (i.e., it began to smell up the place). The family placed Smith in a temporary vault in Evergreen Cemetery in nearby New Haven while they constructed a tomb in the same graveyard. Meanwhile, guards were stationed at the vault in the unlikely event the decomposing Smith happened to revive. When Smith's grave was completed, it was a masterpiece of engineering. Beneath a large mound, a cement shaft led from the underground coffin to the surface and a bell was placed in Smith's hand so that he might sound an alarm if he proved to be not such a corpse after all. There was also a breathing tube. Best of all, a fourteen-inch-square window of thick glass was placed atop the cement shaft. The window was placed over Smith's face so he could see the sweet world above. But it also meant that people visiting the cemetery could look through the window and peer down at Smith's skull six feet below. Naturally you would love to go on a road trip and see for yourself, so be cautioned: because of the age of the glass and the moisture that collects beneath it, Smith's remains have not been visible for a long time. No doubt for a while he provided a very interesting spectacle.

Extraordinary Epitaphs: Vermont

Supposedly written on an otherwise blank gravestone in Stowe: "I was somebody—who, is no business of yours."

⊱•⊰

A double gravestone in Hardwick:

Willie	MARSHALL	His wife, Delia Longe
1872–1944		1876–
He never did.		She always did her best.

⊱•⊰

Edward Oakes died in 1866; his gravestone in West Cemetery, Middlebury, bears two heartfelt sentiments from his widow that create an unintended meaning in juxtaposition: "Faithful husband thou art at rest / Until we meet again."

⊱•⊰

Epitaph on Mary Hoyt (d. 1836) in Bradford: "She lived—what more can there be said / She died—and all we know she's dead."

Augustus's Grave

Augustus M. was described as an "exceedingly eccentric man," and he certainly seems to have been. He died at age eighty-four in Hinesburg, Vermont, in January 1874. Twenty years before, he had had his grave dug on his farm; it had been kept in storage ever since, lined with a rock wall and filled with earth, awaiting the day when it would serve its purpose. In autumn 1873, he ordered the dirt removed from his grave, stating—quite correctly—that he would be filling it before winter ended. Augustus had a habit of sleeping on his side with his knees drawn up, and in 1866 he had a custom-made coffin built so that he could sleep in this position through eternity. Before Augustus died, he instructed that his pallbearers be four young black men who had worked for him for years, as had their father. Following Augustus's instructions, they carried his coffin to his grave, lowered it, filled in the hole, and then walked back to his farmhouse. They were each handed a letter containing their payment.

How a Person May Be in Two Places at One Time

Laura C., a young actress, had made considerable headway in her chosen career; she had appeared onstage with the famous Louisville performer Mary Anderson, had been a leading lady for Frank Mayo, and had had a role in the then-famous play *Davy Crockett*. Her older sister Venie also achieved success onstage in Edward E. Rice's burlesque production of *Evangeline*, America's first musical comedy.

Laura also was a Spiritualist. She took ill and died in Baltimore on November 10, 1884, when she was only twenty-one. On her deathbed she said, "I know my mother will be with me tonight." Her last request was that her body be cremated—a newfangled and controversial procedure at the time—and that half her ashes be buried with her sister Venie in Baltimore, and the other half with her mother in Burlington, Vermont. Her wishes were followed to the letter at the crematorium at Lancaster, Pennsylvania, on December 3. The remains of Laura C. were carried to two locations in two tin boxes.

At Least the Slogans Weren't Set to Music

It was reported in 1902 that an undertaking firm in Fair Haven had taken to putting up roadside signs advertising their wares. One read: "Undertaking as it should be undertaken."

Another read: "Caskets of every design. Open day and night."

A third bore the proud boast that the firm owned the "Finest rubber-tired hearse in the state."

The Swan Knows When It Is Dying: Vermont

In 1935, William S. had a tombstone erected at Washington, Vermont, reading: "William Eben S., 1873–1937." In November 1936, he became a fugitive for transporting stolen goods over state lines. He died in Nowata, Oklahoma, in February 1937.

Death Row Dramas: Vermont

For abusing and poisoning her adopted niece Alice, Emeline L. Meaker of Burlington was given the strictest of sentences in November 1881: she was to spend roughly fifteen months in prison—the last three in solitary—until the last Friday of March 1883, when she would go down in history as the first woman legally hanged in Vermont.

Mrs. Meaker slept soundly on her last night in the jail at Windsor, and after an enormous final breakfast worthy of a lumberjack on the morning of March 30, 1883, she was allowed to examine the gallows that would soon take her life. She checked it out from top to bottom with a dry, calm curiosity that struck bystanders as more than a little strange.

After inspecting the gallows, Mrs. Meaker ate a hearty lunch. Soon afterward she was led to the gallows, the steps of which she mounted without the slightest show of emotion. (One reporter noticed that she "evidently did not like the crowd.") To Sheriff Atherton she handed a note: "I have nothing more to say, only I forgive you for hanging me." Then she mouthed to the crowd: "May God forgive you all." Calm right to the last, she dropped through the trapdoor, died with "scarcely a struggle," and was buried in the prison cemetery.

As an interesting side note, Meaker was deaf and all communication with her had to be accomplished by writing notes.

4

RECONDITE RHODE ISLAND

Grave Robbers and Body Snatchers: Rhode Island

WHEN CABLE B. DIED IN PROVIDENCE IN JUNE 1883, HE WAS BURIED IN the cemetery on the state farm, as was fit and proper. In November, friends had him disinterred so they could bury him elsewhere. When the grave was opened, laborers found that someone had made off with Cable's head, as was unfit and improper.

Extraordinary Epitaphs: Rhode Island

Dr. William P. Rothwell of Pawtucket was so noted for his generosity in picking up the tab for his friends that his phrase "This is on me" became something of a personal catch phrase. He always said that he didn't want any tears at his funeral, and to make sure visitors to his grave got a good laugh, he arranged to be buried under a boulder on which was inscribed "This is on me." Dr. Rothwell died on June 14, 1939.

><

Two identical gravestones side by side in Little Compton leave one speculating as to the untold story behind them. One reads: "In memory of

Lidia, ye wife of Mr. Simeon Palmer, who died December ye 26th 1754." The other: "In memory of Elizabeth who should have been the wife of Mr. Simeon Palmer, who died Augt 14th 1776."

Adapting to Their Environment

In November 1879 a family of immigrants, evidently having nowhere better to go, moved into a vacant tomb in a cemetery near Providence. They were discovered after a week's residence, and it was noted that they stored their dishes on the empty coffin shelves.

Amused to Death

Joshua W.'s wife thought it was awfully funny that night in December 1878 when he mistakenly cured pork with sugar rather than salt. Once the Newport woman started laughing, she couldn't stop and, according to the press, she "kept on laughing until, in spite of the efforts of her husband and others to prevent it, she actually laughed herself to death." The *Louisville Courier-Journal* deadpanned a curious moral from the incident: "Will people *never* learn the terrible danger of buying unsalted pork and keeping white sugar about the house at the same time?"

Yankee Practicality

Elizabeth W. lived in Pawtucket. Her grandfather died in 1899, leaving her an estate of $80,000—with the stipulation that she must marry her grandfather's male heir.

When Elizabeth was nineteen, the male heir died before she had an opportunity to marry him. It may have seemed that her chance of inheriting that eighty grand was irrevocably lost, but she was blessed with ingenuity. She went to Binghamton, New York, and married an eight-month-old boy—with his parents' consent—on April 4, 1901, thereby making him the heir and securing the fortune.

A news report elaborated on the bizarre situation: "[She] possesses the youngest husband in the world. As the marriage was only done to fill the conditions of the will, it is expected that it will be annulled as soon as the estate has been settled and [she] has endowed her young husband with a share of the property." Until then, we presume, she occupied herself by changing her husband's diapers.

Ominous Indeed

In 1903, an unnamed tobacco company offered prizes to smokers who sent coupons from their cigarette packs. An also unnamed, leather-lunged sixteen-year-old boy from Woonsocket sent in 10,000 coupons for his prize. The company sent it, but the treasurer included a uniquely frank word of advice: "If you smoke 10,000 more cigarettes you will win a coffin."

5

CREEPY CONNECTICUT

The Sexton Witnesses Something Worth Writing Home About

IN JANUARY 1879, AN UNNAMED WOMAN WAS BURIED IN STRAITSVILLE. A week later, a man and woman claiming to be siblings of the deceased approached the sexton and asked if he would open the grave. He assumed that they wished to positively identify the remains, and at their request he went through the not inconsiderable trouble of digging up the frozen ground, unearthing the coffin, and removing the lid. Then he got a front row seat to the following spectacle: the visitors lifted the body out of the coffin; examined her shroud and burial clothing, taking care to remove all the pins; threw the pins and the corpse's ring into the snow; rolled the body over in the snow several times; placed it back in the coffin; screwed the lid back in place; helped the sexton lower the coffin back in the grave; announced that they were perfectly satisfied; and left the grounds without a word of explanation.

Premature Burial: Connecticut

Some lucky New Englanders barely escaped awakening in their caskets. Catherine M., a sixty-two-year-old who lived in South Norwalk, went sleepwalking on August 26, 1908, and fell headfirst down a flight of steps.

She fractured her skull and broke her neck, and certainly seemed plenty dead when the doctor examined her. For three hours she lay while her mourning husband and children called in the undertaker. When that worthy arrived with his measuring tape in hand and profit margin in mind, Mrs. M. sat up, yawned, and said, "My head aches this morning and I guess I will have some catnip tea." She was on the road to recovery, but had she revived a day or two later, no amount of catnip tea could have saved her.

Carl L. of Hartford was working on the Middletown Bridge on April 7, 1914, when he touched a live wire. He collapsed, seemingly dead, as 2,300 volts coursed through his body. His coworkers carried him to the undertaker's establishment, where Carl woke up on the slab, rubbed his eyes as though arising in his own bedroom, looked around, realized just where he was, and ran out of the place with a speed that did great credit to one of the formerly deceased. His only memento of the experience was a burn on one hand.

Extraordinary Epitaphs: Connecticut

A pink granite stone in Old North Cemetery, Hartford, reads: "Those who cared for him while living will know whose body lies resting here. To others, it does not matter. September 1, 1882." According to cemetery records, the identity of the plot's occupant is a mystery.

On October 29, 1910, John de Martin of Stamford was killed by a hit-and-run driver in Bridgeport. The widow had an account of the accident inscribed on his tombstone in the hope that the guilty party would read it, be overcome with remorse, and turn himself in to the police.

Phineas Gardner Wright died at age eighty-nine at his home in Putnam on May 2, 1918. He was prominent enough to get his obituary in the *New York Times*, which stated that he had built a monument to himself. The newspaper did not mention that the marker, in Grove Street Cemetery, featured the likeness of Wright and the words "Going, But Know Not Where."

━━━◦━━━

Most epitaphs sanitize the facts of death by studiedly refusing to mention them. A select few, however, do. An unpleasant epitaph on Dr. Isaac Bartholomew (d. 1710) in Hillside Cemetery, Cheshire: "He that was sweet to my repose / Now is become a stink under my nose. / This is said of me / So it will be said of thee."

━━━◦━━━

A similar sentiment, but with a strangely jocular tone, is found on the gravestone of five-year-old Milla Gaylord (d. 1806) in the West Woods Cemetery, Hamden: "Soon ripe / Soon rotten / Soon gone / But not forgotten."

━━━◦━━━

And on Aaron S. Burbank (1818–1883) in Winsted: "Bury me not when I am dead / Lay me not down in a dusty bed / I could not bear the life down there / With earthworms creeping through my hair."

Guardian of the Grave

Strange doings transpired in a cemetery near Milford on the grave of a three-year-old who died in 1878. The tomb was guarded night and day by a white swan that barely left the site, even to eat. Anyone who approached was greeted with warning hisses; sometimes it struck a defensive posture as if intending to attack trespassers. The swan's mate died of grief after attempting unsuccessfully to convince it to return to the lake with her. Hundreds of the curious came to the graveyard to see for themselves the child's grave and its self-appointed guardian.

Train in Vain

"None of us can know how we might act in a supreme moment of revealed fate," begins the old newspaper article. In other words, no one knows how one's going to face death until one's facing death. But we know how John

C., a pistol maker of Norwich, faced his end because that was the topic of the article. John was walking along the railroad tracks on the night of November 1, 1878, when he got his foot caught in a double switch in the tracks—just as the northbound train headed his way. The article relates that John "faced the engine in a defiant way, and almost smiled as it struck him."

Moral: Never Imitate a Circus Freak

Joseph G., scion of a noted family in Hartford, took a fateful trip to New York in 1889. There he saw a freak called the Human Ostrich putting on a show in the Bowery. The HO's shtick consisted of eating nearly anything placed before him; Joseph, with the impetuousness of youth, watched the act and thought, "I can do that too." Then he went home to Hartford. His parents could not help noticing that every once in a while their son would gulp down a live fish or bullfrog, or a slate pencil when he could get one. Joseph ended up getting a fateful job at the Machine Screw Company.

In December 1890, Joseph was caught shoplifting in a cigar store and sentenced to a year in jail. His cellmate watched him eat a tenpenny nail.

In late March 1891, Joseph complained to the jailers that he was ill and requested a visit from a priest. When he arrived, Joseph gave a confession the like of which the priest had probably never heard before. For the past two years, Joseph said, he had had an appetite for all manner of indigestible things, such as steel filings, screws, and tacks—all snacks pilfered from his job at the factory.

Joseph told the priest that tacks and screws were scarce commodities in the jailhouse, so he had been forced to modify his cravings to the occasional savory-looking nail or tempting piece of tinfoil. At last the gods favored the famished man, and he found a screw an inch and a half long, which he swallowed.

After he made his confession, Joseph was taken posthaste to Hartford Hospital, where he could neither lie down nor move without provoking intense pain. In April he was reportedly pounding on death's door, but he appears to have held on until August 1893.

News Flash!

George H., who wrote for the *New York Herald*, was a newshound to the core. When he received fatal injuries in a train wreck at Stamford, Connecticut, on June 12, 1913, he told would-be rescuers to save other victims and spoke his last words: "Call up my paper right away. Tell them there is a big wreck here. It's a big story. Tell them I'm sorry I won't be able to work because I'm all smashed up. Call up mother too."

The reader will note George's somewhat askew sense of priorities: he thought of his big scoop first and his mother second.

Death's Little Ironies: Connecticut

Oscar P. of Bridgeport survived the sinking of the *Titanic*—yet he drowned in a pond six feet deep in Beardsley Park on March 23, 1925. His body surfaced on April 18.

Final Communications: Connecticut

A man who committed suicide in April 1878 left a note that sounded akin to surrealist poetry: "When the devil has time to kill flies with his tail, then will I believe in the love and truth of a woman."

Location Is Everything

Samuel L., cashier at the Birmingham National Bank of Derby, killed himself on November 17, 1913—not due to malfeasance, as one might expect, but because he was in poor health. His suicide was remarkable for its location: he entered a vault in Oak Cliff Cemetery and shot himself in the head. His body was found lying on a coffin.

A Lifetime Membership in the Suicide Club

In 1886, five citizens of Bridgeport—all depressed German immigrants who possibly had been reading too much Schopenhauer—formed an organization they called the Suicide Club. (Or perhaps they were inspired by Robert Louis Stevenson's story "The Suicide Club.") The club's charter was simplicity itself: they pledged that one member per year would kill himself until all were gone. Survivors met every January. History does not record if they took minutes, had a secret handshake, or gave members official cards that entitled them to discounts at amusement parks.

The members of the club were true to their word. One killed himself in 1887; another in 1888; a third in 1889. At the meeting scheduled for January 1890, only the secretary and the president were among the living. Each tried to convince the other to kill himself in the coming year. The ideal solution, they decided, was to initiate a new member who would serve as the tiebreaker. They had their heart set on a mailman who had expressed interest in joining. But the impatient letter carrier let them down by killing himself before signing up.

The club's secretary, Wendell B., was heard to cry: "A cloud hangs over me! I am doomed!" He sold his property and gave the money to his wife—not a good sign. On April 8, 1890, Wendell proved himself a member in good standing by cutting his throat in New York.

No word as to whether the president of the club exterminated himself as promised in 1891; judging from his debate with Wendell, it sounds like he developed cold feet. It appears the club attracted two more pledges, however, because when a cabinetmaker, John K., hanged himself on November 7, 1891, the press reported there were still three remaining members.

⊱⋅⋆⊰

Certain people outside of Bridgeport found the concept of clubs in which recruits egged each other on to self-destruction appealing, and other suicide clubs sprang up in New England and across America. For example, wealthy young Barlow M., a member of the New York chapter, shot himself in the heart in a boardinghouse on October 3, 1892. He left a note for the coroner: "I have committed suicide as per club. Please give verdict to such effect and oblige."

⊱⋅⋆⊰

Morris Allen C., president of the Dallas, Texas, suicide club, fulfilled his membership obligations by shooting himself through the head on West Madison Street in Chicago, on July 8, 1892. He had tried to kill himself twice before with morphine, but the third time was the charm. The aftermath of Morris's suicide was refreshingly strange: he left a letter requesting that the Whitechapel Club of Chicago roast his remains on a funeral pyre. Cremations were rare in America at the time, especially ones performed pagan style, but the Whitechapel Club was up to the task. On the night of July 16, eight members built a pyre eighteen feet long, eight feet wide, and twenty feet high on the south shore of Lake Michigan, the most isolated place they could find in the city. They carried Morris's robed body to the pyre and placed it on top. The cremators marched around the woodpile three times while singing a dirge; after lighting the fire, they played Ernst's "Elegy" on harp and zither. Others sermonized and delivered recitations. When all was over five hours later, they scooped up the ashes of Morris with trowels and placed them in an urn.

⊱─━◦━◦━⊰

So many men offed themselves in Lake County, Indiana, in autumn 1893 that a coroner's jury investigated and determined that a secret suicide club was responsible for a dozen deaths.

⊱─━◦━◦━⊰

On November 19, 1895, Frank S. ordered a glass of beer in an Indianapolis saloon, poured morphine into it, and drank it down. He was taken to the hospital in the nick of time and resuscitated. He explained that he had joined a suicide club the night before and that the members had tossed dice to determine who would be the next to go. Smith won (i.e., lost).

⊱─━◦━◦━⊰

L.W., suicide clubber from New York, poisoned himself in a Chicago saloon on June 1, 1902. A letter in his possession suggested that he did the deed in reaction to the suicide of another club member earlier in the same week.

⊱─━◦━◦━⊰

Bernard B. of Derby, Connecticut, was in good health and employed. One night in September 1903, he told his roommate confidentially that he was a member of a suicide club with headquarters on Catherine Street in New York: "I have been elected to die. I have sworn not to try to escape my fate at the appointed time. Indeed, it would be useless, for if I do not kill myself they of the club would kill me." The next morning, Bernard threw himself under the wheels of a passenger train on the Naugatuck railroad line.

⊱─━◦━◦━⊰

One of the biggest, most ambitious suicide clubs on record was founded at Amityville, Long Island. It had more than fifty members. As of May 1931, the membership had been reduced by half—and not because of failure to pay dues, either. The organization received unwanted attention when a member, Edward S., died of an apparent self-inflicted gunshot wound on May 13, 1931. Police felt he had some assistance from his sister Louise.

Long Way Down

Workers cleaning out a 102-foot smokestack in Ansonia on April 11, 1910, found a body with two broken legs under a pile of soot at the bottom. A little detective work revealed that the dead man was Frederick S., who had last been seen alive the week after Christmas 1909. It appeared that Frederick had climbed unseen to the top of the smokestack while in a suicidal humor and jumped in. The authorities called Frederick's triumph "probably the most remarkable suicide in the history of the state."

Did the Dead Disrupt the Democrats?

The advantage to having a jailhouse ghost is that it adds spice to the prisoners' humdrum lives. The disadvantage is that they can't run away from it. Inmates at the New Haven County jail saw a ghost repeatedly in 1884. It came and went as it pleased and wore a black robe. Its appearance was always heralded by "a feeling of deadly horror" that spread through spectators.

The most detailed report came from a prisoner who, one November night, was awakened by a deep, unholy groan. He peeped through the bars of the cell window and saw nothing outside that would account for it. Convincing himself the sound was made by two tree limbs rubbing together, he returned to his cot. Soon he heard it again—louder and closer. He ran to the window and saw nothing. He heard the noise a third time, and on this occasion the jailhouse spirit materialized in the corner. It stood with one hand raised above its head and the other clutching the ghost of a long rope. It floated through the air and perched on the windowsill. The prisoner stared at it for several minutes and then found voice enough to ask what it wanted.

The wraith answered in fine, purple language strongly suggesting that while alive, it had been in the habit of reading dime novels: "You ask why I come to visit the scene of my incarceration during the last few weeks of my existence. I want revenge and I will have it. Retribution has burst open my tomb, that I may again appear upon earth to torment my persecutors.

While I lived here you were my friends, my companions at work, and now that I am gone, remember me. Tell my enemies to beware!"

The inmate then recognized his visitor as the shade of James "Chip" Smith, a drunken Birmingham outlaw who shot police officer Daniel J. Hayes on December 23, 1880. Smith was hanged at the jailhouse on September 1, 1882.

But that's not the end of the story. On the night of November 10, a few days after the prisoner saw Smith, the Democratic Party of Birmingham held a parade that was disrupted by strange noises—which nobody bothered to investigate—issuing from a lot just beyond town limits. The next day at noon, villagers found the corpse of Michael R., father-in-law of the murdered Officer Hayes, under a fence in the lot. His neck was broken, he was badly bruised, and one eye was nearly gouged out. Of course it was only a coincidence, but onlookers might be forgiven if they thought Chip Smith had returned to pummel his enemies as he had promised.

Be Careful What You Read

Patrick D., who worked at Pratt and Whitney's shop in Hartford, was a carpenter with a taste for literature. On the night of Monday, December 22, 1884, he pulled a book off the shelf and commenced reading to his wife a poem on the topic of death. (News reports didn't give the verse's title or author, perhaps with good cause.)

Mrs. D. found the poem disturbing and begged him to stop reading it. He laughed at her fears but agreed and did some writing instead.

An hour and a half later, Patrick heard the kitchen door open—but it didn't close. He went into the kitchen to investigate and saw the ghost of his elderly mother dressed in black from head to toe, including a dark shawl. Sadly, she pointed at her trembling son, turned, stepped through the open door, and disappeared outside into the darkness. The door then closed on its own accord.

Patrick wasted no time running to his wife and exclaiming, "I have just seen my mother!"

The carpenter found the experience upsetting but went to sleep as usual. On the morning of December 23, he went to work at Pratt and Whitney's and fifteen minutes later was fatally injured when a circular saw threw a piece of planking at his abdomen. He died of peritonitis on the night of the twenty-fourth.

Drastic Measures

Charles B., a former shoe dealer in New Haven, had a reputation for treating his wife shabbily. When she died in January 1887, a neighbor thought he'd murdered her and informed the medical examiner that her death should be investigated. Nothing was done about it.

To Charles's consternation, his wife, though dead, did not leave home. Her ghost appeared often, curiously at about double her natural size and toting what seemed to be an infant.

Charles was not the only one who witnessed the ghost. He invited a teenaged girl who lived next door to come over one night and see it. She took him up on his offer—bringing a servant girl with her—and sure enough, "a huge figure like a shadow did appear on the wall carrying a babe in its arms."

"That's my wife," remarked Charles.

The teenaged neighbor approached the shadowy figure and slapped at it; the ghost responded by moving to another section of the wall. She repeated the experiment with the same result. The servant also saw it.

By April 24, 1887, Charles could stand the haunting no longer. On that date he shot his dog, made himself comfortable in an easy chair, and—using a mirror to make sure his aim was perfect—shot himself in the head. Everyone concluded that he committed suicide to get away from his wife's ghost. If true, he apparently had not considered that killing himself might be a way to join her, *permanently*.

Oh, Rats!: Connecticut

Miss Lavina H. of Myrtle Hill, age eighteen, was a custodian at the Baptist Church of North Plain. On the night of February 21, 1892, she climbed alone into the belfry to repair a broken bell rope. Once in her cold, dark, and lonesome perch, she found the cause of the problem: rats had gnawed the rope in twain. While contemplating this, she heard a squeak behind her. Turning, she saw shiny, evil little eyes observing her from the shadows. She made an ineffectual pass with her arm, but the number of rats multiplied rather than diminished. In a second, dozens of hungry rodents were nipping at every uncovered portion of Lavina. Her only defense was to summon help by pulling what was left of the rope. Arthur R. and two other men passing the church ran to the belfry and pulled her out. During the rescue, Arthur himself was badly bitten. As for Lavina, the rats tore her face, arms, and shoulders to tatters, and chewed off a long braid of hair from the back of her head.

Battle Royale in a Lighthouse

Tending a lighthouse is a lonely business and is not suitable for just anyone, as is well illustrated by what once happened at the Stratford Shoal Light in the middle of Long Island Sound, between Port Jefferson, New York, and Bridgeport. In 1905, Gilbert R. was the chief keeper; his two assistants were Merrill H. and Julius K.

One fine summer day, Julius returned to the lighthouse after enjoying shore leave. He arrived stinking drunk on three quarts of whisky. After imbibing so much alcohol—perhaps because of it—Julius lost his mind and attacked fellow assistant keeper Merrill with a razor attached to a pole. Merrill got away but had to spend the next several days staying out of his coworker's reach. And yet Merrill couldn't completely leave the madman to his own devices, because Julius started chipping away bricks from the side of the lighthouse with a hammer and chisel in the belief that someone was out to get him.

Merrill kept Julius from destroying the tower, but then the lunatic tried to smash the light itself with an ax, and it was all Merrill could do to prevent him. When this mania wore off, Julius adopted a new one: his latest heart's desire was to seek solace in death's chilly embrace.

For seven days until he was rescued, Merrill singlehandedly had to fight for his life, prevent Julius from killing himself, and save the light from destruction. He also had to find time to sleep and eat.

Where head lightkeeper Gilbert R. was all this time, I have not learned. But when he returned, he helped subdue and bind his crazy underling. Julius was dismissed from his government job—as opposed to being promoted and given a pay raise and a pension, which is the modern way of doing things.

Time Capsule

In the mid-1870s, merchant John W. was attacked and robbed at his general store in Colebrook. So traumatized was he by the incident that he lost all interest in continuing his profession. He closed the store, locked its doors, shuttered its windows, and never set foot in it again.

The former shopkeeper died in the spring of 1907. In September the store was opened for the first time in more than thirty years and its old-fashioned contents auctioned. More than a thousand people attended, some coming from many miles away in cars, by horse-drawn cart, and on foot. It was like stepping a generation into the past. Vintage cigars were sold for $1.30 a box; tallow candles went for $1.50 a box; leather boots with red and green tops and brass toes, $2.50 a pair; hoop skirts and stove polish, $0.50.

Those Final Moments: Connecticut

Before walking to the Connecticut State Prison's gallows on April 14, 1898, Charles Boinay recorded a clarinet solo. He hoped his music would live on after he was gone.

Death Row Dramas: Connecticut

John Cronin was in the vanguard. The average, workaday murderer was executed in the antiquated way: standing on a gallows trapdoor with a noose around the neck. But Cronin had the honor of a unique stringing up.

On December 18, 1894, Cronin mounted the gallows at Wethersfield for having killed Albert Skinner at South Windsor on October 6, 1893. The condemned man sat in a chair attached to a hidden counterweight from which small shot slowly drained. When it was empty, Cronin was yanked upward with the rope around his neck, as opposed to the humdrum downward trajectory. He was declared dead nine minutes later and taken to Blue Hills for burial. Though the device used to hang him unquestionably accomplished its intended purpose, somehow the upward-yanking "automatic gallows" failed to catch on.

6

MORBID MAINE

Well-Preserved Folks: Maine

A CEMETERY SEXTON ENTERED A LONG-ABANDONED FAMILY VAULT IN Waldo County one day in 1890 and encountered a coffin in a perfect state of preservation—so perfect, in fact, that the sexton gave in to curiosity and opened it. Surely he expected to see a body inside, but he was surprised all the same: instead of a moldering skeleton, the coffin's tenant was a boy around twelve years old, wearing perfectly arranged clothing complete with a little blue tie and a collar; his hair was meticulously combed. If not for his sunken eyes, one would have thought him to be merely asleep. The child was in such splendid condition that the sexton grew suspicious. Had someone slipped a fresh body into the neglected vault without his knowledge?

Every member of the family who owned the vault was long since dead, so the sexton tracked down the executor of their estate and took him to see the corpse. "Good heavens!" cried the executor when the lid was opened. "That's the body of a young son of the family who died more than thirty-five years ago!"

The two vowed to keep the boy's identity a secret out of fear that some entrepreneur who had his finger on the public's taste in entertainment might steal the body and put it on exhibition.

Extraordinary Epitaphs: Maine

One day in 1902, brothers Herbert and Fred Plaisted were fishing in a boat in China Lake at South China, Maine. From the shore seventeen-year-old Harold Williams fired a rifle in their general direction—not directly at them, but twenty feet to the side of their boat. Nevertheless, the bullet ricocheted and killed Herbert. The Plaisted family erected a monument reading "Shot by the son of Elhanan Williams"—to which the Williams family and their friends objected strenuously, on the grounds that the epitaph failed to make clear that the death was unintentional.

―――○――

Joseph W. Holden (d. 1900) sleeps in Elmwood Cemetery, East Otisfield, beneath this remarkable tribute: "Prof. Holden the old Astronomer discovered that the Earth is flat and stationary, and that the sun and moon do move."

―――○――

In Pine Grove Cemetery, Kennebec County: "Beza Wood, Mar. 14, 1792–Nov. 2, 1837. Here lies one Wood encased in wood / One Wood within another / The outer wood is very good / We cannot praise the other."

―――○――

On Nicholas Eve in the Parish Burial Ground at Kittery Point: "Old and still."

A Legal Question

When E.C.D.'s wife died, he buried her in a cemetery plot belonging to another family—with that family's permission, naturally. But later E.C.D., of Androscoggin County, Maine, decided that he wanted to bury his beloved elsewhere and had her exhumed—without getting permission first.

A lawsuit ensued that was finally settled in January 1901. It was ruled that Mr. D. had trespassed on his wife's grave and was ordered to pay twenty dollars in damages. The chief justice explained: "A dead body after burial becomes a part of the ground to which it is committed, and an action of trespass may be maintained by the owners of the lot, in possession, against one who disturbs the grave and removes the body, so long at least as the cemetery continues to be used as a place for burial."

The Suspicious Saga of Joseph Dyer

In September 1884, Joseph Dyer, a twenty-year-old from Cape Elizabeth, fell off a wagon, was killed instantly, and buried in Evergreen Cemetery in Portland. But in early November 1885, his former girlfriend Blanche claimed to have been told by unnamed persons that Joseph was actually alive and would be coming home soon.

Blanche's assertion sired a bizarre rumor, which held that Joseph's parents exhumed his coffin secretly on Friday, November 6, and brought it into their residence. A novelist couldn't have contrived better timing: just as the lid was opened, revealing it to be empty, Joseph allegedly walked into the house, saying: "Don't open it, for here I am!" He said he had no memory of what had befallen him after his accident.

Some who believed that rumor theorized that after Joseph was buried, he must have been evicted by body snatchers who discovered that their subject was still living and turned him over to medical students who cared for him until he recovered.

The story caused a national sensation but soon took on the aura of a decided hoax. Locals insisted they remembered Joseph Dyer's accident, but there was no trace of a living Joseph or the Dyer family. The mystery could have been solved in short order if they were found, but reporters who sought them came up empty-handed. Rumor held that the Dyers had moved to Deering.

The whole weird tale originated with Blanche, who had a local reputation for honesty. A new theory maintained that some con artist convinced Blanche that Joseph was still alive to trick her out of money given to her by Joseph before he supposedly died.

Blanche embellished her story with all-new details—seldom a good sign. She said she had attended Joseph's funeral and saw him stretched out in his coffin, but admitted she did not actually see the coffin placed in the grave. She wore mourning until those anonymous friends told her Joseph was alive. She said he visited her on November 7, the day after he made his dramatic reappearance at his parents' home. Her employer's family confirmed that Blanche had a male visitor that day.

Blanche said furthermore that on the following Monday, she received a visit from Joseph and two New York physicians. According to Blanche, one of the doctors said that while attending the funeral, he became convinced that Joseph was alive. Instead of stopping the funeral and alerting others of his suspicions, he waited until the ceremony was over and then dug up Joseph, carted the body away, revived it, and kept the whole strange business secret for over a year.

The truth came out on November 19: the story was born of Blanche's combined imagination and embarrassment. Her boyfriend, Charles A., had courted her under the pseudonym Joseph L. Dyer. If we read between the lines of the old news reports, it seems Charles abandoned Blanche and rather than admit it, she pretended her sweetie had died. Why the elaborate ruse about his resurrection and why the locals "remembered" the relatively recent death of a fictitious man from a nonexistent family are imponderables best tackled by psychoanalysts.

Home Cooking

For burning the corpse of his sister Harriet in the furnace of their home, Frank B. of Saco was held for a sanity test on June 11, 1938. He insisted that it was her wish to be cremated at home—"And it didn't cost me a penny!" he crowed triumphantly.

Final Communications: Maine

An unnamed blond woman shot herself in a Bar Harbor hotel on August 10, 1936. She left an arcane written explanation: "If I can't be caviar, I won't be rice pudding."

A Tragedy in Maine

The Lynwood K. family of Oxford was once prosperous. But then Mr. K., a farmer, contracted a lingering illness that rendered him unable to work. He died on February 11, 1911. The next day the widow fatally shot their fourteen-year-old son, Gerald, in the head as he slept and then took her own life.

It was the sort of domestic murder-suicide that has played out thousands of times. One feature made the case unusual: when investigators searched the house, they found a strange document in Mrs. K.'s dresser drawer: a "compact" she'd signed with her husband about a month before he died, though by then he was so weakened by illness he could only sign it with an X.

The contract was a mutual agreement that, when Farmer K.'s inevitable end came, the widow would follow suit by "doing away" with herself and their son. There was also a letter requesting that husband and wife be buried in a double-sized casket and that it, along with their son's casket, be placed in the same underground vault. This was done.

Snow on Fire

Twenty-five-year-old John Snow hailed from Poland; he immigrated to America and married Ida Brann of Coopers Mills. He eventually took the unenviable lead role in a sort-of ghost story.

Snow was an abusive husband and a ne'er-do-well. His mother-in-law, Ruth Brann, several times gave money to help him get established in assorted businesses, but all failed.

In addition to his many other flaws, Snow had a violent temper. Mrs. Brann and his sister-in-law, Mrs. Eva Eaton, were afraid of him. In August 1923, he was placed under a $500 peace bond on charges of wife beating and threatening to kill a man named Davis for mowing grass on Mrs. Brann's field.

John Snow and his wife separated. By Christmas 1923, he was living alone in Gardiner while his wife; baby daughter, Marion; mother-in-law; and sister-in-law all lived in a cottage a mile from Coopers Mills.

Snow had been hired as a woodsman by Deputy Sheriff Frank Jewett, who lived a few miles away at Whitefield. On the morning of December 22, Snow showed up for work in a blubbery mood, weeping over how much he wanted to be reconciled with his wife and child.

Deputy Sheriff Jewett went to Gardiner to do some Christmas shopping. While he was gone, Snow asked if he could borrow the deputy's car. Jewett's fifteen-year-old son, Kenneth, told him no. Snow did not take kindly to the rebuff and shot the teenager in the head. Then he shot the deputy's wife, Lucile Jewett; bloodstains in the pantry suggested that he shot her there and hid her body under a bed. Snow's body count might have been higher but two other Jewett sons were shopping with their father and a daughter was visiting a neighbor at the time.

Snow stole the car and drove to the home of his estranged family in Coopers Mills. Eva Eaton's seven-year-old was playing outside when Snow arrived, an activity that very likely saved his life.

Snow went into the cottage but didn't come out. When the Eaton boy tired of playing, he went inside and found his mother, his aunt Ida, and his grandmother Ruth Brann all shot in the head and Snow dying from a self-inflicted gunshot. The killer had not harmed his five-week-old daughter, who lay in her crib. Evidently, his motive for killing his wife was that she had refused to return to him.

Deputy Sheriff Jewett was found in Gardiner and told that a blood-bath had occurred in the house at Coopers Mill. He did not realize until later that his own wife and son also were victims.

The tragedy was compounded on December 28, when the killer's infant daughter died of pneumonia at a state institution. The child became ill from exposure when taken to a neighbor's house in the wake of her father's killing spree, so her death was directly related to the crazed wood-cutter's actions. Snow's final tally was seven, including his baby. The victims from his family were buried in Jefferson, but villagers refused to plant the wretched Snow in hallowed ground. On December 24, his body was deposited without ceremony in a solitary unmarked grave on the farm where his wife had lived. "There were no grief-stricken mourners at his graveside," remarked the *New York Times*, "merely stolid town officials who performed a perfunctory duty in compliance with the health regulations."

The cottage where four people had died was boarded up. The intention was to just let it rot, uninhabited forevermore.

You might think the story of John Snow would end with his ignominious burial, but you would be mistaken. The people of Coopers Mill and nearby Jefferson were angered that he'd escaped earthly justice, and they celebrated Christmas morning by exhuming his body, dragging it across the ground, breaking into the cottage where he'd massacred his family, tossing his carcass inside, and setting the house on fire. It burned to the ground and the coroner contemplated Snow's charred remains later that memorable Christmas Day. Authorities figured out the chain of events when they found a trail in the snow that led directly from the smoldering remains of the cottage to the mass murderer's open grave. It was strongly hinted in the press that even if the culprits were identified and tried, no Lincoln County jury would convict them.

But what has all this to do with ghosts, you ask? The county attorney explained the villagers' actions to the press by noting an old Maine superstition that if the body of a murderer were burned, the ghosts of his victims would find peace. So it was a way of keeping restless spirits at bay—plus, it felt really good!

Head Injury Hijinks: Maine

When Clem W. of Portland was fifteen years old, around 1849, he went to his father's pasture to catch a colt, which gave him a swift kick in the head. The outer wound healed, but from that day onward Clem was harmlessly insane. In autumn 1894, local doctors who examined Clem's head found that his brain pressed against a broken piece of skull. They removed the fragment and relieved the pressure on Clem's brain. He recovered his sanity right away and the first question he asked was: "Did the colt get away?" For Clem, time had stood still. He remembered nothing from the forty-five years that had passed after the horse's kick.

Silent John

When he was young—circa 1858—John A. was a bright spark in Portland. He was in the dry goods business, popular with peers, a scholar who collected books, and seemed "quick and successful in business," in the words of one who knew him. In sum, John was a man with a bright future ahead.

Then a change came over him, inexplicable perhaps even to himself. He abandoned his prospering business and became a hermit in his rented rooms at the Elm House. He said very little, if anything, to fellow boarders. He never went outside the boardinghouse and left his suite only twice a day to take meals at the communal table. Eventually he gave up even that limited contact with the human race and would come downstairs, take what food he wanted, and return to his rooms with it.

John lived at the Elm House until his money ran out in 1864, and then it was the Portland Almshouse for him. The idea behind the nineteenth-century poorhouse was that paupers had a free place to live but were expected to work to earn their keep. John did not mind the indignity of being taken to the almshouse, but when he got there, he made an announcement: "I swear I won't work."

And he didn't. Two decades later he had neither done a lick of work nor left his room. His only exercise in all that time had been to get food from the kitchen three times a day and take it to his room, and to go the washroom once a week for clean clothes.

Poorhouse officials knew him to have spoken only twice. Once he confessed to a minor fault. On another occasion an officer of the institution requested permission to enter John's room and he replied, "I am engaged, sir."

In 1884 a reporter described John as he appeared in the twentieth year of his institutionalization: "He is now an old man of 64, very neat in his appearance, clean shaved, erect, with a fine, intellectual face, an eye that is still bright, and a step quick and vigorous. . . . He never reads, and seems to have forgotten a world that has forgotten him."

7

DREADFUL DELAWARE

Grave Robbers and Body Snatchers: Delaware

GRAVE MARAUDERS WERE AT WORK IN THE ENVIRONS OF BRIDGEVILLE IN 1904. First they opened the resting place of Turner G. to swipe his jewelry. Then on October 11 someone dug up Mrs. Annie O.'s grave on her family farm. But in her case, it appears the thieves were out to thwart justice in addition to gaining financially. She'd died sitting in a chair the previous July; rumor held that she'd been poisoned and that her body was about to be exhumed and examined. Somebody must have believed it, because he stole not only her jewels but also her intestines, heart, and hands. Had she actually been murdered, traces of poison could have been detected in her bowels, heart, and fingernails. The hands and heart were found hidden in the grave dirt, but the ghoul must have decided Mrs. O.'s bowels were a prize worth keeping.

Winning the Argument

When Mrs. Josephine D. of Wilmington died in May 1893, her husband Jacob wanted to have her buried in Lombardy Cemetery. However, her father, Theo W. of Cheyenne, Wyoming, insisted that she be laid to rest in *his* family graveyard at Oxford, Pennsylvania. (The late woman's father and husband never got along.) Mr. D. won the argument and Mr. W. went back to Cheyenne. But the fuming father was not about to have his wishes thwarted, and before he left town he broke into the grave, hauled his daughter's body away, and buried her in Pennsylvania. On May 16, Mr. D. received an anonymous letter informing him of his wife's actual where-abouts and he issued a warrant against her father, to be served when he got off the train in Wyoming. The state of Delaware did not take grave robbery lightly, and the paternal ghoul faced a possible $200 fine or two years in prison.

Extraordinary Epitaphs: Delaware

Alexander McClyment, a former assemblyman from Dover, buried his three wives in that city's Presbyterian Cemetery. He seems to have con-sidered writing their epitaphs as opportunities to wax poetic. He also appears to have become more disgusted with each loss.

On Sarah, who died in 1811: "Oh, Monster! My heart is torn asunder by this ghastly wound!"

On his first Elizabeth, who died in 1816: "Insatiate archer! Would not one suffice?"

On his second Elizabeth, who died in 1825: "Thy shaft fell thrice; and thrice my peace was slain!"

Battle of Wills

When the ship carpenter Charles M.'s wife died at Wilmington, the undertaker sent him a bill for $27. Charles didn't pay it. Years later, in December 1888, Charles's daughter also died. He went to a mortician and demanded service. Unbeknownst to the carpenter, however, the Under-takers' Association kept a list of, er, deadbeats, and Charles's name was on it. The undertaker requested that Charles pay his outstanding bill; not only did he refuse, he was furious that his antagonist even had the temerity to ask.

In retaliation, the funeral director declined to bury the child's body. Charles went from undertaker to undertaker but found that he had been blacklisted. In desperation, the stingy father applied to the poorhouse for a coffin, but the superintendent would not give him one after discover-ing that Charles had plenty of money. In the end, the miser was reduced to burying his child at a local Catholic cemetery on Christmas Day in a wooden shoe box covered with cheap flannel.

Why didn't the professional carpenter just build a coffin for his daughter? Good question! I don't know!

No Prank

In 2005, the Associated Press reported the case of an unnamed woman in Frederica who hanged herself from a tree next to a highway. She did this a few days before Halloween and her body swung from the limb at least three hours before spectators realized it wasn't a prank.

Phantom Limb: Delaware

In 1915, Lewis J. of (irony alert!) Blades, Delaware, accidentally cut off his hand with a circular saw at a mill. The hand was buried—whereupon he suffered mightily from pains and an itching sensation where his palm used to be. Physicians could not help, so Lewis took friends' advice and exhumed his hand, which had been underground six weeks, and found it to be clenched into a fist. Lewis straightened out his digits and placed a weight on them so they couldn't curl up again. The pain instantly left and stayed away.

8

MACABRE MASSACHUSETTS

Well-Preserved Folks: Massachusetts

IN MAY 1924, WORKMEN IN SWAMPSCOTT CEMETERY IN LYNN OPENED the grave of a man whose pilgrimage had ended in 1876. The casket had a glass window strategically located over the occupant's face, and the workers marveled that the man looked as though he had fallen asleep only a few days before.

Premature Burial: Massachusetts

Alden H. died at Freetown on July 7, 1886, and was scheduled for burial on July 11. But mourners noticed that he retained body heat and a flushed color. It was decided to keep him aboveground until putrefaction made death positive, and H. remained unburied for a week after his presumed passing.

Extraordinary Epitaphs: Massachusetts

In Wayland: "Here lies the body of Dr. Hayward, a man who never voted. Of such is the kingdom of Heaven."

A graphic epitaph in Van Duesen Cemetery, Great Barrington: "Oh would that I could lift the lid and peer within the grave and watch the greedy worms that eat away the dead."

⊢⊶⊷⊶◦⊶⊷⊶⊣

Unintentional humor (which is the best kind!) on the monument of Mrs. Job Brooks in Hill Burying Ground, Concord: "After having lived with her said husband upwards of sixty-five years, she died in the hope of a resurrection to a better life."

Reuben's Chair

Reuben James Smith was a man who knew what he wanted! And what he wanted was a marble sarcophagus of his own design and construction, which he had built in Mount Prospect Cemetery in Amesbury. The zenith of his eccentricity, however, was unknown to the public until his funeral, which took place on January 26, 1899. Smith's favorite recliner was brought to the apartment where he had formerly lived, and the funeral was held there, with Rev. Joseph Lambert presiding. Smith rested in the chair, wearing his favorite felt slouch hat. The recliner was taken from Reuben's room to Reuben's tomb and placed inside. Hundreds of villagers trooped by to see the mortal remains stretched out on the comfy chair in a most lifelike manner. After all had their gawk, the door was sealed by bricklayers and the key ceremoniously destroyed.

Bones and Brats

In November 1884, a gang of Boston juvenile delinquents came up with an initiation ritual that would be the admiration of modern street punks. At the time, there was on Walter Street in the Roxbury district a small, long-forgotten cemetery that consisted mainly of two brick vaults, a few century-old headstones, and plenty of camouflaging vegetation. A policeman in pursuit of the little toughs noticed a hole in the masonry of one of the vaults. He reported his find to Health Inspector Hicks, who went to the graveyard to check it out for himself.

Once there, he heard faint cries seemingly coming from underground. Upon closer inspection, he found a hysterical ten-year-old boy in the crypt where, at the insistence of his "friends," he had spent a chilly night in the skeletal company of some of Boston's former residents. Whether his companions, who had been using the tomb for a hideout, intended to return and rescue him was an unanswered question.

After getting the badly frightened and hungry boy out of the vault, Hicks looked inside and found congenial surroundings, including broken bottles, playing cards, and dime novels mingled among bones and broken coffins. He hired a mason to brick over the hole and the miserable brats had to find a more wholesome place to play.

Body Snatching BS

Estelle N., age about thirty, died of a spinal ailment and self-imposed starvation in Egremont in 1858; afterward she was buried in Coventry. That was the last heard of her until December 1884.

At that time, a rumor got started that a man on his deathbed, Dr. H.W. of Connecticut, confessed to his brother that while he was a student at Albany Medical College back in 1858, he and other students had stolen Estelle's body from her grave and brought their trophy to the school. Much to their discomfiture, to say nothing of hers, Estelle revived while they were dissecting her. The experience drove her insane, and they had her committed to the asylum in Schoharie County, New York—secretly, of course, because to admit it would be the same as confessing to grave robbery. Allegedly, she was still alive in 1884 and dwelling in the madhouse.

The story improved with each retelling. It was stated further that Miss N. had not been taken to an asylum after all, but rather to Bellevue Hospital in New York City, after which she lived at the Schoharie County home of a man who happened to be the uncle of one of those medical students. There she regained her sanity and eventually married her benefactor's nephew. Perhaps her husband was one of the body snatchers who had snatched her body!

The yarn was exposed as a hoax when indisputable facts came to light: firstly, there was no insane asylum in Schoharie County. Secondly, Dr. W.'s brother denied that the physician had made any such incredible deathbed confession. Thirdly, another doctor pointed out that if Estelle N. had been buried alive, she would have suffocated before the medical students got their paws on her. Fourthly and most conclusively, Estelle's grave was opened and she was right where she was supposed to be. But the story was a sensation while it lasted, and the world needs sensations.

A Sepulchral Scrooge

The residents of Holden were surprised to see smoke issuing from a tomb on October 23, 1904. They found the wealthy, and ironically named, miser Pennyman D. inside, warming his hide beside a small fire. Pennyman insisted that he had a right to live there since it was his family's tomb. He pointed out that the place was warm, cozy, large enough, and—best of all—rent-free.

For the Greater Good

With improved technology comes progress, and with progress comes the occasional inconvenience—such as reeking skeletal remains being scattered willy-nilly on public property. In August 1887, the Edison Electric Light Company dug a trench along Boylston Street in Boston. At the top of a hill they uncovered a cemetery. Feeling that scientific advancement could not wait, the workmen broke open the graves and flung their contents to the side of the road among other impedimenta such as rocks and dirt. "Some of these bones have been hung upon the fence of the common, where they are the subject of scurrilous jests," observed the *Evening Record*. One enterprising laborer sold a skull to a Harvard medical student for fifty cents. The advantage was that Bostonians soon had modern electric lights with which they could read about such depredations in the papers without straining their eyes.

Simultaneous Departures: Massachusetts

Historian Daniel Allen Hearn noted a striking example of simultaneous spousal death that occurred in 1743. On April 14, at the same hour during which Margaret Fennison was busy being hanged at Boston's Cambridge Common for infanticide, her seafaring husband Bartholomew was accidentally knocked overboard and drowned.

In Which Freethinkers Test Their Theories

The date was December 12, 1896. Neighbors were getting worried; for the past several hours there had been no sign of life from the apartment at 47 St. Botolph Street, Boston. Also, the odor of gas was getting stronger and stronger. When a crowd investigated, a porter broke down the door and a wave of gas fumes billowed out, forcing everyone to step back.

When they could enter the apartment, they found the bodies of May Louise Collins of Midway, Kentucky, and Samuel Putnam, originally from New Hampshire; the woman's body lay across the man's. Both had reputations as writers and lecturers on freethinking or religious skepticism. In fact, Putnam was president of the Free Thought Federation of America, and at least one of Collins's friends said she was obsessed by the topic. In short, the police had a pair of dead atheists "all dressed up and no place to go."

Closer inspection of the apartment, which had belonged to Collins, revealed that the noxious fumes came from an open gas fixture—next to which was a second fixture that was lit. It was fortunate indeed that the building had not exploded.

The deaths seemed steeped in mystery. Was it an accident? Had Mr. Putnam, age fifty-eight, and Miss Collins, age twenty-one, been lovers? If so, had they committed mutual suicide via asphyxiation? There were no notes indicating suicide, but it seemed plausible to some because Collins wrote that she thought people should have the right to kill themselves if they wanted. Or was it a case of murder-suicide? Collins had a habit of battling insomnia by drinking whisky laced with chloral; had she drugged Putnam and then turned on the gas?

The medical examiner's official verdict was accidental death by inhaling gas fumes. Bottles of liquor at the scene suggested that the freethinkers had had too much to drink and were unaware that lack of oxygen was stealing their lives away—they simply lost consciousness and died in their sleep.

Putnam was said to have spent a lot of time at Miss Collins's apartment. However, her friends declared that she had high personal moral standards, and one of the men who'd found the bodies assured the press that both had been fully clothed. Unfounded rumors that Putnam had fallen in love with Collins and murdered her persisted, no matter how much her friends defended her character. For example, Collins's brother Nathaniel remained convinced there had been foul play.

Putnam's body was cremated while Miss Collins was stored at a Boston undertaking establishment pending word of her family's wishes for disposal of her remains. A crowd of gawkers who were curious to see a genuine dead atheist got in and stared at her features, "which were calm and peaceful in death."

On December 15, Collins's body arrived in Lexington, Kentucky, by express train. She was the daughter of Dr. Thomas C. Collins and her family, "one of Kentucky's oldest and most respected," had been broken-hearted a few years before when she'd publicly announced her rejection of Christianity and written articles promulgating atheism. She received a "Godless burial" in Lexington Cemetery on December 16—"without song, without prayer, and without any promise of a future life," wrote a reporter.

Dr. Collins was too distraught to attend services. Over time, he adopted May's beliefs, or rather her disbeliefs. It was reported in January 1897 that he was expiring from grief. On October 2, 1898, he ended his existential misery by tying himself to a buggy and driving into a pond near Paris, Kentucky.

May, a known proponent of suicide, might have said, "Well, why not?"

The Last Diagnosis

Dr. W.R. died of rheumatic heart disease in Boston on February 1, 1905. As he expired, he wrote a note diagnosing his own case, assuring the coroner it was a natural death, and making notes on what it felt like. It read: "Nothing suspicious. I died of rheumatism of the heart. My effects go to my wife, Annie, Hickory, N.C. The pain is terrible. The rheumatism has reached the vital organs."

Boys at Play: Massachusetts

July 28, 1912: Twelve-year-old Henry T. of Lawrence was proud of his brand-spankin'-new .22-caliber rifle. Louis D., age eleven, sneered at Henry's prize possession, saying the gun was "no good." He added, "I bet it couldn't kill anything."

"Give me written permission to shoot you and I'll show you whether it is any good," said Henry, who even at age twelve clearly had a good legal mind.

Louis scrawled on a scrap paper, "I gave him permission to shoot me," and signed it. Moments later Louis was dead with a bullet in his heart.

⊱ ⊰

Nine-year-old Edward S. was accidentally burned at the stake by six pals while playing "cannibals" in Brockton on March 9, 1935. Edward told his mother before he died that his playmates had tied him to the tree against his will; she at first refused to let the boys serve as pallbearers but then changed her mind for reasons that do not appear.

Death's Little Ironies: Massachusetts

Boston fireman Thomas D. spent Christmas Eve 1914 fighting a fire on Pearl Street. A floor collapsed in the building and he barely escaped with his life. Six hours later, Thomas walked in his sleep at the firehouse and stepped through the hole in the floor whence was located the sliding pole. His injuries proved fatal.

The Elizabeth Barrett Cook Mystery

Elizabeth Barrett Cook of Brookline was only twenty, a member of one of Boston's oldest families, and engaged to be married to a graduate of the Massachusetts Institute of Technology with the dashing name of St. George Tucker Arnold. She was due to inherit two separate fortunes upon her twenty-first birthday. In addition, she was on a Mediterranean vacation: on December 3, 1931, she departed from Boston with her mother, Mabel E. Cook, on the liner *Providence*. They intended to return home on the *SS Chinese Prince*.

It might have seemed an idyllic life, but on February 4, 1932, Elizabeth got tragic news while the *Chinese Prince* was docked at Naples: a cablegram stated that her fiancé was dead and that she should "on no account return" to Boston. (The exact wording of the message was never released.) On February 9, during her voyage home, Elizabeth Barrett Cook herself died. She was buried when the ship docked at Gibraltar.

Naturally an investigation was held, during which several curious facts emerged, few of which make any sense whether considered separately or in aggregate:

- The fake cable was signed "Helen James." Miss Cook had known nobody with that name.
- Elizabeth's aunt, Mrs. Albert C., divulged that on a previous occasion the heiress had been sent another cruel hoax cablegram—and under remarkably similar circumstances. In June 1931, while traveling from Paris to Naples, she received a message claiming that her mother had died.
- The fact that Elizabeth had twice been the victim of cables falsely announcing a death seemed suspicious, and some people— including her friends—thought she had sent them to herself to earn sympathy from fellow passengers.

- The heiress did not unpack her luggage aboard the ship despite the anticipated long voyage home.
- Elizabeth evidently had a vivid imagination and craved attention. She told travelers a romantic tale of the tragic death of her sweetheart Malcolm—but there was no such person. One passenger, Robert B. of Philadelphia, recalled that Miss Cook said she had gone to Johns Hopkins Medical School and Radcliffe College; in reality, she had attended neither.
- Another theory held that she believed the cable announcing the death of St. George Arnold was genuine and had committed suicide in a fit of despair. One passenger aboard the *Providence* told the *Boston Post* that at one point during the voyage, Miss Cook threatened to kill herself but had been "dissuaded by women onlookers." Reportedly, a bottle of ether and a number of sleeping pills were found in her stateroom.
- The ship's purser said that he knew the cable was a fake.
- The mystery only deepened when the *S.S. Chinese Prince* arrived in Boston on February 20. A passenger declared that Miss Cook had received *two* cablegrams, not one.
- Five passengers stated that Miss Cook seemed happy and normal, and they believed that she died of pneumonia. Myrtle Eileen S. of Grover Hill, Ohio, who had comforted Elizabeth in her final hours, said the young society girl "was suddenly stricken with what appeared to be a heavy cold," the result of wearing a low-cut gown on a cold night.
- On the other hand, passenger Robert B. said the port surgeon at Gibraltar told him "positively" that Cook had poisoned herself.
- Captain Howard U. of the *Chinese Prince* handed the mysterious cablegrams to the British Consul General in Boston. A meeting was held at the British Consulate, attended by the Captain, several attorneys, Miss Cook's uncle Albert C., her fiancé St. George Arnold, and a Consul General. The meeting lasted an hour, and when it ended the attendees maintained a stony silence about the proceedings.
- The Consul General announced to the press on February 21 that he was certain Elizabeth Cook had arranged to send the cables to herself which were then delivered by the ship's purser. The messages—which she had received while the ship was docked

in Naples—were in fact Italian telegrams, not trans-Atlantic cablegrams. Why on earth she would do such a bizarre thing, the official could not conjecture.

- Had Miss Cook actually died of pneumonia? As doubt spread about the circumstances of her passing, British authorities at Gibraltar exhumed her body and did a chemical analysis on her internal organs. Their official verdict was released on March 16: they could not determine cause of death, though her stomach was normal.

And the case ended forever at that inconclusive point, like an Agatha Christie mystery with the final chapter missing. There are plenty of clues and possibilities, but few solid facts.

Final Communications: Massachusetts

As Fred C. attempted to asphyxiate himself with gas on December 28, 1929, he couldn't resist writing a friendly note to the medical examiner of Brockton: "Hello, Dr. F. Just give me credit for doing a good job." His boast proved hollow when police rescued him.

Not Civic Minded

George D., a weaver of North Adams, concluded at the end of July 1894 that life was a burden and drowned himself. The problem for the community lay in his choice of location: he jumped into the Dry Brook reservoir, which provided the town's drinking water. He wasn't discovered for three days, and by then the village's water was heavily flavored with George.

An Honest Effort

Walter H. sent his own typewritten obituary and biography to the Boston newspapers on January 8, 1903. Just as the papers got his message, he sipped morphine in a Tremont Street drugstore. Bystanders called an ambulance immediately. Walter was rushed to the hospital and did not die, but not from lack of trying. He was depressed over a woman.

Unartistic Use of a Chisel

On December 28, 1923, W.J.D. of Winthrop fancied it would be a lark to drive a chisel into his own head with a hammer as he observed the proceedings in a mirror. The police termed it "a peculiar case of suicide," and they were correct.

Hey, What's in the Box?

If one wishes to go to Eternity's Foyer, why not do it in a way that will make good reading in the headlines? That seems to have been the philosophy of a drifter named Stephen L., who arrived at the Worcester City Hospital on the point of death on June 1, 1935. A search of his rented room revealed two intriguing artifacts. One was a notably indecisive suicide note Stephen wrote while dying:

> To Whom It May Concern: Whenever a man usually takes his life it is always proper to give the reason. My reason is because, first—I have no job. I have no one in this world except a woman I love terribly, and she is too good for me. I am ashamed of myself because I am a failure and not a success. God bless Rose. Goodbye. I feel the effects now. The room is going around and around. I can barely see what I am writing. Maybe it is the end. Who knows. I don't care. It is very pleasant. Yes. No. [The rest was indecipherable.]

The other item was a cardboard box beside his bed. It contained a sizable, foul-tempered, and energetic black widow spider, which had been mailed to Stephen from Los Angeles. The seller had included a card informing Stephen that for a mere five dollars more he could purchase an even bigger black widow and its offspring.

Stephen died at the hospital on June 3. Had he actually made a bid to enter the record books as the only man to commit suicide via black widow spider?

Sadly, no. The Rose mentioned in his suicide note was Rose C., a student nurse in Westerly, Rhode Island, who admitted that she had given Stephen 125 sleeping pills when she visited him on May 30, two days before the landlady found him comatose in his bed. He actually died of a narcotics overdose. So what was he doing with the arachnid in the box? Apparently he just wanted people to *think* he had died after being kissed by a spider. It was a good story while it lasted.

The Phantom of Cotuit Gets Close and Personal

Cotuit is a village connected to Barnstable; in 1884–85, as now, its industries consisted of fishing and summer tourism. But one thing Cotuit appeared to have in those days that it seems to have no longer is a pesky ghost. It was seen by many residents whose "veracity is beyond question," but they couldn't agree whether the spirit was male or female.

Whatever gender it was, it appeared exclusively at night in the forest between the north end of Cotuit and West Barnstable. Mrs. George C. told a correspondent for the *Boston Globe* with carefully preserved New England twang: "Yes sir, I've seen it once, an' my husband's seen it sev'ral times. Others has seen it too."

Most ghosts seldom approach the living closely, but this one seemed to take special delight in getting up close and personal. On one of the occasions when Mrs. C.'s husband saw it, he was sitting down to light a pipe when it "nearly passed over him." It appeared to be a tall woman in black, with a veil to match. Mr. C. was not one to take being run over by a ghost lightly and he remonstrated with it, but it didn't answer and was gone in a flash.

On another occasion, Mr. C. was friendlier and said, "Good evenin'," when it passed very close to him. Again it refused to respond.

One night, Mrs. C. and her mother were walking down the road when they saw what the former described as "a woman, dressed all in black, her head covered with a black veil, just as my husband said. She was standin' by a tree when I saw her, an' the next minute she was gone. It had brushed right by mother."

Millard A. said: "I saw it at about the same place as the others. It looked to me like a tallish woman. I couldn't say how it was dressed. I stopped when I see it, an' the next minute it rushed right past me an' disappeared." Millard added that he did not address the ghost, perhaps realizing it would be an exercise in futility.

Eugene C. saw the being one night while walking with Ezra H., and again it invaded the personal space of the living: "When we see it, it was right up to us, an' it looked like a tall woman dressed in black, her head and face covered with a black veil. It rushed right by me an' was gone in a flash."

Levi N. spotted the spirit on January 4, 1885, while driving his peddler's cart from Oysterville. A large rock flew out of the bushes, hitting Levi's horse. Another stone zipped by the peddler's head and dropped into the wagon, tearing a hole in the canvas. The rock tosser appeared to be "a tall man with a long coat." Whether it was a belligerent ghost or a human prankster, it imported its own missiles: "The stone which dropped in the wagon weighed all of a pound, and appeared to be a piece of grindstone. It was different from any kind of stone you would expect to find in these woods."

Willie S. of the schooner *John Stroupe* and Willis N., captain of the schooner *Nellie Paine*, were riding into Cotuit one night when they approached the place where the peddler Levi N. had been the target of thrown rocks. Suddenly a tall man stood in the road before them. They shouted for it to get out of the way of the galloping horses. The figure stepped to one side—just barely, for the wagon passed so closely the two men had the impression they touched it.

The journalist who reported these events made a point of noting that Cotuit was a village of teetotalers. The "ghost" may well have been a practical joker with nothing better to do than hide in the dark forest on cold winter nights and wait for passersby to frighten, but if so, he was a foolhardy soul who, simply by getting so close to his victims, was just begging to take a few lead slugs in the belly.

A New England Cannibal?

The town of Otis was alarmed by one of its citizens in June 1879—a former sailor identified at first by the *New York Times* only as Smith, which did not significantly narrow down his identity. (A later report called him John Smith, which was much better.)

This Smith fellow lived with his French wife of eight years in a hollow on top of one of the highest mountains in the region, in a log hut described by a reporter: "A more dreary, desolate, and uncomfortable spot cannot be imagined."

Mrs. Smith did all the farmwork, leaving her husband free to pursue his whimsical activities. He worshipped squirrels, gnarly trees, and a wooden statue he called Boudish whose face he washed every Sunday morning. He built Boudish partway up the mountain but had to replace him repeatedly because people kept stealing him.

As if he didn't already seem like a character straight from an Edward Lear limerick, Smith impressed all with his gastronomic feats. He ate pies "plates and all"; he swallowed live fowls with an élan to be admired by any circus geek; dead snakes; toads; rotten eggs; fish fresh from the hook; and any kind of meat, including the bones. A party sent by the *New York Times* tracked down Smith and one of their number offered him a drink of whiskey. The old sailor bit off the bottle's neck and chewed it up before the impressed reporters.

But this is what alarmed the folks in Otis: Smith claimed to be from Rhinebeck, New York, but said he spent twenty years among a South Seas cannibal tribe and could not quite shake the eating habits he'd learned from them. (They didn't consume *him*, he said, because he tasted too much like tobacco.) Rumor held that he ate a man in New Jersey, which he denied. But he did admit that he offered to work free for Chester M. of Blandford for six months if Chester gave him one of his daughters for dining purposes. Smith claimed his palate craved youths "who are fat, handsome, and don't use tobacco or wear whiskers." The children of Otis gave Smith a wide berth, especially after he unsuccessfully chased some of them.

Surrounded by Razors and Throats

On November 3, 1923, a lunatic escaped from the Massachusetts State Hospital. (The press declined to provide his name but mentioned that he was considered dangerous, which was a big help.) Authorities spent the next ten days searching for him. They located him in Worcester; he had spent his time on the lam working in a barber shop. They apprehended him before he had a chance to go Sweeney Todd on customers.

Egregious Executions: Massachusetts

Samuel Frost of Petersham celebrated Independence Day 1875 by making himself independent of his brother-in-law Franklin Towne—specifically, Frost borrowed a considerable amount of money from Towne to purchase a farm and did not want to pay it back. He bludgeoned Towne in a barn and buried the remains there. But Frost was hardly a criminal mastermind. Neighbors and farmhands became suspicious when Frost was suddenly debt free, and the mephitic stink that emanated from the barn further provoked unfavorable comment. Frost broke into a sweat, sure that the police would soon be on the way. And so they were—but when they dug up the barn floor, the evidence was gone. Frost had dug up the ripe corpse, cut it into pieces, and buried the parts in sacks all over the farm. Then to make sure the coppers were fooled but good, he spent the next three weeks repeatedly exhuming and reburying the sacks in new locations around his property. He was finally caught red-handed pulling off his disgusting bait and switch. He was executed on May 26, 1876. According to some accounts, the overly tight noose yanked off Frost's head and sent it bouncing before interested spectators; according to others, the head merely hung by ligaments as blood sprayed everywhere like a sanguinary lawn sprinkler. But in either case, Frost learned that crime does not pay.

Brutes of Husbands: Massachusetts

Middle-aged shoemaker Michael Doran and his wife, Catherine, lived in South Weymouth. They married in 1866 and were compatible enough to breed fifteen children. But in 1883, Mrs. Doran separated from her husband due to his jealous streak. On February 11, 1886, Doran murdered his wife in this atrocious manner: after stabbing her in the neck with his shoemaker's knife he caught her streaming, steaming blood in a cup and drank it. When the cops showed up, he admitted all.

><

On Christmas Eve 1891, Frank L. Moulton, a "dissipated barber" of Lowell, murdered his wife, Alma, after a quarrel. It started when Mr. Moulton wanted more room in bed and the missus refused to yield any space. She slapped him; he choked her; they got out of bed, dressed, and continued the battle. Mr. Moulton picked up a flatiron and hit Alma over the head three times, pounding her head to a shapeless jelly. "I did the job and it's a damned good one," proudly remarked Moulton to the police.

><

Ellen Holmes seemed to disappear from her Chicopee home on September 1, 1891. Actually, she was in her home the whole time. Her husband, Walter W. Holmes, told neighbors that she had run off with another man but, knowing his past history of domestic violence, they were suspicious. On Election Day the neighbors invaded Holmes's house—presumably after having done their civic duty by voting—and unearthed his wife's body. The couple's nine-year-old son, Harry, revealed that Mr. Holmes had beaten his wife senseless over some trivial matter and buried her in a crawlspace, thinking her dead. The coroner found sand in her lungs, proving she had been buried alive. Holmes was given the hanging he richly deserved on February 3, 1893, during which he was almost decapitated by a badly placed noose. It is doubtful that he needed an overcoat in the next world.

><

On September 1, 1908, Honora Jordan accused her husband, Chester, of infidelity at their home in Somerville. He replied by throwing her downstairs and beheading her with a cleaver, burning her head in a furnace, chopping her body into pieces, disposing of some of the fragments in the furnace, and packing the remainder in a trunk, which he then incompetently tried to dispose of. Chester Jordan went to the electric chair on September 24, 1912. Before turning to murder and mutilation, he had been a vaudeville comedian.

Perpetrating an Eyesore

An inconsiderate litterbug with a taste for cheap sensation cut a body to pieces in early January 1887, and instead of hiding the pieces in the forest like a decent person, he scattered them throughout the suburb of Lexington. Boston had not witnessed such a parade of disembodied human parts since Professor Webster murdered Dr. Parkman in 1849.

First, a bundle of blood-soaked clothes was found on January 4; next day, a farmer discovered a man's head and an arm buried in the snow. The head was pretty gashed up and appeared to have been parted from its owner's body with an ax. Nearby was a bloody copy of the *Boston Evening Record*, dated December 23, 1886.

A mile away, searchers found the mutilated, naked torso in a gully. The legs were crudely removed, probably with the same ax that had taken the head. The killer tossed the trunk of the body over a wall and made a halfhearted attempt to hide it under a rubber horse cover.

On January 7, the left leg was found in a field. A number of cuts suggested that the murderer had attempted to remove it at the knee but given up.

The remains were identified as George A. Codman, a bachelor who was also the Somerville milkman. James Edward Nowlin, Codman's seventeen-year-old employee, told the authorities a suspicious story. He said the milkman left town in a sleigh with a stranger named Frank, and that Codman had taken all his money with him.

Nowlin—described as being "a fine-looking young man, with rosy cheeks and bright blue eyes, the picture of health and physical beauty"—was arrested on January 6 and confessed to murdering his boss in the stable by stabbing him in the back with a carving knife, after which he dismembered the body and scattered the pieces. His motive was to rob Codman of his savings, which Nowlin estimated to be $400 but which turned out to be $275.

The rosy-cheeked milkman's butcher was hanged at Cambridge Jail on January 20, 1888.

The Jeweler Digs Holes for His Wife—and Himself

Mrs. Edith D. of Tuckahoe, New York, was missing. No one had seen a trace of her since August 10, 1932. Since suspicion usually falls on the spouse in such cases, the police kept a cynical eye on the missing woman's husband, forty-four-year-old jeweler Charles Edwin D. When neighbors asked him where she had gone, he said she'd burned to death in a car wreck in Canada. He even told that story to the police. Many people believed him. Would a sensible person tell such a bald-faced, easily disprovable lie to law enforcement authorities?

The couple kept a summer cottage on the banks of Great Herring Pond in Plymouth, Massachusetts. The police—who for some reason were not willing to take the widower's word about the car crash—found a mattress cover there with three large portions cut off. Encouraged, they dragged the pond for three consecutive days in mid-September with no results. The jeweler breathed more easily.

Edith D.'s dog had been kept in a Plymouth kennel all this time. Police set it free at the cottage, hoping it would lead them to evidence of foul play. But the dog merely romped about the property and licked the investigators' hands.

Charles D. was arrested on suspicion of murder but released by a district court judge on September 12 because the state had no corpus delicti— that is, they could not hold Charles no matter how strange his behavior seemed because they had not found his wife's body. After his release, he immediately rented a room in a Quincy boardinghouse, adopted the name "Ralph Anderson," shaved his dapper waxed moustache, and cultivated a shabby appearance. Nothing suspicious about that!

But a stained mattress from Charles's household was analyzed, and on September 14 came the announcement that the stains were human blood.

Searching the couple's Tuckahoe home, investigators found a letter dated September 9 from the Cooperative Bank of Hingham, Massachusetts. Edith—or someone pretending to be her—wrote to them requesting that her stocks be transferred to someone called Grace D. They also found a deed dated August 2 in which Edith transferred some property to "Grace D. of New York City." Detectives looked at each other and asked: Who is this Grace D.? She turned out to be Grace A. of Middleborough,

Massachusetts—attractive, blond, twenty-four, and the daughter of a rich manufacturer—who admitted she had "been friendly" with Charles. Her wealthy new boyfriend told her the same old story about his late wife's death in a car wreck. It looked like the debonair jeweler was going to have to do some fast talking.

He chose a different course. Charles promised to speak to a conference of reporters on September 16. Instead, on that day he shot himself in the head in the bathroom of his rented apartment.

Six hours later, a National Guardsman digging up a recently laid cement floor in the cellar of the couple's summer cottage found Edith in a "well-constructed vault, two and a half feet deep," proving the jeweler had been handy around the house. She had been shot in the head with a .38 revolver—likely the same one with which Charles ended his own life. Detectives found a letter Edith had written to a friend several days before she was murdered—an eerie note in retrospect: "Charlie has not been himself for at least six months. He has acted like a crazy man on account of that woman. He would go down into the cellar and dig and then come up and not say a word. He has been working down in the cellar all the time."

She was unaware that her irritating husband was digging her grave.

On September 17, Charles's attorney revealed that his client had left a letter to be opened after his suicide. In it, Charles claimed that his wife had shot herself, and he had buried her body in that convenient hole he just happened to have been digging in the cellar because he thought "the world will not believe my story."

I don't know what happened to the couple's dog.

Postcards from a Killer

The Black Dahlia Avenger, the Zodiac Killer, the Unabomber, and the BTK Strangler were all psychopathic killers, but each was unable to derive enjoyment solely from murder. They also boasted about their deeds by sending taunting letters to the police and the newspapers, inadvertently giving the authorities more clues to work with. The Black Dahlia Avenger and the Zodiac managed to get away with this risky game; the other two were too clever for their own good and presently languish in jail, having learned that they were not smarter than the police.

We are accustomed to such behavior in our distressing day and age. But in 1912 it was almost unheard of for a killer on the loose to communicate with the police. In the fall of that year, the Buffalo Police Department received an anonymous postcard from Boston, dated September 11: "I am sick of trying to fool myself. I am a homicidal maniac. I killed Joey J. of Lackawanna, N.Y. I strangled him as I did others. Please advertise the fact. Post it or write for the information. Come to [illegible]."

The writer's blatant craving for publicity ("Please advertise the fact") echoes the words of many modern serial killers. The superintendent of the Buffalo PD was intrigued by the postcard, since a six-year-old Syrian boy named Joseph J. had disappeared while playing at his home in Lackawanna on October 12, 1911. Gordon P., one of his playmates, last saw him walking away with a man who gave him candy. The neighbors assumed Joseph drowned, but his body had not been found. The boy's father, merchant George J., insisted that his son was kidnapped and called in help from the police, private detectives, and even the United States Secret Service, all to no avail. For a while he received anonymous letters warning him to call off the search.

Now, almost a year later, came the mysterious card stating that the boy was dead. But was it genuine or the product of a cruel practical joker? The writer gave no evidence to support his claim, so the police chief chose not to publicize it.

The ignoring of the card must have troubled its author, for a few days later the chief of the Lackawanna Police Department received a postcard bearing the same anonymous writer's penmanship: "Boston, Mass., Sept. 17, 1912.—If you only knew the remorse in my heart, on account of the murders I have committed as the result of my homicidal mania, even you and George J. would pity me. I am writing this just getting over another drunk to try and forget the ones I killed, but like Banquo's ghost, it will not [stay] down. I am fast going to pieces mentally and spiritually."

A third card from Boston arrived a month later, postmarked October 23: "Am so sick of this business that I shall go to Buffalo next Sunday and will call you on the telephone. My brain is worse, and all I think of is murder, and I love to kill. Shall kill some kid before I leave here Sunday." On the specified date, the writer neither called the police nor murdered any children, but on November 7, George J. received a postcard in the familiar hand "giving revolting details of the murder of his son," according to the press. Two days later the child-killer took pen in hand and sent the police some particulars that they could check out.

Joseph J. will be found in the bottom of outhouse back of saloon near Doyle's, on the Ridge Road. A drunk-crazed brain done the deed, and remorse and sorrow for the parents is bringing the results, which will soon come to the end. The demon whisky will then have one more victim, making four in all. Drag the closet. The next morning [after murdering Joseph] I tried to kill a little newsy, an Italian, who always stands in the morning at Seneca Street and the hotel called—I forget, but about 121 Seneca Street. The boy knows me well. Ask him. I wish to pay the price, but will not let the Boston police get me for my family's sake.

Once his postcards began receiving widespread attention in the national press, the killer—basking in his sudden notoriety—became as verbose as the Zodiac would be several decades later. He wrote again, claiming credit for the murder of another boy: "Wednesday night, December 10, 1902, I enticed Michael K., a newsboy at Eighty-Sixth Street and Central Park West, New York City, into the Park opposite the entrance to the Arsenal Police Station. I strangled him and just escaped the officer who found him as I came back. . . . Three times have I taken life, twelve times have I tried, and cannot help it."

On the night mentioned by the writer, the strangled body of eleven-year-old Michael K. was found lying on a bridle path in Central Park. The killer carefully placed a stack of Michael's newspapers under his head as if it were a pillow. The body was still warm when found by a policeman. At the time of the murder, suspicion fell on rival newsboys and a Greek peddler whom local newsies enjoyed annoying—though the little ruffi-ans did not include Michael K. Though the postcard writer failed to offer specific details that he could not have found in newspaper reports, police had the chilling feeling he was telling the truth.

The onslaught of nameless postcards continued. One mailed from Boston on November 9 offered the murderer's peculiar excuse that he "unfortunately had too much money" and revealed that he was a mem-ber of a prominent fraternity and was "honored and respected." In addi-tion, "My son is married and happy. Can I under the circumstances give myself up? I can, of course, but there are still more murders I have not told you. Shall I come?" Given what we now know of serial killers, this card is of particular interest. Was the writer providing false clues about his personal life to throw police off the trail, as Dennis Rader (the BTK Strangler) did in some of his letters? Was the writer actually prominent in his community, or was he a pathetic loser indulging in a fantasy of being powerful and esteemed?

In some postcards the writer dropped hints that he might give himself up when he probably had no intention of doing so. On November 12, the killer sent a card postmarked New York City, in which he promised to go to Buffalo on November 13 and said he would visit the police department promptly at eleven a.m. "So shall expect you to be in your office," he added with Zodiac-like mock politeness. The card appeared to be signed either "R. Oenission" or "R. Deneission"; the psychopath's difficult penmanship made a precise determination impossible. In either case the word matched no surname in the known universe, but some erudite detectives realized that the mystifying word was *Deumessori*, Latin for "the Reapers of the Gods." Detectives noticed that the killer's handwriting, while always distinguishable as coming from the same man, sometimes was neat and legible and sometimes nearly indecipherable. The writer admitted that he killed when under the influence of alcohol, so they sought a well-educated suspect with a drinking problem. The police took him at his word that he was a man of means.

The Lackawanna police finally searched the saloon outhouse for Joseph J.'s body, as described in one of the postcards. On November 16 they found the "horribly mutilated," dismembered, and badly decomposed body in a cesspool eight feet deep. It was now certain that the writer had personal knowledge of the boy's murder, and the police took seriously his additional claim to have killed Michael K.

The day after Joseph J.'s dismembered body was found, the Rochester lawmen arrested middle-aged George S. of Boston, who vaguely resembled the man last seen with the boy. The police became suspicious when they found George leading a twelve-year-old newsboy to his room. But the boy admitted he had visited George before, so whatever went on between them, George apparently was no murderer. On the same day, Lackawanna authorities received a letter from the killer, postmarked Boston, November 15, and written on the stationery of the Tremont Hotel, an establishment that—perhaps not coincidentally—was located near the Boston Newsboys' Club. The murderer promised he was about to come to Lackawanna to surrender, but skeptical police noted that he had made that vow several times before. They refused to divulge the other contents of the letter.

Joseph J.'s funeral was held in Lackawanna on November 18; all the businesses of the city closed during the service, which was attended by hundreds of traumatized schoolchildren. The boy's mother "collapsed at the cemetery and is reported to be in a serious condition," according to a wire service report.

In the meantime, the police came up with a strategy for catching the murderer that has been duplicated with success in modern times: they reproduced the killer's postcards for public viewing in hopes that someone would recognize the penmanship. One person who saw the facsimiles was John H., chief millwright at the American Chemical and Agricultural Works in Buffalo. He thought the handwriting resembled that of a man who had applied for work there in September 1911. He had been overqualified and worked at the plant only four days, but he'd written John a cordial letter a few months later. By sheer luck, John still had the letter on file; it was written in New York and mailed from Whiting, New Jersey, on February 1, 1912. The writing was so similar to that on the postcards that John immediately took his suspicions to the chief of the Buffalo Police Department.

On November 18, the authorities in Whiting arrested balding, bespectacled John Frank Hickey, whose appearance could not have been more innocuous. He was forty-seven years old, had been born in Lowell, Massachusetts, and worked for years in various locations as an itinerant contract laborer and construction expert. The *Boston Evening Transcript* described him as "a man of considerable literary attainment." What literature Hickey wrote does not appear in the record, unless the reporter was referring to the incriminating postcards and letters. As the police suspected, he was an educated man and an alcoholic. He was found working in a field at the Keswick colony, a philanthropic institution still in existence dedicated to rehabilitating those with addictions. When told he was being arrested for murder, Hickey merely smiled and said, "That is a serious charge."

Keswick records revealed that Hickey was an inmate at the institution from December 4, 1910, to April 2, 1911. He recommitted himself on Wednesday, November 13, only about a week before his arrest. The matron at Keswick described Hickey as gentle, docile, and industrious, and she expressed shock that he had been arrested. When jailed at Toms River, New Jersey, Hickey told the sheriff: "I am innocent of any murder. I have committed no crime. I am willing to go to Buffalo, and shall make no trouble for the New York State authorities." At the same time he admitted to his lawyer that he had been in New York City at the time of the Michael K. murder and in Buffalo when Joseph J. disappeared. He also told his attorney that he was divorced and had a twenty-one-year-old son. (One of the anonymous postcards to the authorities included the line "My son is married and happy.") Hickey refused to reveal where his son lived: "I don't want anybody to know that. What is the use of having him worried?" It was heartwarming to see that Hickey was capable of being concerned for the welfare of somebody's son, even if it was his own.

The defense attorney had his work cut out for him. The killer's post-cards had been written in his client's distinctive handwriting, and one of them correctly described the resting place of Joseph J.'s remains. Most of the cards had been mailed from Boston, the city where Hickey had lived before he admitted himself to the Keswick colony. In addition, the author-ities in Lawrence, Massachusetts, revealed that he had been arrested there on August 5, 1912, for drunkenness and attacking a small boy. After this scrape with the law, Hickey had quietly slipped out of town.

The district attorney, wasting no time, called witnesses before the grand jury in Buffalo on November 19. The testimony was convincing, and the jury returned an indictment against Hickey the next day. The prisoner was moved from his New Jersey jail cell to the Erie County Penitentiary in Buffalo. Authorities feared that he would be lynched if he were jailed in Lackawanna. So detested was Hickey that the police had to lead him from the county jail to the city hall courtroom by means of an underground tunnel. The last time the tunnel had been thought a necessary precaution for saving a prisoner from mob violence was when Leon Czolgosz assas-sinated President McKinley.

Hickey kept up the pretense of innocence for ten days. On November 29, realizing the strength of the case against him, he disregarded his attor-ney's advice and confessed. In one of his postcards, Hickey claimed he had perpetrated three murders, but in another boasted of thirteen—"twelve besides the murder of [Joseph J.]." In his confession he admitted to only three homicides, and one of them was accidental. The first had taken place nearly thirty years before, in his hometown of Lowell, on Septem-ber 1, 1883. In those days Hickey worked in a drug store. The bane of his existence was Edward M., the town drunk—an American archetype that never seems to turn up in Norman Rockwell paintings. Edward made a pest of himself by daily begging the young clerk for a shot of whiskey. Hickey got so fed up that he gave Edward a drink laced with laudanum, hoping to make him sick. Instead, the Mickey Finn killed the weakened inebriate. The citizens assumed that Edward had drunk himself to death and no inquest was held. Hickey maintained that remorse over the incident drove him to drink, which in turn spawned his violent impulses.

The murders Hickey admitted were those of Michael K. and Joseph J. It turned out that he was a suspect in the Michael K. murder right from the beginning, having been picked up by the police shortly after the body turned up in Central Park. Hickey had even confessed while in a drunken state, but recanted the confession when he sobered up and was turned loose due to lack of evidence. The full details of his child murders are unknown, as the district attorney considered them too repulsive to release.

Authorities suspected Hickey was responsible for many more killings that he chose to keep silent about. Given that serial killers generally rack up a long string of murders before they are caught, the police likely were correct. The reader will recall that when writing his first postcard, when he had little fear of getting caught and therefore was probably telling the truth, Hickey confessed to killing Joseph J. and "others." (On the other hand, in another note he claimed only three victims: "Three times have I taken life.") In particular, Hickey was suspected of having murdered twelve-year-old Lawrence F. of Allegheny, Pennsylvania, in December 1909 and nine-year-old Edward A. of Kane, Pennsylvania, a year later. Lawrence was given whiskey and strangled in an abandoned house, and Edward A.'s remains never were found. Hickey was also thought to be the killer of a boy named Alexander H., whose body was found in a barrel in Cleveland, Ohio, on May 3, 1907. Hickey was probably innocent in the Edward A. case, at least, as he spent most of December 1910 at the Keswick colony.

Although Hickey denied committing any homicides except those of the drunkard Edward M., and the children Michael K. and Joseph J., he did confess to assaulting and torturing many boys in Massachusetts communities, such as Quincy, Boston, and Lawrence. Like Jeffrey Dahmer some eighty years later, he scraped up the nerve to attack only when fortified by drink. The district attorney said: "Hickey apparently is a man with a dual personality. He is intelligent. He is overcome with remorse and says again and again that he can't comprehend what possessed him to commit the crimes. He asserts he became a maniac only when filled with whisky." However, Hickey never became so full of remorse that he turned himself in, as he promised to do in his communications to the police. He seemed more troubled by the accidental murder of Edward M. than his intentional crimes. "I do not know what this thing is that comes over me," he said. "This obsession strikes me when I am sober and I take drink to get over it. Then I kill some boy. I see Edward M.'s eyes before me. That comes over me at any time, night or day, drunk or sober." He acknowledged that he'd made four suicide attempts over the years.

Before Hickey's trial, the press reported a sad exchange between the tailor Henry K., father of Michael, and the police superintendent. Mr. K., a French immigrant, wrote to ask if he could see the prisoner: "I am not happy since the child was lost. No matter where I go or what I do, my child is always in my mind. Maybe justice will cool me up, when [the] murderer is dead." The superintendent replied that he could visit Hickey as long as he submitted to a search at the jail: "We shall do everything possible to comfort you if you come here. Your letter shows that you still grieve for the dead boy. Be comforted, because God takes care of us all and He knows everything."

When Hickey was arraigned on December 2, he pled not guilty despite his voluntarily signed confession. He was remanded to jail and his trial for the murder of Joseph J. was set for December 16.

The newspapers noted that the judge hired "a prominent medical expert" at the request of Hickey's new defense attorney. Seasoned trial observers knew that this probably meant the defense was going to plead not guilty due to insanity. They were correct. At trial, the defense's alienist was the sole witness who testified on Hickey's behalf. Hickey's lawyer told the press: "It would not be fair to an insane man to have him put on the stand in his own behalf." It could not have escaped the crafty lawyer that his refusal to put Hickey on the stand also saved his client from the perils of being cross-examined. The attorney did not deny that his client was a murderer but, as a *New Orleans Picayune* article noted, "when any testimony was given tending to show Hickey's dissolute habits [the lawyer] promptly seized upon it for lengthy cross-examination, evidently to impress the jury with the idea that Hickey's manner of living had resulted in insanity." The suggestion seemed to be that the defendant was crazy enough to murder, and therefore should escape the death penalty, and yet was sane enough to carefully plan his crimes, hide evidence, present an agreeable facade in public, hold down a number of jobs, and taunt the police.

The evidence against Hickey was formidable. A timekeeper at the Rogers-Brown Steel Company testified that the defendant had not come to work the day Joseph J. disappeared; another witness had seen Hickey on the day in question drinking heavily at McGovern's Saloon, located near the child's house. A Lackawanna man testified that he'd seen Hickey in a candy store with Joseph and his friend Gordon P. on the fatal day. Gordon picked Hickey out of a lineup. Then, of course, there was the little matter of the numerous postcards written in Hickey's hand and his voluntary confession. In addition, two alienists testified for the prosecution that they found Hickey perfectly sane and faking his would-be insane outbursts. It seemed certain that the district attorney would win the verdict he sought, murder in the first degree with the death penalty. For his part, J. Frank Hickey seemed confident that he would soon be taking his leisure in the electric chair. "I have made my peace with God," he said after his initial confession. "I am ready to pay the penalty for my crimes demanded by man."

Yet, when the penalty was decided on December 21, the jury found Hickey guilty only of murder in the second degree and sentenced him to no fewer than twenty years and no more than life at hard labor in the state prison at Auburn. It took twenty-six hours of deliberation to reach this vague and idiotic verdict. Even worse, Hickey's trial nearly ended with a hung jury. They made a decision only after the judge refused to discharge them and ordered them to reach a verdict. Some jurors wanted to declare Hickey not guilty due to insanity; it appears they thought it cruel to sentence a crazy man to death, but not cruel to sentence him to a term in prison rather than an asylum. The disgusted judge took the unusual move of publicly berating the jury, commenting that it was "extremely to be regretted that justice could not be done the defendant. The public and the court don't feel satisfied with this result." He refused to give the customary thanks to the jury, congratulating only the nine men who had voted for the death penalty.

The district attorney vowed to the press that he would see J. Frank Hickey retried, perhaps for the murder of Michael K., and that next time around he would get a verdict worthy of his crimes. Soon the attorney had to change his tune. Because Michael K. had been murdered in a different jurisdiction, Hickey could not be tried for that crime until he finished his jail sentence for killing Joseph J.—and nobody knew exactly when that would be since the jury had sentenced him to such an indefinite term. The *Boston Evening Transcript* reported that the district attorney believed "society must be satisfied without further punishment of the murderer."

9

NUMINOUS NEW HAMPSHIRE

Grave Robbers and Body Snatchers: New Hampshire

Someone abstracted Mr. Beckwith from his grave in Old Cemetery in Acworth two weeks after death—long past the point when one might think his remains useful for educational purposes. To cap the insult, almost thirty years later vandals destroyed his gravestone. Friends of the deceased put up a new stone that told the tale:

> This stone tells the death of Bezaleel Beckwith,
> Not where his body lies.
> He died Oct. 21, 1824, ae. 43.
> The 13th night after his body was stolen from the grave.
> Now twice buried the mourner cries,
> "My friend is dead, his body gone."
> God's act is just my heart replies.
> Forgive O God what man has done.
> Erected by friends of the deceased
> In Acworth in place of one destroyed
> By some ruthless hand in Apr. 1853.

Extraordinary Epitaphs: New Hampshire

On Lizzie Angell (d. 1932), Forest Hill Cemetery, East Derry: "I don't know how to die."

Franklin B. Evans Proves Useful

One of the biggest sensations Northwood, New Hampshire, ever had occurred when elderly Franklin B. Evans strangled his thirteen-year-old niece, Georgiana L., on October 24, 1872, and then removed her internal organs with a knife and gravely inspected them—he said he performed the mutilation to satisfy his curiosity about human anatomy. For these crimes he was hanged on February 17, 1874. As was usually the case with executed criminals, his body was sent to Dartmouth Medical College so students could practice their dissecting skills upon his person. Because their subject was something of a criminal celebrity, the students were not content to simply dissect and dispose of him. Someone took a stereoscopic photograph, which still exists of Mr. Evans stretched out on the dissecting table. Once the students completely skeletonized Evans, they wired his bones together.

Even that was not the end of Evans's belated usefulness. Medical students are noted for possessing a somewhat suspect sense of humor, and the ones at Dartmouth had no lack of creative ideas involving employing Evans's skeleton as a decoration. In the words of one newspaper, "Many a morning it has been found suspended from the village flagpole, or sitting contemplatively upon the front steps of some timid citizen. It attended the chapel services one morning, hanging from a lofty hook. It has been constantly used to scare freshmen." The graduating class of 1878 posed in a group photo with Evans in the center.

Death's Little Ironies: New Hampshire

On July 11, 1914, a Boston and Maine Railroad freight train hit a buckboard wagon containing sixteen persons returning from a Sunday school picnic at Rochester. Six were killed. The party had not heard the train's whistle because they were singing "Nearer My God to Thee" just before the impact.

Phantom Limb: New Hampshire

In July 1882, railroad worker Josiah W. had an accident that resulted in the loss of both feet. He spent the night unconscious in a hospital, unaware that his feet were gone. When he awoke in the morning, he complained that his toes felt all cramped up, and requested that someone move them. At the time, his toes were indeed "cramped up"—his feet were stored in a bag by his wife, who intended to take them to Fremont, New Hampshire, for a decent burial.

A man who lost an arm in Manchester in the fall of 1881 gave it to an undertaker for burial. It was placed in a box, lying on the back of the hand, for several hours. Meanwhile, the amputee felt great discomfort as though the missing arm had been placed in an awkward position. Suddenly, inexplicably, the pain ended. It was later discovered that the undertaker had repositioned the arm "in an easy and natural position" at exactly the same time the injured man's pain ceased. The amputee said he could tell in just what position the arm originally had been placed in the box, because he could somehow feel it—and he was proved correct.

In another example, the same undertaker was given for burial an arm removed below the elbow. The amputee moved to another town, but a year later he visited the undertaker, saying that he felt a pain in the missing arm as though his fingers were folded up against the palm. He requested that the undertaker exhume the arm. This was done and the fingers were in the position described. The fingers were straightened, the arm reburied, and the victim felt no more phantom limb.

Just Like Howard Hughes, Sort Of

Samuel P., his wife, and five sons lived in a farmhouse on the side of Teneriffe Mountain, near West Milton. There were no neighbors for miles, so things got lonely at the farmhouse.

One son, twenty-two-year-old Joseph, met a farm girl while on a trip in 1862 and fell in love. One fateful night, Joseph worked up the nerve to tell his father about it. Samuel angrily replied, "Stop talking and go to bed!"

Joseph did as he was told. The next day he refused to get out of bed—and the next day, and the day after that. In fact, the obedient lad stayed in bed on his father's orders for fifty years until he died in 1912 at age seventy-two. He didn't even get out of bed when his father died in 1881 and when his mother did likewise in 1889.

Joseph refused to cut his beard or trim his nails, so by the time he answered the Last Call he resembled Howard Hughes, only without all the money.

Two other brothers, Ephraim and Samuel Jr., also never married. The farmhouse, scene of so much oddness, burned to the ground on November 23, 1936. Two smoke-blackened chimneys were all that remained.

10

PECULIAR PENNSYLVANIA

Grave Robbers and Body Snatchers: Pennsylvania

DR. PHILIP SYNG PHYSICK (1768–1837) WAS PRESIDENT OF THE
Philadelphia Medical College and one of the most prominent surgeons of his
day. But "the Father of American Surgery," who gained medical knowledge
from performing dissections and autopsies, did not fancy the idea of his
own body being snatched from the grave and subjected to such procedures.
He left a clause in his will requiring that "grave watchers" be hired to camp
at his burial site for two months after he died. The Physick family followed
orders but were so suspicious that they spied on the grave watchers.

⊢•⊷•○•⊶•⊣

At the unholy hour of four thirty a.m. on December 4, 1882, Philadelphia police stopped a wagon driven by Frank M., "Dutch" P., and Levi C.
as they headed for a medical college. The cargo consisted of five bodies
just lifted from Lebanon Cemetery, a black graveyard. Next morning the
police arrested two more men, including Robert C., the cemetery superintendent. The reader may gauge the unpopularity of body snatchers from
the fact that when the five were being taken to their court hearing on
December 5, Fourth Street was crowded with angry blacks who wanted
to lynch the accused. Under oath, the ghouls admitted to a scheme by

which bodies taken to the cemetery's receiving vault were shipped off to medical schools and empty coffins buried instead. The snatching was done in collusion with the graveyard's proprietors; in fact, records showed that within the few months preceding their arrest, 155 bodies allegedly had been buried one at a time in the same grave.

As the resurrectionists left the courthouse, they were greeted en route to the jail by a furious mob, including women as well as men. The terrified prisoners were saved from a most unpleasant death only by a squad of club-wielding policemen.

⊱────⊰

Martin V. B. H. was a wealthy farmer of Mowersville with a reputation for eccentricity. After he expired in 1886, a rumor grew that he had been buried with money. There are people who are willing to perform any Herculean labor if they think it will be profitable, and some persons of that description opened H.'s grave one night in mid-July 1888. It was no easy chore; the monument over the grave had to be undermined and moved, and then the coffin was pulled out of the ground and broken open. Imagine the disappointment of the grave robbers—no valuables within! All that hard work resulted in nothing but an empty hole and profanity! They expressed their frustration by mutilating Mr. H.'s decomposing face and snapping a cane that had been interred with him. Just so the expedition would not be a total loss, they made off with the coffin's silver plate and handles. As Mr. Dylan sang, the vandals took the handles.

⊱────⊰

Dr. Ellwood K. was buried in Philadelphia's Laurel Hill Cemetery in December 1935. On the morning of March 14, 1936, employees found the physician lying on the ground outside the family crypt. Understandably, grave robbers took his jewelry. Not so understandably, they also stripped the doctor of his clothing.

Morbidity Is the Mother of Invention

The fear of live burial weighed so heavily upon the mind of John P. of Williamsport that he amassed a collection of morbid newspaper articles about persons who had met that very fate. But he wasn't content to rely on the fallible inventions of others and decreed that there would be no underground burial for him at all. He designed and built for his family an eye-catching aboveground tomb in Grandview Cemetery, which featured round doors (not unlike Hobbit hole entrances) that could be opened from the inside with the turn of a knob. Of course, it would work only if the entombed family members could get out of their coffins in the first place, so John ordered that their coffins would be left half open rather than nailed shut. National news syndicates ran stories about John's pride and joy, including pictures, in April 1902.

Extraordinary Epitaphs: Pennsylvania

An epitaph reported in 1873 to be somewhere in the Keystone State: "In memory of Tabitha, beloved wife of Joseph Wright, Thomas Andrews, Eben Halstead, Edward Murray, and Charles Dean, by her devoted husband, Cyrus Morgan."

><+>-0-+<

In a sad and lonely graveyard at the foot of the Laurel Hill Mountains, about nine miles from Uniontown, there is a sandstone marker that tells a fittingly tragic story (all its eccentricities of spelling and capitalization are verbatim):

> In memory of
> Polly Williams,
> Who was found murdered
> by her seducer at the
> white rocks, august 17th, A.D.
> 1810 aged 18 years
> Behold with pity you that Pass by
> Here doth the bones of Polly
> williams ly
> Who was cut of in her tender bloom
> By a vile wretch her pretend
> ed groom

The White Rocks are part of the summit of the Laurel Hill Mountains. They are full of treacherous fissures—and in one of these, thirty feet deep and near the base of a beech tree—was found the battered body of Polly Williams. Had she accidentally fallen into the crevasse? The townsfolk thought not, because dents in her head corresponded to the shape of a bloody rock found near her body. The popular theory was that her "seducer" and intended groom, Phillip Rogers, threw her down the fissure and, finding that she survived, precariously climbed down the formation and completed the job by hitting her with a rock.

Rogers was arrested and tried, but despite the certainty of the stone-cutter's opinions, he was acquitted due to lack of evidence. He lived the rest of his life in Greene County, married three times, and had twenty-two children. But he never escaped his neighbors' suspicions that he'd gotten away with murder, and they made him miserable by singing a popular ballad about Polly's demise whenever he was within earshot.

▷•┼◦•┼◦•◦┼•◄

In Greenmount Cemetery in York, there stands a marble granite monument on the grave of the wife of a prominent merchant from long ago. It reads: "A victim of chloroform poisoning and shock. The result of a doctor's negligence." A reporter sought out the widower in 1905 and asked him what the deal was, and got only a melancholy, vague reply: "It is all the truth. Some tombstones may lie but that one does not. It is a long and sad story which I do not care to repeat."

▷•┼◦•┼◦•◦┼•◄

Samuel McCracken, a wealthy resident of Morrisville, made a contract with the local cemetery association requiring that his monument could never be removed. Unable to tell that he was obviously up to something, the association members agreed. Soon afterward, on April 16, 1862, McCracken committed suicide by slashing his throat. When his grave marker was erected, the community beheld his sacrilegious epitaph: "If leading politicians and priests all go to heaven, then I am bound to stop at some other station."

There followed decades of turmoil among the townsfolk. Some wanted the stone removed, but the cemetery association was legally bound to leave it be. Others wanted to remove it with or without the association's permission. Some ambitious folks suggested that every corpse in the cemetery except McCracken's be exhumed and moved to a different burial place. Such draconian measures were never undertaken and he remains where he was originally planted.

Mrs. McCracken's epitaph reads: "In memory of Phoebe, wife of Samuel McCracken, who died March 30, 1860. She died a firm believer in Christ, her Saviour."

⊱•❉•⊰

On Daniel F. Cole, who died on March 22, 1921, in Wellsboro: "I Wonder Where He Went." Cole actually has two gravestones: an ordinary rock with this crudely chiseled inscription and a spiffy, professionally lettered tombstone with no epitaph. Evidently someone was bothered by the first monument.

⊱•❉•⊰

The old Ross Park Cemetery in Williamsport exists no longer, but according to a correspondent of the *Federal American Monthly* (June 1865 issue), it once contained the gravestone of Henry Harris (d. May 4, 1837), which related that he was killed when a horse kicked him in the stomach. The monument included a rather absurd carving depicting this action scene. It added, touchingly, that Henry "went to the world where horses don't kick, where sorrows and weeping is no more."

An Obsolete Occupation

The steady march of technology renders certain jobs obsolete; for example, those who wish to make a living as a town crier, a blacksmith, or a buggy whip salesman are bound to be sorely disappointed.

Another career outmoded by progress is the "layer-out of the dead," also known as the watcher over the dead. Before embalming was widespread and funeral directors took certain unpleasant chores out of the hands of laymen, relatives of the deceased usually washed and dressed the body, bound its jaws and arms, and held an uproarious wake if so inclined. But most importantly, they had to keep an eye on it for signs of life just in case the doctor was mistaken, or else the departed could be buried alive.

There were professional layers-out who took over the unenviable task for a fee. One of these—a woman—spoke candidly with the *Philadelphia Times* about her job in 1881, including the duties involved and some of her hair-raising experiences.

The duties included mingling with the family and, presumably, providing them with words of good cheer; negotiating temporary loans in case the family was short of cash with which to purchase items such as crepe, black armbands, widow's weeds, and flowers; washing the body; arranging the same in the coffin; artistically organizing floral decorations; and even doing some housecleaning if the lady of the house was too grief-stricken to attend to such things. If the defunct were a suicide, it was part of her job to disguise all evidence of self-inflicted wounds, such as knife cuts or rope burns.

But what you really want to hear about are her hair-raising experiences, so read on.

On one occasion, the layer-out said, she was busily scrubbing the body of a young woman "when the supposed dead girl sat up and screamed as lustily as if nothing had ever ailed her." It took the layer-out some doing to convince the girl's family that she was actually alive. The expert corpse cleaner noted to the reporter, "Sometimes I imagine I can feel the heart beat in a body I am washing, and in such cases I immediately send for medical aid."

Once, the layer-out was hired to attend to a prosperous elderly woman, only to find that the latter's head had been shaved and she had a sewn-up incision in her throat—clearly, the work of doctors who had performed a postmortem. The grieving family let their strange employee in on the secret: the matron had wandered away from the house, got drunk, and drowned. Her family had no idea where she had gone. When her body surfaced, the authorities thought she was a pauper; thus her remains were taken to a medical college and prepared for students to dissect. Fortunately, her husband read a newspaper account of the inquest and recognized the unknown subject as his missing wife. He went to the coroner's office and demanded her return. The sheepish doctors-in-training removed her from a pickling vat with assurances that it was all an honest mistake, and the widower could at least take comfort in the fact that they had not yet gotten around to cutting her into fragments. He brought the body home and paid the layer-out to work her magic on it. She told the reporter with pardonable pride: "I fixed her up so nicely and no one outside of the family ever imagined as they took their 'last look' that the poor lady had been at the bottom of the river, in the morgue, in the pickling vat, and escaped but by a few hours the dissecting table."

The layer-out said that everyone in her trade had undergone some bizarre experiences. However, "We become so hardened, I might say, that we don't mind them."

Entrepreneurial Embalmer

Dr. S. L. of Erie claimed that he had discovered the ultimate embalming fluid. Local businessmen had such confidence in his product that they—after first sagely consulting with scientists—formed a company in 1883 to invest in it, with capital stock fixed at $250,000.

Dr. L. perfected his technique in 1882 on the body of a child named Stephen F., son of a pauper madwoman. The doctor displayed showmanship in the most graphic and impressive manner imaginable by keeping the corpse on open display in a casket in his office. A reporter from the *Erie Letter* described this early example of product placement in words that cannot be improved upon: "It is exposed to the atmosphere, but the health authorities agree that there is no more danger of contaminating the air than if the body was a piece of marble. It lies dressed in purple and fine linen furnished by charitable people, its little hands crossed, and with the last smile it wore in life still upon its face."

The manufacturers of Coca-Cola and Kentucky Fried Chicken, to name two corporations that have secret formulas, make it a point of interest that their formulas are kept in separate bank vaults and are known to only a handful of persons. Little do these companies realize that their secrecy was anticipated by Dr. L. and his investors—but no mundane bank vault for them! They kept the embalming fluid formula in a hermetically sealed casket. One member of the group was elected to keep the casket away from prying eyes, under a $100,000 bond. He was instructed to open the casket and read the formula to other stockholders only in the event of Dr. L.'s untimely death.

John W.'s Bogus Journey

On the morning of Monday, February 16, 1885, John W. of Center Township abruptly fell ill and expired before the doctor arrived. John certainly seemed dead, anyway: his body became cold and rigid, his face turned a waxy pale, and his jaw hung open most unattractively. The family, the pastor, and the physician (when he got there) were all certain that his tale was told.

The family mourned around his body; his oldest son took the death particularly hard and wailed for his father to return. Many hours later, he was still inconsolable. "Won't you speak to me one more time?" he cried to his dead father.

Imagine the sensation that ensued when the corpse's lips moved, his eyes popped open, and he said in a reproachful tone, "Oh, why did you call me back?"

After the initial wave of unbridled, soul-paralyzing terror wore off, the family gave the formerly defunct man restoratives. When he recovered, he told them that when he'd died he'd slipped into a trance in which he was aware of everything happening but could not speak. What befell John sounds uncannily like modern reports of near-death experiences:

> He next remembered of being in a dense darkness and being led by two invisible forms, moving as though floating in the air, with nothing above or below. Then it seemed to get lighter every moment, and he saw two beautiful, shining forms on either side of him. He experienced a feeling of perfect peace and heard the most soothing and delightful music. The feeling of rest was the most noticeable thing in his new state, until it was disturbed by a voice in pain calling him. He felt a thrill of regret, then all became black, and he seemed to be back in the old pain-racked body again, and opening his eyes he found his son and family crying and calling on him to come back.

Mr. W. lived until February 17, when he died again. This time he did not return.

Paying Their Disrespects

It all started when a Lithuanian priest, Father Burba, was sent to head the church at Plymouth, Pennsylvania. Local Polish immigrants wanted one of their own countrymen to have the appointment.

The Poles, headed by a ringleader named Martin W., sent threatening letters to Father Burba, telling him that if he fulfilled his duty of granting certificates of burial, they would see to it that he filled a grave himself. Burba took their threats seriously, and by January 1890, two deceased children of a Lithuanian, John K., had been left unburied. Their decomposing remains were placed in Sobieski Hall (a room above Joseph P.'s store on Main Street) on January 17, for lack of a better place. It was an outrage against religious feeling, common decency, and all that was right and proper—and it probably didn't help Mr. P.'s business, either.

Ill will was so strong between the two factions that when the children were buried at last in the cemetery on January 21, the ceremony had to be performed under police guard. The undeterred Poles crept to the graveyard that night with digging tools and unearthed the coffins of five Lithuanians, including the children.

They left three caskets intact, but the children's coffins were broken open. The bodies were pulled out, mutilated with pickaxes, dragged over the ground, and flung over the fence. The Lithuanian community heard about the atrocity as it was occurring, and soon the graveyard was flooded with thousands of angry, armed Lithuanians in a lynching humor. The Poles fled, whereupon the Lithuanians gathered up their compatriots' remains and reburied them with all the dignity they could under the circumstances.

Jessie Dies, and Then Things Get Weird

Poor Jessie B.! The daughter of a storekeeper, she was the belle of Northumberland until she went insane in 1885 at age eighteen. She was sent to the asylum at Danville in January 1890, but returned home after a month's ineffectual treatment.

On February 25, 1890, Jessie's last night on this sweet earth, she was overtaken with maniacal energy. She played "beautiful and weird refrains" on the family's upright grand piano—and then she smashed it and other furniture as well. She retreated to her room, and all was quiet. Her family assumed she had worn herself out and gone to sleep.

They learned the awful truth next morning when Mrs. B. took breakfast to Jessie's room and found her dead in bed. "Her features bore a look of agony and were horribly distorted," wrote a reporter who knew that his readers craved such details. The doctor came and pronounced her dead of "congestion of the brain"—a vague nineteenth-century catchall medical term for any number of ailments but usually meaning a stroke. The undertaker showed up an hour later. By then Jessie's face had turned black. He countered this circumstance by squirting a gallon and a half of embalming fluid into a vein.

Whatever was in that embalming fluid, it was good stuff. Ten hours after the treatment, Jessie's grieving mother entered the parlor to gaze once more upon her daughter's countenance and nearly fainted: Jessie seemed to be coming to life again! Her face had regained its natural color; her cheeks were apple red; and her grimace was gone, replaced with a winning grin.

Mrs. B. was convinced Jessie was merely in a trance (and had somehow managed to survive taking over a gallon of embalming fluid into her body). The undertaker and a doctor reexamined the corpse and assured the family that she was most decidedly dead.

Jessie's mother still had her doubts. When the funeral was held three days later, the house filled with mourners, the minister preached a sermon, and then Mrs. B. told everyone to disperse as there would be no funeral after all. She was certain Jessie was alive and refused to bury her.

Days passed. Jessie remained in the parlor. Friends and relatives dropped by to pay respects and to stare. The body had not decomposed in the slightest.

On March 25—by which time Jessie had been deceased an entire month—the undertaker gently persuaded Mrs. B. to permit the burial, on the grounds that it was such a lovely day. The formerly dismissed pallbearers were recalled and they carried Jessie to her waiting grave in the cemetery on the northern side of town. She remained lifelike and smiling right to the end, and as far as anyone knows she still is.

Bizarrely Buried: Pennsylvania

A Rumanian immigrant, Jacob J., died at Sharon in April 1903. He was too poor to afford a casket, so his friends—who had some pretty singular ideas—undertook the undertaking. They crafted a homemade coffin out of pine boards and painted it bright green. Before nailing it closed, they put a skin-tight cap on Jacob's head and filled the coffin with apples and other fruit.

⊳⊷⊙⊶⊲

William K. of Felton was buried on January 31, 1925, just as he had requested: with his head resting on a Bible rather than a pillow, wrapped in an American flag instead of a shroud, and using a railroad handcar as a hearse. Actually, the handcar wasn't William's idea. It was necessary to transport pallbearers because of the deep snow.

That Irresistible Urge to Pinch a Mummy's Nose

For years, an Englishman named Mack lived in Wayne. Gossip held that he was the heir to an unclaimed British title.

When Mack died of exposure in 1895, his unclaimed body went to the undertaker, who gave it a charity embalming and determined to hold onto it until Mack's family claimed it.

As of April 1904, the unclaimed body was possessed by a second undertaking firm. Over the years thousands of people trooped by to see it. The original embalmer had preserved Mack so well that the undertakers received offers from museums who wanted to buy and display him. A reporter wrote: "The skin retains its natural color and the sandy mustache and hair remain as in life. The nose has become unnaturally sharp from having been pinched by people who doubted if the man was really dead."

A Face Full of Benson

Dr. Charles Coleman Benson, born an Englishman, resided in Philadelphia with his wife, Isabelle. Despite his reputation for eccentricity, he was a candidate for a prize offered by the French Academy of Medicine for pioneering work in finding a cure for tuberculosis.

On the morning of March 12, 1910, Mr. and Mrs. Benson sat down opposite each other at the breakfast table in their Filbert Street apartment and drained a glass of poison apiece. The doctor left a note reading: "My dear wife and I have decided that we do not wish to longer live. We have committed suicide. We ask for decent attention and wish our bodies cremated and the ashes scattered to the air. To those who will attend to our funeral we will give all the property remaining to us. I have two patents pending in the Patent Office, and much medicine and drugs, also some little furniture."

The duty to fulfill the doctor's request that he and his wife be cremated and their ashes "scattered to the air" fell upon Mrs. Ada S., their landlady, who made her way to Chelten Hills Cemetery one cold, snowy, blustery morning with two urns containing the powdered remains of the Bensons. Ada climbed a hill, opened one urn, and scattered the ashes in the breeze. But when she tossed the contents of the other jar into the gale, the howling wind tossed the ashes right back on her. She was whitened from head to toe with the ashes of a Benson. Overcome with the disgustingness of it all, she fainted in the arms of a cemetery attendant.

Some People Will Do Anything for $20 Million

The relatives of Henrietta Garrett—heiress to a snuff tobacco fortune who died in Philadelphia in 1930—had no idea what became of her final will. The only one on record was dated 1921 and disposed of only $62,500 of her fortune.

It was no trivial matter, either: her estate was worth $20 million and by 1937, 23,000 persons in the United States and abroad were vying for a slice of it, claiming to be heirs. The chief claimant was Mrs. Henrietta Ferguson of Haverford, Pennsylvania, who was unhappy because the only known will provided her with a relatively measly $10,000—but she had a pretty good idea as to where the missing will was located.

Mrs. Ferguson swore that she and Mrs. Garrett's maid had witnessed the signing of the final will in 1924. The maid was dead by 1937 and could not be interrogated. However, asked Ferguson, was it not possible that the maid secreted the will in the millionaire's casket? In August 1937, she requested a court order to have Mrs. Garrett exhumed. She reasoned: "The remains of Mrs. Garrett lay in a casket in a darkened room four days after her death, the open casket offering a convenient receptacle in which to hide her will."

Cooler heads might have argued that if the maid had wanted to get rid of the will, she would have simply destroyed it rather than go through all the melodramatic trouble of hiding it in a coffin, but the court was swayed by Mrs. Ferguson's dubious logic and granted permission to commence digging.

The late Mrs. Garrett's headstone was removed on October 25. Her casket was unearthed and opened the next day. Result: no will, though the court-appointed examiner conceded that the coffin was in such a sorry state that any documents hidden within would have been destroyed.

As of April 1938—when a man in Newark, Delaware, claimed to be the son of Henrietta Garrett—the question of the missing will was still unsettled.

Vicissitudes

In his heyday, Samuel C. was rich—his father left him an estate worth $2 million. In addition, Samuel was a nationally famous art dealer and broker whose most famous client was J. P. Morgan.

But fame and good fortune do not automatically make one a good businessman, and Samuel lost his wealth via bad speculation in art and real estate. When he died of pneumonia at age seventy-five in Newark, New Jersey, on January 12, 1921, Samuel was worth eighty-seven cents.

The pauper was laid to rest in a $10,000 mausoleum in Stroudsburg, Pennsylvania, which he had had constructed back in the days when he could afford it.

Keeping Them Around: Pennsylvania

Neighbors hadn't seen the elderly tax collector and retired manufacturer Rogan S. and his wife, Elizabeth, in a while. So one day in October 1939, the New Brighton health officer broke down their back door. He was greeted by Mrs. S. In one room the officer found Mr. S.—eighty-five years old and two weeks dead, sitting in a chair under a gas light with a never-to-be-finished book nearby.

Rogan must not have been a very energetic individual because Elizabeth did not realize her husband had been deceased a fortnight until it was pointed out to her. "I thought there was something wrong," she mused. "He wouldn't talk to me."

Seeing the Mule from the Inside

Joseph R., only fourteen years old, was a child laborer who drove a mule in the Murray mine shaft at Wilkes-Barre. On August 9, 1888, a runaway train of five loaded boxcars hit him with such force that the boy's head was driven into the side of his mule. It required two miners to pull Joseph out of his predicament. He received a fatal skull fracture; the mule died almost instantly.

David H. Loses His Superpower

David H., age seventy-eight, was the top snake charmer of Pottsville. He could handle poisonous snakes with abandon and was "credited with the possession of a strange power over the reptile kingdom." He made a living for several years by capturing rattlesnakes, which he sold to museums and circuses. He also sold a nostrum he called rattlesnake oil.

One day in September 1890, a noticeably intoxicated David entered the barroom in a hotel carrying a cage with an enormous rattler in it.

"Watch this, gentlemen," slurred he, "and I'll show you how to bite a rattlesnake's head off!"

He opened the cage and produced the snake. But the serpent, not wishing to be the fall guy in David's attempt to duplicate an act of circus geekery, chomped him on the right wrist. The old man hurriedly put the snake back in the cage and slunk from the barroom, possibly out of embarrassment.

No one saw a trace of David for three days. He was found curled up in misery in the tall grass surrounding a foundry, much more dead than alive, purple from head to toe, and sporting an extravagantly swollen right arm. He lived five more days in this unenviable state, conscious to the end and begging all present to put him out of his misery.

The Swan Knows When It Is Dying: Pennsylvania

In April 1911, Frank L. of Lambertville started telling anyone who would listen that he was going to pass away at noon on Thursday, May 25. He was in good health, so his friends and relatives laughed at him—admit it, you would have too. As the day drew near, Frank came down with a minor illness; his family physician sent him to Saint Francis Hospital in Trenton, New Jersey, for treatment. Frank's case did not seem to be serious, but he said to the doctors and nurses, "I will die at noon on May 25," so they gave him extra attention.

The anticipated day came. Frank was in good health at 11:30 a.m. At 11:45 a.m. he grew pale and weak. He died at noon. An autopsy disclosed that he'd expired from acute dilation of the heart. This surprised the doctors, as it was not the ailment for which Frank was receiving treatment.

Don't Drink Lizards

Once upon a time, Mrs. Anna J. of Marcus Hook swallowed a live lizard that got in her drinking water. Thereafter, she was plagued constantly with the sensation that the lizard was crawling up from her inner depths and lodging in her throat. (This fear was probably psychosomatic; surely the lizard could not have long survived in the hydrochloric acid of her stomach.) She worried so much about being strangled from the inside that she died on the night of July 24, 1900, insisting that the reptile was in her neck. The coroner found no evidence of choking, so it seemed that Mrs. J. worried herself to death.

A Skeptic with a Good Arm

Florence A. of Philadelphia, age fifteen, thought it great sport to scare people by dressing like a ghost. On the night of August 19, 1900, she donned a sheet and tried her hand at spooking some people in a vacant lot at Fifty-Seventh and Ludlow Streets. The crowd scattered—with the exception of a skeptic with good aim, who hurled a brick at the ghost's head. Then Florence became the genuine article.

Aiming for the Apple: Pennsylvania

In another case of a William Tell imitation gone badly, Pittsburgh detectives encountered a baffling death scene on December 12, 1939. Fifteen-year-old Boy Scout Norval H. lay mortally wounded from a gunshot wound in an upper room in scoutmaster Daniel H.'s house; an apple on a string dangled from the ceiling, suspended by its stem; and the scoutmaster lay dead with a rifle by his side. Putting the clues together, detectives theorized that Daniel accidentally shot Norval during a William Tell challenge and then shot himself out of remorse.

It Worked

A group of Italian sewer laborers were eating lunch and warming themselves in a shack in Carrick, a borough of Pittsburgh, on a cold day in November 1906. One of them thought it would be a good idea to warm ten sticks of frozen dynamite near the fire.

Practical Jokers at Work

March 11, 1907: John D., twenty-year-old laborer, was asleep in front of a hot coke salamander at the Pressed Steel Car Works in McKees Rocks. One of his coworkers, standing on a crane overhead, thought it would be richly funny to pour oil down on the salamander—when the oil ignited, the flash would scare John awake! His expressions of surprised terror sure would be funny! But the cranesman's aim was bad, and most of the oil hit John, saturating his clothing. When the inevitable flash came, the sleeping man was turned into a living torch. The cranesman abandoned the scene, hopefully with a newly improved sense of humor.

———

Richard S., Harold S., and Michael G. were coworkers in a dye house in Chester. On November 11, 1927, Richard and Harold put a lump of something they thought was saltpeter in Michael's coffee "just as a little joke." The substance actually was poison. Michael flew away like a dream shortly after drinking it, and before the day was over, his very funny coworkers were arrested and held without bail.

Bookworm Becomes Worm Food

Is it possible to "read yourself to death"? William C., a boarder who lived in Chester, might have done exactly that. Reading was his favorite (and only) indulgence, and he developed a habit of staying up all night reading. His landlady remarked, "He invariably slept but three hours out of the twenty-four."

Years of failure to rest properly put a strain on William's heart, and in July 1912, his roommate found him dead in bed with, appropriately, a book in one hand.

Death's Little Ironies: Pennsylvania

Harry S. was general manager of the Westinghouse Union Battery Company in Pittsburgh. On February 22, 1928, he died when he fell through a third-floor window at the Pittsburgh Athletic Club. Detectives discovered that before Harry fell, he had been reading *The Clock Strikes Two*, a mystery novel by Henry Kitchell Webster. The corner of page 273 was dog-eared—indicating it was the last page Harry had read—and featured this bit of dialogue: "Forty years ago my daughter fell in love and wanted to marry against my will. She tried to escape from a room I'd locked her into and in trying fell and was killed."

In other words, it looked like Harry had been reading about a fatal fall moments before he took a real-life plunge. Broken vines outside the window suggested that his fall was accidental, not suicide.

In 1913, Emory T. was informed by doctors that he had only a year to live. On the other hand, the Philadelphian had just inherited $250,000 in an era when the average yearly salary was $800. He reasoned thus: since his life was nearly over, why not spend his windfall just as fast as he could within that precious year?

Why not, indeed? The doctors were wrong, and Emory did not take what Thomas Wolfe called "the last voyage, the longest, the best" until fifteen years later. In 1928, he was not only dead, but dead broke in Atlantic City.

On June 10, 1933, Isabel T. of Philadelphia accidentally gave a child named John B. a teaspoonful of poison rather than the medicine she had been reaching for in the dark. Isabel was the matron of the Society for the Prevention of Cruelty to Children.

Death's Door

Robert C. returned to his Pittsburgh home early in the morning of January 5, 1919, only to find that he had locked himself out. No problem! He got a hatchet, chopped a hole in the door, and tried to crawl through. The flaw in his plan became evident when he got stuck halfway in and froze to death.

The Moon as Murderer

Such things were not supposed to happen. Else F. told her father, Rev. Frederick F. of the Tabor Lutheran Church, that she was going for a walk. Then, despite having no history of personal trouble except for a "serious nervous disorder," she disappeared.

The next day, February 24, 1932, two boys found the attractive twenty-two-year-old Tennant College student frozen in a deserted shack in a field in Burholme Park, Cheltenham Township, near Philadelphia. She was naked except for a thin band of silk. Her clothes were found hanging on a bush two hundred yards from the shack.

The death scene was a real puzzle. Had Else been molested? No. Murdered? No sign of it, despite some bruising. Committed suicide? No sign of that either. Died of exposure? Maybe—but why would someone strip naked on a freezing winter's night and lie down in a shack?

Else's family doctor and at least one prominent psychologist, Dr. Thaddeus Bolton, agreed on an explanation that seemed like a throwback to the medieval era: she'd died of something they called "moon madness." As explained by Dr. Bolton, head of the Psychology Department at Temple University:

> The theory I advance is based on observations of a natural condition among near-insane and nervous persons. The attacks of extreme nervousness frequently re-occur at regular intervals—about twenty-eight to thirty days apart. Coinciding as they do with the full moon, it has long been thought by many that the moon's rays are responsible. I understand that Miss F. was of a nervous disposition, that she was worried over her studies and her failure to pass certain examinations. When she left her father and started to walk

through the woods it is possible that she became agitated thinking of her schoolwork. Then as night came on and the moon rose, she became lost, and with the full moon shining over her head she may have lost her reason. The rest follows. She undressed under the delusion she was preparing for bed, then lay down in the cold. Since it was bitter cold that night, it is not difficult to see how quickly death came.

In other words, the sight of the full moon exacerbated Else's nervous disorder and lured her to the shanty, where she felt compelled to disrobe and wait until she perished miserably from exposure—which appears to have been the official cause of death.

Leave 'Em Laughing

Pittsburgh dentist Nathan S. couldn't figure out what was wrong with the mask he put on patients' faces to administer anesthesia, but it had rendered one customer unconscious. On November 13, 1937, the dentist deemed it a good idea to put the mask on himself and try it out—while no one else was around. He made notes as he slowly journeyed to the Forever City: "Sight is good—hearing is decreasing—eyesight is decreasing—is bad—smell is—"

He died in his dental chair of an overdose of nitrous oxide.

But the story doesn't end there. A few hours after the dentist's demise, a *Pittsburgh Press* reporter couldn't resist the chance to test the "death chair" for himself. The journalist described the experience using the third person: "At first there was a sweet, almost sickening smell. The reporter breathed harder and perspiration rolled down his arms and legs. He began to swoon. . . . The reporter swayed as if intoxicated. Faces whirled about him. A light-headedness. [He] was not conscious he had arms or legs."

His curiosity nearly cost his life, but unlike the dentist he had the good sense to make sure a rescuer was standing by.

Final Communications: Pennsylvania

Joseph D. killed himself in his home on Lombard Street, Philadelphia, on March 9, 1887. He left behind a curious note indicating that, in his last moments, he considered Shakespeare's line "All the world's a stage" a less fitting analogy for existence than a clown-infested circus: "Having no more use for this old hulk, I lay down to die just as I lived. This world is not a stage, but a circus, clowns, supes [supernumeraries], and ringmasters doing all the work, and the big bums getting all the money."

David E., an inventor residing at Wilkes-Barre, was driven insane by his failed attempts to build a perpetual motion machine and shot himself three times in the head out of sheer frustration on November 23, 1882. His suicide note was remarkable for its unfashionable antipathy toward religion:

> I do sincerely prohibit any and all of the reverend devils to babble and lie over my old body. Bury me in my old rags as I am now; sell this coat of mine or give it to whom you please. I die in my atheistical faith as fearlessly as the heathen dieth in the faith of his existence. I believe not in conscious existence nor sensitiveness after death. It is the end, the final end, of men as well as the common animals. Ye will judge this and blame it: nevertheless, it is truthful. I considered and concluded that to commit suicide would be the best thing that I could possibly do. I am but eluding misery and pain. It is clear and evident that I am in the uttermost poverty and distress, having no health nor strength to be a slave any more. I believe it prudent to leave this tyrannical and oppressive world and to be a pauper no more. I owe no person anything; therefore, what things are here shall be yours. It would please me if they were of much greater value. Farewell.

James Smith, self-described socialist, gassed himself to death in his land-lady's Philadelphia establishment on the night of January 31, 1913, making himself officially a bad tenant. His motive, as revealed in his suicide note, was that he did *not* want to work: "I hereby will my body to the first medical college that wants it; also $2 to you, providing you turn over the other $25 to the local Philadelphia socialist party. I am sorry to have troubled you this way. I did this to cure an acute attack of shovel-stiff laborhoboitis."

The *Phoenix Gazette* callously headlined the story "One Jim Smith Less."

Tommy W. had been a vaudeville comedian for twenty-seven years but never became a headlining star as he had hoped. When he gassed himself to death in his Philadelphia home on November 9, 1930, he left a note revealing his thirst for fame: "And if anybody wants to know where I am, just tell them that at last I'm with the big timers."

Not Recommended

James M. of Philadelphia chose to commit suicide via self-choking on January 3, 1892, by forcing his rosary down his throat. Surgeons extricated a crucifix and a string of beads with forceps, but he died of internal bleeding on January 6.

Getting a Grippe

Influenza was a common and horrifying disease in the nineteenth century. Sometimes people called it *la grippe*, as if giving it a fancy French name would somehow make it more bearable. Euphemisms did not help in the case of George G., a businessman from Nineveh, Pennsylvania, who suffered so greatly from the miseries of the disease that he decided to join his fathers on February 18, 1892. He got out of bed, broke a window, stuck his head through the shattered pane, and rubbed his throat against the jagged edges. In effect, he tried to saw off his own head. He was found on the floor, unconscious and very bloody. A doctor sewed up his throat, but when no one was looking, the beleaguered businessman ripped out the stitches. Thus ended the days of George G.

Death of a (Well-Dressed) Salesman

E.F.D., a traveling salesman, committed suicide in the Westminster Hotel at Scranton on December 12, 1895. Obviously a believer in going out in style, he drank two bottles of laudanum while reclining in an easy chair with his feet propped on a shelf. He was found fully dressed, complete with gloves, overcoat, and hat.

Party Poopers: Pennsylvania

Edward P.'s friends held a dinner party in his honor at a house in Pittsburgh on December 21, 1922. During the last course, the guest of honor said, "I want to put a piece on the player piano," and excused himself. A few moments later, his friends heard the strains of "Let the Rest of the World Go By"—followed by a gunshot. The partiers found Edward leaning dead against the piano.

Near the close of the year 1928, Esther V. of Towanda committed suicide by drinking poison. Days later, fellow Pennsylvanian Louis M. brandished a bottle of the same kind of poison at a New Year's Eve party. "Anybody dare me to drink it?" he asked. "Go ahead," scoffed the revelers, acting on the assumption that he had replaced the poison with water. But Louis hadn't, and as the nonplussed partygoers watched, he downed the bottle and went into convulsions. He confronted our last enemy on New Year's Day 1929.

Aping the Master

In 1893, nine days after the premiere of his Sixth Symphony, the Russian composer Tchaikovsky committed suicide. (According to some, he might have died of cholera.)

On July 21, 1907, Pittsburgh musician Margaret K. played the Sixth Symphony on her piano and then fatally cut her throat, apparently out of sympathy with the piece's creator.

Too Much Joy

Tola S., age thirty-five, was to be married to Paul B. of Wilkinsburg on the night of October 25, 1928, in Philadelphia's Calvary Episcopal Church. Instead, only four hours before the wedding, as guests gathered for the ceremony, she went to a second-floor bedroom full of wedding gifts and blew out her brains. She left a note reading, "I have nothing to live for; please forgive me."

Further explanation came the next day: the bride-to-be had killed herself because she was *too darn happy*. Her friends and family believed Tola was worried that her happiness had hit its peak with her nuptials and that her life could only be a downhill slide from there. She felt the only sensible thing to do was to die while in a state of exultation.

Rising from a Pond

In the summer of 1876 came a report of a ghost that spent America's centennial year by scaring the fool out of passersby. This Spirit of '76 couldn't have chosen a spookier location to haunt. It may have been the shade of Jacob W., an elderly man who had been murdered a mile and a half from the haunted site.

The ghost lived (if that is the proper verb) in a picturesque pond in the "Pond Fields" northwest of Caernarvon Township—an uninhabited wilderness in Berks County's highest elevation. It was seen on the night of July 23 by a group of young men on the way home from a service at Bethel church. A "frightful object" arose from the pond. Said the *Reading Eagle*, "After making a few deep, low-sounding cries, it arose and began to perform all kinds of antics around them. They shouted at it, but did not frighten it in the least." One of their party, Greeley S., shot it several times with a revolver, "which had no more effect than if shot into a stone fence."

The youths fled without even looking back. They were rendered speechless from fear for a while and found themselves unable to describe what had frightened them except to say that it looked horrible.

Ghost on the Tracks

In 1873, a vagrant was run over on the tracks of the Reading Railroad, just below the Port Kennedy station. The accident resulted from the engineer's negligence. Afterward, trainmen saw a ghost at the site until autumn 1880, when it seemed the appearances had ceased.

But the ghost was only biding its time. On Christmas Night 1882, engineer Charles W. on the 9:00 freight train saw "an apparition of unusual size." According to a *Philadelphia Times* article from January 1883, it had made a visitation every evening since then. Usually it stood on the tracks, frightening engineers, who could not help running it over, and allegedly was run over several times a night.

Trainmen were a hardy lot, and the various engineers, brakemen, and firemen on the line made a habit of leaving their stations with plenty of brickbats and ammunition in case they saw the ghost. These precautions were futile. On the night of January 1, 1883, brakeman George N. was standing on the platform of a train approaching the spot where the supernatural mischief generally happened. In the locomotive's headlights, George saw a man standing near the tracks. He pulled the emergency cord and the train stopped. George hopped off and confronted the figure, which he described as a man standing with one hand over his face and pointing at the train with his other hand. A blast of cold air hit George with sufficient force to knock his hat off. George stood stunned and speechless until the conductor opened a door and warned him he'd catch a cold if he stayed out there.

George was not one to be made a fool of by a ghost, and the next night he carried an iron bar. The spirit did not show, but the night after that it returned. George conked it over what should have been its noggin and a passenger fired twice at its face with a revolver. The ghost vanished, not perturbed in the least.

One Saturday night in January 1883, engineer Charles W. saw it standing in the middle of the tracks ahead, but it looked so much like a flesh-and-blood person that he slammed on the brakes and set the whistle blowing and the bell ringing. But there was insufficient time to stop, and the train ran over the figure on the track. "We've killed someone, Jim, and we had better go back and pick up the pieces," Charles said to the conductor. They stopped the train—but there were no pieces to pick up.

Scared to Death

Robert M. of Wanamie worked for years as a pump runner for the Lehigh and Wilkes-Barre Coal Company. It was noted in his obituary that he was a Civil War veteran and "not easily frightened." Yet something scared him to death. That something was a ghost—or what he took to be one.

One day near the beginning of August 1896, Robert had been doing whatever it is pump runners do when he heard a weird noise issuing from the bowels of the mine. He paid no attention to it at first, but then he was overcome with an uncanny feeling. He heard the sound again and looked up. He had the sensation that someone was nearby. He saw a floating white man-sized object in the mine. Robert addressed it, but it did not answer. After it disappeared, Robert made a search and found nothing that could account for the sighting.

The veteran thought the apparition was a harbinger of death. He quit his job that very day and took to bed, sick—but the doctors couldn't find anything wrong with him. Robert turned away from their medicines and grew weaker, certain that he was doomed to die shortly.

The end came on August 16, 1896. Had he beheld an authentic ghost or had he frightened himself to death after seeing something with a natural explanation? Either way, Robert M. was just as dead.

Headstone

Martin M. of Mill Village spent December 27, 1885, watching workmen digging a ditch along railroad tracks. As the laborers tossed shovelfuls of dirt and stones, Martin noticed a particularly strange-looking rock. Upon closer inspection, it turned out to be the petrified head of a child. "The forehead, cheeks, and nose were well shaped and perfect," said a press account. "The eyes were sunken, but perfect in shape. A piece was broken from one ear, but the other was whole and of good shape."

Head Injury Hijinks: Pennsylvania

Marion D., who operated the rolling mill for the Philadelphia Iron and Steel Company, had a slight workplace accident on June 29, 1878: an iron clamp weighing fourteen pounds flew off the shaft of a rapidly revolving flywheel and hit Mr. D. in the forehead, knocking a crescent-shaped, three-inch-long piece of skull out of the laborer's head and carrying a considerable dollop of brain tissue with it. The chunk of dislodged cranium must have hit the floor with a resounding *splat* that chilled the marrow of all bystanders. The flying clamp also loosened Marion's teeth and injured his jaw so badly that he could not open his mouth for three weeks.

Marion was carried home and examined in turn by a trio of physicians who declared his wounds fatal. But he fooled them all: nine weeks after his gruesome mishap, soft tissue had formed over the hole in his head. The pulsations of Marion's brain were visible in the somewhat-healed hole.

By April 1880, Marion had entirely recovered physically; his mind was not quite the same as before, but as a contemporary account noted, "His mental characteristics, although materially changed, are considered by the physicians wonderfully good when the facts of the case are taken into consideration." Marion's recovery was favorably compared to that of Phineas Gage, the hero of the still-celebrated "American Crowbar Case"—so named because Gage, a railroad worker from New Hampshire, survived after a premature exploding powder charge sent a tamping iron through his head.

In fact, Marion did Phineas Gage one better. Gage kept the tamping iron as a souvenir of a memorable occasion, while Marion kept that fragment of skull in his pocket as a portable conversation piece.

Oh, Rats!: Pennsylvania

A farmer, Jessie L. of East Pennsboro, was irritated by the rats that ate his hens' eggs, devoured his corn, and invaded his granary with rattish impunity. Upon inspecting the granary one day in March 1875, Jessie found that there was only one hole the vermin could use for an entrance. He sprinkled corn meal on the floor, waited a while, nailed the hole shut from the outside, and entered the building with his trusty terrier and a club. But there were three unforeseen flaws in Jessie's plan. One became evident when he got inside and heard the latch on the outside of the door fall into place. Master and dog were now locked in.

Another flaw was that there were more rats in the structure than Jessie had anticipated. *Lots more.* The rodents were infuriated when they found their egress blocked and retaliated by leaping on the farmer and his dog. Jessie swung his weapon left and right, up and down—then came his third mistake: it was too dark to see what he was doing, and he accidentally killed his own dog with a blow from the club. Sensing an advantage, the rats swarmed over the farmer, biting his hands and shredding his clothes. An especially intrepid one nipped his nose. Luckily for Jessie, a neighbor heard his shouts and opened the latch. The farmer bounded out of the granary, leaving his dead dog behind.

After cleansing his many, many wounds, Jessie decided rat killing was best left up to the professionals: cats! He borrowed twelve and put them, along with three of his own, in the granary. Then he went to bed and probably dreamed about his bewhiskered enemies. In the morning, he opened the granary door and found ten dead cats, one blind cat, two cats with one eye apiece, two unharmed cats, and 119 slain rodents. Nothing was left of the dog but bones and hair and perhaps its immortal soul. The famished rats had consumed the canine while Jessie was out collecting cats.

Buried on the Installment Plan

Philadelphians were impressed with Peter J., a Civil War veteran passing through town in the summer of 1878—to be more precise, they were impressed with *what remained of him.* For it seemed, due to his multitudinous battle injuries, that more of him was missing than was actually present. He had lost both legs below the knee; his right arm was amputated below the elbow; he had parted company with half of his left ear and nearly all of his teeth; two fingers were gone from his left hand; and his right eye was gone. Peter made a living as a traveling musician specializing on the barrel organ. He kept placards reading "Chancellorsville," "Lookout Mountain," "Fredericksburg," "Manassas," and a dozen other historically significant locations to remind spectators that he had lost pieces of himself in battle. A reporter for the *Philadelphia Bulletin* recorded the words of the incomplete veteran for posterity:

> I'm bein' buried in installments, and there'll be a lively time gettin' me together again.... That 'ere right leg, what used to fit on that stump, is

decently buried down at Culpeper Courthouse, in a little grave just behind the barn. The boys plant flowers on it every summer. The left leg, which you see is gone, is down in old Virginny, near to Richmond, and has a tombstone over it saying: "Here lies Peter J.'s left leg, which he lost in the Seven Days' fight. *Requiescat in Passem* [Pacem]." They put a little flag on it on Decoration Day. That 'ere right arm is preserved in alcohol in the army hospital at Washington, and them two fingers which is off is buried close to a big tree at Gettysburg, where an appropriate mark has been raised. I was down to see my little grave last fall, and was a-weepin' over 'em for some time. Them 'ere teeth is buried in Georgia, and I'm afeared nobody is takin' care of 'em; and that 'ere piece of ear was shot away to nothin' at Old Oaks Battlefield. You are lookin' at me [missing] eye, are you? Well, that's doin' good service in portato field in Albany.

The crowds were impressed with the greatly abridged old soldier's account of his piecemeal deterioration and donated to him generously.

Dubious Doctors

One fine morning long ago, Mrs. Connery of Fairmount Avenue, Philadelphia, noticed that her baby's knee was badly swollen. She called in T. B. Miller, MD, billed as the ex-dean of the Philadelphia University of Medicine Surgery. This august personage examined the infant and declared that it had somehow broken its leg. He wrapped the limb in bandages, applied liniment, and left, with the reassuring promise that he would be back.

Dr. Miller returned the next day with five other doctors because he felt a consultation was necessary. The learned physicians concluded that the baby's leg had mortified and must be amputated—with a saw!—to save its life. Dr. Miller said they would visit the Connery household with bone saw in tow on the following Monday. As they left, the mob of medics recommended that the baby be strapped down in its crib.

Mrs. Connery was not a doctor, but she was pretty sure such radical surgery was not warranted for a swollen knee, and she took her child to a doctor at Jefferson College for a second opinion. Several more doctors examined the leg and concurred that it was merely sprained, and amputation was decidedly not recommended.

The worried mother sought a third opinion, this time from a man who had a reputation as a faith healer. He looked at the baby and said the child had somehow stuck a pin in its leg. "You go home and work the swelling from the right side to the left and it will come out," he said. The faith healer, it turned out, was correct: the baby's leg was neither gangrenous nor even sprained. Mrs. Connery kneaded her child's swollen knee until a needle poked through, which she extracted with tweezers. The baby made a full recovery.

However, on Monday, Dr. Miller and his band of colleagues appeared at the Connery household as promised, toting far more knives than seemed necessary, plus additional equipment—some of which seem more appropriate tools for a carpenter or the Three Stooges than a doctor—including hammers, chisels, extra saws, and a bottle of ether. Mr. Connery informed them that the child was on the mend and their services were not needed. One of the consultants, miffed, said that he came to amputate the child's leg, and by cracky that's what he aimed to do. He shouted that he had set the baby's leg and saved its life and demanded a $25 payment. The irate father showed them the door, and they left grumbling, taking their saws, hammers, and chisels with them.

If the reader thinks that the doctors exhibited eccentric behavior, bad diagnostic skills, and poor bedside manner, thereby hangs the rest of the tale. When the story got around, investigators found that neither Dr. Miller nor any of his five cohorts were real physicians at all. They were all lunatics who had bought bogus medical school diplomas!

The problem was widespread in Philadelphia by the late 1870s. One man, William B. Smith of Fifteenth Street, developed an abiding interest in human anatomy and read everything he could find on the topic. He even attended Philadelphia University for a couple of years, but no one could say whether he graduated. He was injured at his place of business, lost his reason, was sent to Kirkbride's Asylum for the Insane three times, and had done a stint in the Pennsylvania Institution for the Insane. Despite Smith's madness, in 1853 his family bought a gift of a diploma from the Philadelphia University of Medicine and Surgery in his name, which gave him the right to practice medicine. Fortunately for the city's ill and lame, "Dr." Smith never actually saw any patients.

The authorities wanted to know where all these fake diplomas were coming from. In June 1880, they found that some of the medical colleges themselves were bogus. One investigator who spent $150 bought five degrees, including two doctors of medicine, one doctor of divinity, one doctor of laws, and one doctor of civil law. On June 9, the number one culprit was arrested: Dr. John Buchanan, dean of the Eclectic Medical College of Pennsylvania, which later changed its name to the American

University of Philadelphia. Under an alias, Buchanan was also dean of Livingston University of America. Two other faculty members were arrested and another six abandoned the city.

When the authorities raided Buchanan's premises, they found a half ton of blank diplomas, just waiting to be filled out with the names of purchasers. Correspondence indicated that Buchanan's concern had sold three thousand bogus degrees and that the American University in particular had been operating as a diploma mill since 1867.

Bondsmen put up Buchanan's bail. He thanked them by vanishing like a shade and leaving them holding the bag. The onetime physician faked his own drowning and fled to Canada. He did this not only to escape the law, but also to cheat his bondsmen. But Buchanan proved better at shamming sheepskins than hiding from the authorities. On August 24, he turned up in Windsor, Ontario, cowering under the alias Fairchild. On September 10, he worked up the courage to cross into the United States and was quickly arrested at Saint Clair, Michigan.

His trial was short and none too sweet. On December 6, he was found guilty, fined $500, and ordered to pay the cost of his prosecution and spend ten months in prison for trying to defraud the government.

"Dean" Buchanan confessed to his fraudulent career in March 1881 and told authorities the names of persons he had done business with and the names of "wholesale druggists in Philadelphia who have sold his diplomas." He admitted that over the years he had corresponded with five thousand persons interested in purchasing phony medical credentials. According to a news account, in Buchanan's confession he related "how diplomas were signed by the faculty; how, in one instance, three professors, for $5 each, signed 500 diplomas and how, for $350, diplomas which were to be sent abroad were certified by the Spanish consul. In all, about 10,000 names are tangled up in his disclosures."

He estimated that there were twenty-five diploma mills in America and Europe serving individuals who wanted to be doctors without undergoing the inconvenience of actually attending medical school. He thought 20,000 fraudulent doctors were currently operating (no pun intended) in the United States and another 40,000 in Europe. Buchanan also sang like a canary on such topics as abortion, snake oil patent medicine, and grave robbery—an activity in which he personally had participated. As icing on the cake, he explained how he'd faked his suicide.

In October 1881, after his ten months were up, Buchanan was resentenced to a year in jail and a fine of $1,000 for his leading role in running the nation's most notorious diploma mill. It was a lenient sentence considering how much incalculable pain and suffering undoubtedly was caused by the lunatics and incompetents who practiced medicine under his phony diplomas.

After serving his sentence, the dubious doctor kept his nose clean for a while. But on January 19, 1885, he was again arrested in Philadelphia—along with his new business partner, Dr. Rebecca Russell—for selling diplomas that bore the forged signatures of "some of Philadelphia's most prominent physicians." Perhaps Buchanan thought nobody would notice.

Phantom Limb: Pennsylvania

Willie C., a nine-year-old lad from Whitehall, lost an arm in July 1874 after it was run over by a train, that champion limb amputator of times past. He was taken home to recuperate. His severed arm was treated in an oddly cavalier fashion. It was tossed in a pail and then placed in a box and buried in the family garden. Little Willie complained that he felt as though something were crawling on the palm of his missing hand. Interested parties exhumed the hand and found a worm on the palm. They put the arm in a glass jar but had to force it in—Willie felt pain in the missing limb as they did so. Then they filled the jar with alcohol and buried it. Willie complained that his arm and fingers were cramped up and that his pinky and ring fingers were crossed. The interested parties dug up the jar and found the hand in exactly the position Willie described. Let's hope they gave his arm a dignified, spacious burial the third time around.

Why It Is Not a Good Idea to Do Home Experiments
on Someone's Brain

Henry B., black and seventeen years old, was the servant of a Philadelphia physician whose name was withheld—with good cause—in the press when the doctor's secret journal was discovered two years after the doctor's death.

This physician's specialty was brain diseases, with a side interest in psychology and hypnotism. Henry picked up knowledge in the same subjects from his employer and had a theory that some of the brain's cells were unnecessary and could be destroyed to no ill effect. The doctor's journal bore the following entry, dated March 9, 1869: "Henry's theory about superfluous brain cells is certainly novel, and if the boy were not so precocious I would laugh at it. There may be something in it, but how can it be proven?"

His servant's comments gave the doctor a swell idea for an experiment: why not remove part of a living human's brain just to see what happened? Well, why not? The entry dated May 30 reveals that the doctor did try it and was immediately sorry:

> I feel that I have brought down the anger of Heaven upon my head in attempting to tamper with the noblest part of the Creator's handiwork. Henry B., who has been beneath my roof since childhood, still lives. He exists, he breathes, he digests, but that is all. He is no longer an entity, and by my hand. To you, my beloved wife, I confide this horrible secret, and I beg of you to do all you can to prevent my memory from being tarnished because I feel the grave to be near.

The "horrible secret," if the reader has not already guessed, is that the doctor removed a substantial portion of Henry's cerebrum—but with the servant's eager agreement, for he was only too happy to serve as a human guinea pig:

> On the morning of that terrible day, I placed Henry in the operating chair in the back office, first telling him what I intended to do. I administered five ounces of ether, and when he was thoroughly under the influence I used the trephine. A semi-circular opening was made in the right parietal bone, one and a half inches above and in front of the ear. The brain was exposed and then without hesitation I inserted a curette and pushed it forward toward the exterior part of the longitudinal fissure, where, phrenology teaches us, the seat of veneration lies.

After removing an ounce of gray matter, the surgeon waited until the sedative wore off so he could observe the results of his handiwork, which turned out to be unexpected and horrifying: "There was a twitching of the entire muscular system on the left side, and a continual drawing down of the left side of the mouth. . . . His right eye was sparkling and intelligent, but the other was dead and stony, and the contrast between the two was amazingly strange." The subject was unable to speak intelligibly.

Well, this *was* a fine pickle! The alarmed doctor then did what any rational person would do: he figured that he could balance things out if he removed an equal portion of the *other* side of the brain. Henry went under the knife again, this time receiving a hole on the left side of his head. Of the results the doctor wrote sadly, and with marked understatement, "My theory about equalization was altogether unsound." The surgery left the servant a powerless "piece of living clay—a vegetable without a will."

The surgeon was too ashamed to tell anyone what he had done, leaving his wife to wonder why poor Henry had suddenly become a shambling idiot. The helpless servant remained in the household only a few months, until the doctor's remorse became so overwhelming that he sent Henry to the Blockley Almshouse, where he died in 1875.

The doctor's wife never knew about her husband's ill thought-out experiment. She died in 1881, and he joined her in the Land of Dreamless Sleep in 1882, racked by shame right to the very end. Some said his guilt killed him.

Was the story of Henry's secret brain surgery true or merely a journalistic hoax? Let's hope it was the latter, though the wealth of detail makes one wonder—as does the fact that performing surgery as described in the article would indeed result in a stroke and then a vegetative state.

If You Must Crucify Yourself, Get Help

Sixty-four-year-old James Q. of Philadelphia did something that he considered awful. He did not divulge to anyone the exact nature of his trespass but felt he should punish himself for it. So one Thursday night in March 1891, while his family was asleep, he decided the time was right to crucify himself. He mistakenly thought crucifixion was a one-man job.

James marked out the shape of a cross on the floor, sat down and stretched his legs, held a nail on his right foot, and drove it through with a single hammer blow. He performed this feat of self-carpentry in total silence, and his family did not wake up. Then, holding a nail in place against his left foot, he struck it with a hammer. But the glancing blow failed to drive it through and it was imbedded in a bone. James stretched his left hand on the floor, palm upward, and drove a nail through it with his right hand. (How he held the nail in place I have no idea.) The easy part was over. Now came the real difficulty: nailing the right hand, since he had only one free hand with which to pierce it. But he was spared this seeming impossibility when his family awoke and stopped him, presumably by confiscating his hammer.

James's family pried the nails out of his left hand and right foot with all the appropriate sound effects the reader can imagine, but the nail in the left foot was solidly fixed and could not be wrenched free. It seems the family did not consider it a pressing matter, as they waited until morning to alert a doctor. When the physician arrived for his house call, he found the patient trying to pull the nail out with a "rough instrument." The doctor attempted to help with a medically dubious set of pliers. He broke off the outer portion of the nail but the remainder was lodged in the bone.

James's next stop was Pennsylvania Hospital, where Dr. Frank G. cut into the bone and extracted the rest of the nail. The patient underwent this surgery without anesthesia, and during the process he fulminated so violently upon his sins that the police took him postsurgery to the insane ward at Philadelphia Hospital. He remarked that he had been planning to crucify himself for forty years at least and was glad that he finally did it. Ironically, he lived near Carpenter Street.

━┄━▶━○━◀┄━

But at least James *wanted* to be crucified. George R., a Slavic coal miner at Avella, was unpopular with his fellow workers who suspected him of spying on them and reporting "workplace misdeeds" to their superiors at the Pittsburgh and Washington Coal Company. One day George's drunken coworkers took him to the mine and pounded him like plaster. He was saved when the police broke up the mob, but their thirst for vengeance was not slaked. On April 23, 1910, the miners trekked to George's house, carried him to the mine, stripped off his clothes, and forced a crown of thorns onto his head. That was tarts and gingerbread compared to their final atrocity: they nailed George to a cross by driving spikes through his wrists and palms and securing his body with ropes. The intoxicated miners threw rocks at their victim, beat him with clubs, and danced like fools around the foot of the cross. (This sort of behavior might qualify as "workplace misdeeds.") George was rescued a second time but died later at a hospital. The miners were arrested and brought to Washington, Pennsylvania, to save them from a mass lynching.

━┄━▶━○━◀┄━

Then there was the case of the seven boys in Wilmerding, ranging in age from six to eight years, who saw a recreation of the passion play in a nickelodeon in April 1911. They were inspired to recreate the scenes by crucifying one of their playmates, seven-year-old Taylor B. They constructed a cross out of scantlings and went so far as to drive two ten-penny nails through Taylor's palms, but got scared and ran away when he fainted. Luckily for the brats, little Taylor refused to be a tattletale.

No, I don't know why there was once such an affinity between Pennsylvanians and crucifixions.

Will Weirdness: Pennsylvania

Kate P. of 2942 Leithgow Street, Philadelphia, fled this vale of tears on November 24, 1902. She didn't leave her son so much as a shiny new nickel. Even worse, her will forbade him ever to visit her grave, which seems somehow unenforceable and legally dubious: "My son Percy shall have no part of anything belonging to me. Thus I mean to leave him for the language he used toward me and the way he treated me in taking my money and in making terms how I shall live. Also, it is my desire that he never visit my grave. He has broken a good, kind mother's heart and does not deserve having a mother's grave to visit. May God help him to make peace with his conscience."

When Joseph K. of Hazleton died in August 1905, he left $500, which he requested be used to purchase a glass of beer for everyone who attended his funeral.

George W. of Summerdale harbored no love for his son-in-law, as revealed to the world when his will was probated on November 18, 1908: "Fifty cents to be paid to my son-in-law, Charles W., a native of Huntingdon, Pa., to enable him to buy a good stout rope with which to hang himself."

Similarly, when Dr. David R. poisoned himself in Philadelphia in June 1925, not only did he leave his widow Laura only a dollar from his $15,000 estate, he also advised her to kill herself. He recommended hanging and suggested that she buy the necessary rope with her inheritance.

A Professor Revolts

George Herbert S. taught at Lafayette College in Easton until 1897, when he refused to obey instructions from the college president, who fired the professor for insubordination.

The ex-professor didn't take his dismissal with good humor. He cut rare vines, smeared tar on the chapel, destroyed the organ, and threw hymnals down a well. He also intended to burn down every building on campus except the gymnasium, but fortunately did nothing worse than set fire to Pardee Hall, gutting the building.

George was arrested in June 1898, went on trial in February 1899, and was found guilty. I forgot to mention that the vandalistic would-be arsonist had been a professor of moral philosophy.

Creature Comforts

Richard and Lewis Wistar were wealthy bachelor brothers who lived just outside Frankford. In the 1880s, their eccentric thought processes conceived the idea that their farm animals should have better living conditions. To achieve this agreeable purpose, they constructed brownstone mansions for cows; a henhouse complete with walnut staircases, which cost $7,000 (the equivalent of about $160,000 in modern currency); a "palatial stable" that cost $15,000 (modern equivalent, approximately $340,000); and a springhouse with stained glass windows.

The granite pigpen was never completed. Richard got engaged to a woman from New York, but she died in a carriage accident. Afterward he lost all interest in construction.

The brothers remained bachelors and ended their days in Atlantic City. Lewis Wistar died on February 21, 1894; Richard followed suit six weeks later on April 7, 1894, having lost his will to live.

In 1901, the local country club leased the old Wistar estate and its bizarre structures.

Sing or Swing

Velka A., age twenty-three, murdered a fellow Austrian immigrant in Mercer County. Yet his sentence was commuted from the death penalty to life imprisonment on April 16, 1912, chiefly because he had such an enchanting baritone singing voice. Perhaps it was only a coincidence that the governor who signed the commutation was named Tener.

Unorthodox Innards

The doctors told William G. of Philadelphia that his heart was located on the right side of his chest rather than the left and that other internal organs also had set up shop in unorthodox places. William was so upset about being a freak of nature that he committed suicide.

But he did not die debt free: he owed his boardinghouse landlady for back rent and also for small sums of money he had borrowed on occasion. He assured her that when he died, she could sell his bizarre body to a medical school.

She asked the coroner to give her William's body so she could auction it to the highest bidder and recoup her losses. On August 6, 1915, the coroner informed her that he could not legally allow her to take ownership of the body, and if no family members claimed it, it would go to the state anatomical board. The upshot is that William died, the landlady got shafted, but medical science gained.

Who Needs to Hire Lawyers When We Can Always Dream?

Henry W., postmaster of Williams, died in 1916—apparently without leaving a will. No one could find such a document anywhere, and it looked as though an administrator would have to be appointed.

But then the widow had a dream in which she saw the will at Henry's old house in Hyndman. She went there and found it among other old papers. The witnesses had long forgotten about the will but recognized their signatures. It left the entire estate to Henry's widow.

Those Final Moments: Pennsylvania

Ward McConkey went to the gallows in the Pittsburgh prison yard on the morning of May 10, 1883, to pay society for killing shopkeeper George McClure at the aptly named Dead Man's Hollow near McKeesport on August 2, 1881. He walked to the scaffold laughing, and his final words were "Good bye, all ye murderers!"

<hr />

Gangster William Deni shot Patrolman Harry Donahue in Philadelphia in 1934; as he was led to Rockview Penitentiary's electric chair on July 3, 1935, he said, "The big bad wolf got me."

It Pays to Get to the Point

W.H.C. was the telegraph operator for the New York Central Railroad at Brown, Pennsylvania. He was found dead at his desk on November 19, 1903, bludgeoned to death with a bloody spike maul found nearby. His watch and money were gone. The telegrapher knew his murderer, because at 6:50 p.m. he sent this telegraph to a fellow operator at Oak Grove: "Send switch engine quick to me; I am being murdered by—"

The killer was never found. Had the victim lived only a few seconds longer, detectives would have had a pretty decent clue.

Death Row Dramas: Pennsylvania

For his role in a fatal Philadelphia holdup in April 1923, Joseph Trinkle was sentenced to die in the electric chair. A Philadelphian named Walter K. wrote to the governor offering to be executed in Trinkle's place. Walter said he wanted to "startle humanity to a keen realization" of what the death penalty entails—and to prove he was serious about his offer, he even offered to pay his own carfare to the prison.

Walter failed to explain exactly how taking on a guilty man's punishment would prove his point about capital punishment, but in any case the board of pardons sent him a letter patiently explaining that "there is no law in this state that will permit the substitution of an innocent volunteer to take the place of a condemned criminal." They were probably tempted—but prevented by a sense of official decorum—to add, "And your idea is really stupid."

An Unimaginative Hiding Place

The best the folks in Pottsville could figure was that George S. Jr. had quarreled with his mother, who heartily disliked his girlfriend. The disapproving mother disappeared in August 1909, and during her absence young George, age twenty-one, courted Violet H. as much as he darn well pleased.

But the romance ended on September 2, when George's father noticed that the attic door had been sealed closed. Something behind the door stank prodigiously, and the cracks were sealed with paraffin in a losing battle to keep the smell confined to the attic.

Mr. S. forced the door open and found just what you expect he found. She had been strangled. The police hurried to the place where they instinctively knew they would find George Jr.—Violet's house—but they were too late. He blew out his brains when he saw them coming.

A Creepy Story

A troop of Boy Scouts spent the night of July 9, 1932, at Darby Creek in the forest near Media. As the scouts slept, scoutmaster Wilmer B. and his assistant Walter H. explored a trail. Their flashlights shone on a man standing in the woods—an old man "with a flowing white beard," shabby clothes, and a seedy hat. They were so startled by his unexpected presence that at first they thought him an optical illusion.

"You are very brave to be in these woods at midnight," he said. Laughing, he added: "Maybe—maybe you would like to see something? Come with me and I will *show* you."

They took him up on his challenge and followed him some five hundred yards off the trail. The old man ventured through the tangled underbrush so quickly and easily that the experienced woodsmen had difficulty keeping up with him.

Suddenly he stopped at a spot where Norwinden Drive degenerated into a seldom-used dirt trail, about a mile from the state road and a hundred yards from Darby Creek. The bearded man broke into a cackle. He cried, "There! Look!" and pointed at three fallen trees that formed a casket shape. Wilmer and Walter aimed their flashlights at the trees and saw the decomposing body of a middle-aged man lying between them. He was well dressed in an expensive blue shirt, blue silk tie, and herringbone-weave trousers.

"Good Lord!" shouted Wilmer. "We ought to tell the police right away!" Wilmer and Walter swung their lights back at the place where the guide stood, but he was gone. Somehow he had vanished in the thick woods, in total silence, seconds after his final announcement. Thoroughly unnerved, the two men crashed through the forest growth to Springfield Township, where they told the police about their bizarre experience.

The body was in such a remote location that it took Wilmer, Walter, and a search party an hour to find it again. The coroner made some conclusions. The man had been dead three months. It was not a case of suicide; a fractured skull suggested that the victim had been beaten to death and stashed among the trees. Although a revolver (with the serial numbers filed off) lay nearby, the body bore no bullet wounds. A pair of smoked glasses was all he had in his pockets.

Who was the hermit of the forest? How did he know about the well-hidden corpse—and did he have something to do with the murder? Investigators scoured the forest but found no trace of the strange man with the white beard and the questionable sense of humor. They couldn't even find anyone who knew anything about him. Albert J. of Ogontz was suspected of being the mysterious hermit, but he denied it. He was detained but the scoutmasters did not identify him.

The murder victim had expensive dental work and detectives hoped it would be a means of identifying him, but this lead did not pan out. The man was buried on July 11 and his name is unknown.

In the Days before Craigslist

The matrimonial ad said that the man placing it, John K., was forty-one years old, rich, lonesome, handsome, and the owner of a fine house. That sounded good to factory worker Leona M., age twenty, of Coshocton, Ohio. After corresponding with her dreamboat Mr. K. for eight months, she traveled to Fisher, Pennsylvania, to marry him.

Their relationship was rocky right from the start. It turned out that John's advertisement had stretched the truth in a few minor respects. For one thing, he was far from wealthy. For another, he'd subtracted twenty years from his real age. His handsomeness was strictly a matter of opinion. He drank and made unwanted sexual propositions. His house was not exactly palatial. And finally, the farmer was brutish and ill-tempered. But apparently he really was lonesome, just as advertised.

Leona decided to marry him even though he had lied villainously in his ad—the fact that she could not afford the fare back to Coshocton contributed to her decision. But on June 13, 1934, the night before their wedding, she found it necessary to run to a bedroom and lock the door. John broke down the door and "made advances." She refused his entreaties and fought him off.

They argued all night, and in the morning he left to plant potatoes, taking her clothes with him so she couldn't leave him flat. When he returned, the argument recommenced. It ended when he drew back his arm as though to hit her.

Leona seized a gun John had hidden beneath a lounge cushion and shot her intended through the neck. She spent the next couple of months playing a harmonica in her jail cell in Clarion.

She was acquitted on August 30 before a cheering courtroom.

Grumpy Old Men

Henry R. and his friend James C. got into an argument on June 13, 1935, which ended with Henry knocking James down with a hatchet and driving a nail into the top of his head. Henry initially lied to the Kensington police by saying an improbable nail-wielding stranger had burst into the house and committed the deed.

On September 1, a jury found Henry guilty and sentenced him to spend the remainder of his life in prison. Which probably wasn't very long—the killer was seventy-five years old and his victim, eighty-three.

Three Victorian-Era Orphan Girls

It was Christmas Day 1886, and a coal miner, John A.—a married man with five children—was riding in a sleigh with three attractive women, none of whom was over age twenty: Delia (or Della) C., Ella K., and Jennie Q., all students at the Soldiers' Orphan School in McAlisterville. The newspapers delicately stated that John "insisted upon getting out of the sleigh too often, on account of a disease he claimed to be suffering from." Likely this was a subtle, between-the-lines way of informing readers that John had to take frequent urination breaks due to gonorrhea or some other STD.

The miner brought whiskey and shared it with the three gals. "The party drove through town and their conduct was shameful," said the papers, again refusing to tell posterity exactly what that phrase meant. But if John thought he was about to get lucky, he was due for the rudest of surprises. Instead, his demure young companions waited until he was sufficiently intoxicated and helpless. Then they beat him over the head with the butt of his whip. They "inflicted injuries on his person that cannot be mentioned," probably Victorian newspaperese for castration. They knocked him out of the sleigh and dragged him until he let go. They also robbed him of his pay.

A man found John lying in the snow and took the wretched man to a stranger's house. John lingered there for a day in "the most excruciating pain" and died.

Della C. told at least two acquaintances what she and her friends had done to John: "We tied him up with our garters, and dragged him behind until he let go. We left him in the snow." She added, with callous sarcasm: "If he dies I guess I'll buy a black dress and go to the funeral."

The girls spent the next few months in jail at Lewiston, Mifflin County. They went on trial on April 23, 1887, and as was often the case with female murderers of the era—especially young, good-looking ones—the men involved in the legal system appeared willing to jump through any hoop, however irrational, to help them avoid punishment. The defense attorney "spoke touchingly of their neglected training and, to the astonishment of everybody, the district attorney announced that the commonwealth would abandon the case and the girls were acquitted." No explanation was forthcoming other than that the poor dears came from a disadvantaged background.

The Pennsylvania Witchcraft Murder, or: I'm Charmed, I'm Sure

When our Puritan ancestors journeyed from England to the New World, they imported a belief in witches. Usually this superstition manifested itself in harmless ways, but sometimes it resulted in entire communities quaking in terror until cooler heads prevailed, and in the worst cases, belief in witches led to the deaths of innocent citizens. The most famous instance of this paranoia getting out of hand, of course, was the witch trials in Salem, Massachusetts, in 1692, which resulted in the hanging of nineteen souls and the pressing to death of another under heavy weights—but no burnings at the stake, contrary to popular belief. (Two dogs also were killed, but everyone seems to forget about them.) According to historian John Demos, even before the infamous incidents of 1692, there had been many witchcraft trials in New England. By the dawn of the eighteenth century there were almost one hundred recorded cases, resulting in over thirty-eight executions. For example, three women and one man were tried and executed during a scare that gripped Hartford, Connecticut, from 1662 to 1665.

Even in the nineteenth century, belief in witches survived in places, such as New Orleans, isolated pockets in the Appalachian and Catskill Mountains, and southeastern Pennsylvania. It is the Pennsylvanians who shall be of interest in this chapter, for there the conviction seems to have survived the longest, resulting in a sensational murder trial that took place well into the twentieth century.

York County was settled largely by German immigrants, whose collective name—the Pennsylvania Deutsch—has long been misunderstood as meaning "the Pennsylvania Dutch." In the rural sections of the state, men and women who specialized in curses were known as "hex doctors," while those who practiced their own special brand of medicine without a license were "powwow doctors." Members of both groups were considered witches. A female powwow doctor explained in 1928: "There are two kinds of 'powwow.' One is asking the Lord, while the other is termed witchcraft, although in both we use various verses of the Bible." The specific verses of scripture were a secret, for the doctors felt that to reveal them would result in a loss of power and income.

By the late 1920s, most hex doctors were gone from York County, but "powwowers" still plied a good trade. The self-proclaimed witches had a grip on the credulous, who feared and loathed them yet paid for charms and potions and cures for illnesses. District Attorney Amos Hermann's office complained that hundreds were swindled annually by practitioners of witchcraft, especially farmers who feared for their families, cattle, and crops, not necessarily in that order. The powwow doctors had a good thing going: most of their patients would see them on the sly while also seeing a physician—you know, the kind who had a diploma from a medical school and who used impractical methods such as state-of-the-art equipment and modern medicine. Should the patient get better, the powwow doctor received all the credit; should the patient get worse, the licensed doctor received all the blame.

Some of the powwow doctors' quaint practices have been preserved for posterity. To remove warts, they would tie a piece of string around a lump of fat, rub it on the wart, and bury it (the fat) as the physician chanted. To rid the patient of serious disease, the doctors would feed meat, eggs, and vegetables to animals, or bury it in anthills. Once the edibles had been eaten, they would announce that the disease had been passed from the patient to whichever unfortunate critter had consumed the food. "Selling a cold" was the prescribed method for banishing the common cold. To do this, the doctor would chant and then advise the patient to "sell the cold" for a penny. (But who would buy one?) If there were no takers, bury the penny. People came to powwow doctors seeking cures for such minor ailments as inflammation, burns, goiter, and cancer. No doubt many went to their graves firmly convinced that they would have survived if only the doctor had fed more vegetables to a cow.

The doctors claimed the ability to heal broken hearts as well as broken bodies. A popular love spell involved combining flour, cheese, and salt and placing the mixture in a loved one's room. In the event of a breakup, it was recommended that paper that had been wrapped in bloody beef be dried and then cut into the shape of a woman and buried. Three wishes would come true for the patient. In the event that the wishes did not come true, the doctors prescribed waiting nine days and then doing the ritual again three times.

One practitioner of these dark arts was a sixty-year-old farmer named Nelson D. Rehmeyer, who lived the life of a recluse in North Hopewell Township, nineteen miles from the town of York. On the morning of Thursday, November 29, 1928, a neighbor of Rehmeyer's noticed the braying of an angry mule that had not been fed. For the past two days, the farmer's bludgeoned, choked, and roasted corpse had been lying in the kitchen of his isolated and rather scary-looking farmhouse.

The police did not have to resort to charms and magic to find the culprit. Neighbors told them that Rehmeyer's chief assistant/rival was another powwow doctor, thirty-two-year-old John H. Blymire (sometimes spelled Blymyer) of York, who had been committed to the State Hospital for the Insane at Harrisburg in August 1923 over his belief that witches were persecuting him. The authorities questioned him about the Rehmeyer murder and soon had evidence enough to justify an arrest. An acquaintance of Blymire's, John W. Dice—who had served prison time for selling sea monster's tears as a blindness cure—informed the police that Blymire had lately been keeping company with two local youths, Wilbert Hess, eighteen years old, and John C. Curry, fourteen. The police picked up Hess and Curry, and soon the district attorney had a confession from the three prisoners.

There were two principal motives—at least to which they were willing to admit—and seldom has murder been committed for more bizarre reasons. Blymire was upset with Rehmeyer for attempting to put a hex on him, and informed the Hess family (for a then-hefty consultation fee of ten dollars) that Rehmeyer had cast a spell on them as well. Blymire and Hess decided to join forces against their common enemy. There was only one sensible course of action: they must knock Rehmeyer unconscious, cut off a lock of hair from the back of his head, and bury it eight feet underground. Then the spell would be broken. But the trio clubbed Rehmeyer with too much gusto. His hair was so matted with blood that Blymire refused to take a lock, claiming that to undergo the ceremony with a gory clump would do more harm than good.

The other confessed motive was to search Rehmeyer's house for an obscure old book called *Pow-Wows, or The Long Lost Friend.* The *New York Times* managed to track down a copy of this legendary anthology of charms. Magician John George Hohman of Rosenthal, Pennsylvania, wrote it in 1819, and publisher T. F. Scheffer reprinted it in 1856. Hohman edified his readers with a number of folk remedies / magic spells, which he claimed were good for man and beast, covering such problems as curing rabies and epilepsy and encouraging cattle to return home. Charmingly—pardon the pun—Hohman also included a recipe for making "good beer." A paragraph at the beginning of *Pow-Wows* indicates the tenor of the book: "Whoever carries this book with him is safe from all his enemies, visible or invisible; and whoever has this book with him cannot die without the Holy Corpse of Jesus Christ, nor drown in any water, nor burn up in any fire, nor can any unjust sentence be passed upon him. So help me." Needless to say, mere possession of the book did not save Rehmeyer from "all his enemies, visible or invisible."

That the killers took whatever money they could find on the premises suggests a third, more earthly motive. The district attorney theorized that robbery was Blymire's principal motive, and that he used the business about relieving a hex to get the two youths to help him. It's also plausible that Blymire wanted to remove one of his chief competitors in the powwowing business.

According to Hess, the three entered Rehmeyer's house and demanded the book. When the old man resisted, Blymire threw him to the floor to cut off the required lock of hair. Hess beat Rehmeyer with a stick of stove wood and Blymire broke a wooden chair over his head. After Rehmeyer was beaten and kicked into submission, Blymire sought money. Finally, Curry tied a rope around Rehmeyer's neck and pulled until the powwow doctor strangled to death. The three then stole a few more dollars they found lying about, doused the body with lamp oil, lit the corpse, and hurried away. Unluckily for them, the fire extinguished itself and although the body was charred, the ropes tied around its neck, arms, and feet were intact. All the wounds were visible.

Hess confessed the deed to his brother Clayton and his sister-in-law the next morning. Blymire also confessed to Clayton Hess, adding: "If they get me I hope they don't get the other fellows. I am to blame for the whole thing." He may have committed an atrocious murder, but at least he felt better afterward. "Rehmeyer is dead now," he told the police. "I no longer feel bewitched." (A month later, Hess and Curry saw the light during a revival held at the jail by the Women's Christian Temperance Union and renounced their belief in witchcraft.)

Despite his peaceful feelings, Blymire's troubles were just beginning. Police attempted to connect him with a couple of unsolved murders that had occult overtones. One was a witchcraft-related murder that took place in the county on March 24, 1922, when Mrs. Sallie Jane Heagy shot her husband while imagining that witches had cast a spell on her. Although Mrs. Heagy clearly was guilty, the authorities wondered if Blymire had influenced her. Mrs. Heagy wasn't talking, as she had committed suicide soon after her confinement to a mental ward. The other crime was the shooting of pregnant sixteen-year-old Gertrude Rudy, whose mutilated body was found beside railroad tracks on November 11, 1927. Blymire and Rudy lived near each other and had worked at the same cigar factory; Blymire often was seen in the girl's company and neighbors remembered that he had "acted strangely" at her funeral. No compelling evidence was forthcoming, and Blymire was never charged with complicity in either murder.

Since 1926, according to the coroner L. U. Zech, four babies had died in York County as a result of their superstitious parents trusting the witch cult's magic charms. The York County Medical Society called Zech's estimate too conservative and announced that "scores of infants as well as some adults died in this section annually as victims of 'voodooism' and its allied cults." Authorities wondered if Blymire had had a hand in any of these deaths.

Outside reporters found great sport in making York County look backward and primitive. One condescending article that appeared in a Philadelphia newspaper began: "Turn back the pages of history to the Dark Ages or take a trip to York County—it amounts to the same thing." Lest the modern reader get the wrong impression, the vast majority of "Yorkers" did not believe in witchcraft and were deeply embarrassed about the bad publicity the murder brought to their county. The minister who officiated at Rehmeyer's funeral remarked during his sermon that "this murder had given the community ugly publicity that is surely not welcome." The local paper, the *Dispatch*, indignantly stated that thousands of communities around the world had inhabitants who believed in witches and noted that even such a great figure as Napoleon was superstitious. The community's mortification is gauged by the fact that although the crime was the most newsworthy event in the area, the *Dispatch* buried the story deep within its pages.

Blymire went on trial on January 6, 1929; Hess and Curry attended the sessions with their own trials pending. District Attorney Hermann served as the prosecutor, and each accused man had his own defense lawyer. Herbert Cohen represented Blymire, Harvey Gross represented Wilbert Hess, and Walter Van Baman represented John Curry. DA Hermann must have decided it would be easier to get a conviction if he overlooked the men's bizarre motives and instead attributed it to robbery and greed, commonplace motives the jury would understand. Hermann was convinced that the story the trio told was a complete fabrication to cover their true intentions. It was true that the three murderers had gotten away with a pathetic haul of only a few dollars, said Hermann, but they'd expected to find much more, since they'd believed rumors that Rehmeyer was a wealthy miser.

Nevertheless, it was impossible to keep witchcraft completely out of the trial since the beliefs of the defendants and the deceased were inextricably linked with the supernatural. For example, Hess and Curry claimed Blymire had tricked them into helping commit murder by appealing to their belief in the existence of witches and hexes. On January 7, several prosecution witnesses appeared, including Clayton Hess, brother of the accused Wilbert Hess. Clayton stated under oath that Blymire had confessed to the murder two days after it'd occurred by telling him, "I got the witch." Clayton Hess had given his brother, Blymire, and Curry a lift to the Rehmeyer farmhouse on the night of the murder, unaware of his passengers' true intentions. Mrs. Alice Rehmeyer, estranged wife of the victim, who had told the press that her husband's fanatical belief in witchcraft had broken up their home, testified that John Blymire and another man had dropped by her house looking for Nelson Rehmeyer on November 26, the night before the murder. A hardware store clerk testified that Blymire and Curry had bought the clothesline used to bind and strangle Rehmeyer at his store. The case against Blymire was so strong that the prosecution rested after calling only six witnesses.

Defense attorney Cohen realized that things were looking bleak, and on January 8 he tried to enter a defense of insanity for Blymire. In Cohen's words, "[Blymire] believed then, and he believes now, that he had an honest right to go down there and brain the man who 'hexed' him." After all, the accused had spent time in an institution. However, after listening to experts with conflicting opinions about Blymire's sanity, Judge Ray Sherwood ruled that just because Blymire was delusional enough to believe in witches and curses, that did not make him legally insane. Cohen was so shaken by the judge's decision that he asked for (and received) a one-day adjournment so he could plan a new strategy. All he could do in the end was to put Blymire on the stand and hope for the best.

On January 9, the thin, pale powwow doctor testified to his earnest belief in witches. Blymire insisted that he'd murdered Rehmeyer not for money, but to lift a curse—though no doubt the money, such as it was, was a nice bonus. He asserted that his belief in witchcraft was so strong that he would even murder the judge and the district attorney if he thought they had bewitched him. He failed to state whether he would slaughter his defense lawyer under such circumstances.

Blymire testified that he had seen "real" doctors for melancholia, none of whom helped him very much, so he'd visited a number of powwow doctors, including the amusingly named Sam Schmuck and one "Mrs. Noll" (real name: Emma Knopp) of Marietta, said to be the high priestess of the supernatural in that section of Pennsylvania. (The *New York Times*'s reporter provided an ungallant description of this worthy: "Answering to seventy years, she could easily pass for a hundred. She is small of stature, bent and withered, with piercing eyes and hooked nose, looking as if she might have stepped out of a fantastic picture of witches of medieval days.") The powwow doctors concurred in their diagnosis: Blymire was bewitched, and in Mrs. Noll's expert opinion, the culprit was Nelson Rehmeyer. She'd determined this by placing a dollar bill on Blymire's palm and saying a magical incantation. When she removed the bill, Blymire saw the face of Rehmeyer in his hand. Mrs. Noll told Blymire that codefendant Wilbert Hess's family also was hexed. Her prescription was for Blymire to procure a lock of Rehmeyer's hair or to swipe his *Long Lost Friend* book, stat!

Had Blymire and his attorney resorted to the "witchcraft made me do it" defense 250 years earlier, it might have worked. In case the jury did not think belief in witches was a good excuse, Blymire was followed on the stand by a York physician, Dr. Julius Comroe, who testified that the accused was "absolutely insane," and by Dr. Richard Ridgeway of the State Hospital for the Insane, who stated that "as a feeble-minded person, [Blymire] cannot distinguish right from wrong." The case went to the jury later the same day. The members were not impressed with the defense testimony and reached a verdict of guilty with a recommended sentence of life imprisonment.

Blymire's superstitions got him in trouble, but they also provided him with a measure of comfort. After the jury foreman announced the verdict, Blymire yawned and remarked without emotion, "I am happy now. I am not bewitched anymore. I can sleep and eat and I am not pining away. But I think they [the jury] went a little strong. Yes, that's it, a little too strong." Blymire should have been thanking his lucky witchcraft charms, considering that they did not give him the death penalty for committing a murder that was obviously premeditated and unnecessary. Would it really have been so hard for three men to cut a lock of hair from the old farmer's head had that been their true ambition? Some observers wondered why they hadn't just collected it after Rehmeyer made a trip to the barber.

The next defendant, fourteen-year-old John Curry, had his day in court on January 10 after the selection of a new jury. The preternaturally calm Curry denied allegations that he'd strangled Rehmeyer, asserting that he'd done nothing worse than holding the old man down during Blymire and Hess's murderous assault. He claimed that he had tagged along on the fatal night only out of a natural curiosity to "see some of this witchcraft stuff performed." Perhaps he thought beating and strangling Rehmeyer and burning his corpse was just part of the ritual.

Except for his description of himself as a mere bystander, Curry's story dovetailed with Blymire's in most particulars. He repudiated the prosecution's claim that robbery was the motive. In Curry's own words, "Rehmeyer asked Blymire if we wanted his money and Blymire said 'No, we want that book.' So Rehmeyer handed his pocketbook to me and I handed it to Blymire, who put it in his vest pocket." The reader will notice that although Blymire disavowed robbery as a motive while on the witness stand, and even when speaking to his victim, he took the offered money anyway. Curry overlooked the fact that the three further ransacked the house for money after committing murder.

Curry's attorney, Walter Van Baman, urged the jury to inflict neither life imprisonment nor the death sentence on a fourteen-year-old. His speech brought tears to spectators' eyes, but the jury was flinty of heart. When court reconvened on January 11, they sentenced the teenager to life in prison. He was the youngest person to be convicted of murder in the history of York County. Before being taken to the reformatory, Curry remarked tearfully, "I think it is pretty hard, but I guess all I can do is to make the best of it. I hope this will be a lesson to other boys."

Many deemed the Curry verdict an outrage. The famous comedian and social commentator Will Rogers, for one, complained in his syndicated column that Curry should have been given a change of venue and that the jury was punishing the boy for his ignorance.

The third defendant, gaunt and hollow-eyed teenager Wilbert Hess—who believed that Rehmeyer had cursed his family—went to trial on January 11, almost as soon as the Curry trial was over. His attorney, Harvey Gross, showed more pluck than did Curry's, and he vigorously cross-examined the state's witnesses. He moistened the eyes of the jury with a passionate speech lasting nearly an hour and a half, to no avail. On January 12, a third jury found Hess guilty of second-degree murder, with a penalty of ten to twenty years in prison.

Thus ended the greatest sensation York County had ever known. One beneficial effect was that the trials broke the powwow doctors' iron grip on the superstitious. The *New York Times* made note of the concerted effort by "the coroner, the District Attorney, medical society officials, clergymen and lawyers . . . to drive [powwow doctors] out of the county forever." The district attorney promised to prosecute powwow doctors for fraud, despite their clients being too afraid of them to testify. Some thought the harshness of verdicts, especially the life sentence for barely adolescent John Curry, was intended by authorities to send a message that practitioners of witchcraft and black magic no longer would be tolerated. (Hess's attorney pleaded with the jury that it was not necessary to "squeeze the last drop of blood from the hearts of these poor, ignorant people in order to vindicate the honor of the County of York.")

The severity of John Curry's sentence was lessened in 1934 from life to ten to twenty years. While in prison, he became an artist; most of his works were landscapes or depictions of the Crucifixion. He requested a parole in 1934 and again in March 1937. Both he and Hess were paroled in 1939. Hess died in York in January 1979; the commonness of Curry's name renders him more difficult to trace in the records, but most likely he died in November 1974. Despite receiving a life sentence, Blymire was paroled in 1952. According to Pennsylvania death records, he died in May 1972, probably in Philadelphia.

"It will be many months before York lives down the reputation, gained for it by the Rehmeyer murder and its exploitation by metropolitan newspapers, of being a backwoods community," complained the *York Dispatch* in December 1928. The paper's prediction proved correct. For several decades the murder and trial were the most notorious events in York County history. As recently as 1988 the film *Apprentice to Murder*, featuring Donald Sutherland as a character named John Reese, was very loosely based on the crime that, for a while, had Americans again discussing witches in all seriousness.

BIBLIOGRAPHY

Grave Robbers and Body Snatchers:

Louisville Courier-Journal. "Body Snatching." December 6, 1882, 5.
————. "An Ex-grave Robber . . ." July 24, 1881, 10.
————. "Ghouls Desecrate Fremont's Tomb . . ." December 23, 1937, I, 1.
————. "Grave-Robbers Strip Body of Noted Doctor." March 15, 1936, I, 9.
————. "Historic Tomb . . ." April 26, 1904, 2.
————. "Kidnapping the Dead." July 25, 1878, 2.
————. "Torpedoes Hid in Whitney Grave." May 19, 1899, 4.
————. "Woman's Foot Left on Miner's Porch." September 25, 1921, 8.
————. "The Work of Ghouls." November 19, 1883, 2.
————. "The Work of Ghouls." July 14, 1888, 6.
New York Sun. "Grave Robbers at Work." October 25, 1884, 1.
Philadelphia Inquirer. "Ghouls Mutilate a Woman's Body." October 12, 1904, 1.
————. "Tracing the Ghouls Who Opened the Grave." October 17, 1904, 15.
Wallis, Charles L. *Stories on Stone.* New York: Oxford University Press, 1954.

Body Snatching Part Two: When Schemes Went Awry:

Louisville Courier-Journal. "A Body Snatching Doctor's Fate." May 21, 1882, 6.
————. "Death Seems a Live Subject for the Inventor." June 22, 1896, 3.
————. "A Grave Robber Killed." May 19, 1882, 2.

Winning the Argument:

Arizona Republican [Phoenix]. "Grave Robbery." June 11, 1893, 1.

The Sexton Witnesses Something Worth Writing Home About:

Kentucky Gazette [Lexington]. "Strange Outrage at a Grave." February 19, 1879, 2.

Sally Surprises the Shovelmen; and Other Well-Preserved Folks:

Louisville Courier-Journal. "Petrified Body Is Found by Workmen." May 19, 1924, 3.
————. "A Remarkable Case of Petrification." March 25, 1894, 3.
Pittsburgh Telegraph. "Remarkable Petrifaction." October 18, 1873, 3.

Obsequies for the Obese:

Louisville Courier-Journal. "An Immense Corpse." February 26, 1879, 3.

The Miracle Face:

Arizona Silver Belt [Globe, AZ]. "On a Tombstone." October 26, 1895, 4.

Spirit Son:

Louisville Courier-Journal. "Small Talk." August 15, 1878, 3.

Have a Heart:

Piqua Daily Call [OH]. "Ghoul Takes Heart from Buried Body." November 5, 1945, 1.

Premature Burial: Not Just a Myth:

Baltimore Sun. "'Dead' Woman Came to Life." August 27, 1908, 1.
Louisville Courier-Journal. "Alive in Her Grave." April 27, 1889, 5.
————. "Back from the Valley of the Shadow." March 1, 1903, I, 4.
————. "'Dead' Man Comes to Life at Undertaker's." April 8, 1914, 6.
————. "Died after He Was Buried." March 25, 1900, 4.
————. "Feared Burial Alive." November 8, 1909, 4.
————. "He Was Not Dead." August 16, 1891, 6.
————. "Is It Suspended Animation?" July 15, 1886, 5.
————. "Not Dead." December 17, 1889, 5.
————. "Scared the Watchers." August 4, 1889, 13.
————. "Sent to Untimely Graves." February 5, 1881, 6.
————. "Told in a Few Words." December 14, 1901, 2.

Devices to Prevent Premature Burial:

Louisville Courier-Journal. "Can Escape from His Tomb." June 8, 1902, IV, 8.
————. "Death Seems a Live Subject for the Inventor." June 22, 1896, 3.
————. "A New Tomb to Prevent Being Buried Alive." April 6, 1902, III, 4.
————. "Signals from the Grave." September 15, 1895, II, 5.

Almost as Bad as Premature Burial:

Louisville Courier-Journal. "Sent to Untimely Graves." February 5, 1881, 6.

The Joke Was on the Doctor:

Louisville Courier-Journal. "A Day in a Coffin." January 14, 1883, 9.

Extraordinary Epitaphs:

Federal American Monthly. "How Hard It Is to Write Good." June 1865, 648–49.
Laurel Chronicle [MS]. "Infidel Epitaph May Cause Removal from Cemetery." January 21, 1910.
Lexington Dollar Weekly Press [KY]. "Brief Items." April 26, 1872, 3.
Louisville Courier-Journal. "Auto Accident Described on Victim's Tombstone." June 4, 1911, I, 6.
———. "Curt Epitaph . . ." February 11, 1900, III, 4.
———. "Doctor Famed as Host Dies." June 15, 1939, I, 7.
———. "Monuments for Three Wives in a Cemetery." July 31, 1899, 4.
———. "Object to His Gravestone." October 11, 1912, 4.
———. "This Is an epitaph in a Wayland, Mass., Churchyard . . ." October 12, 1900, 4.
———. "Tombstone Accuses a Pennsylvania Physician." July 26, 1905, 4.
———. "Tombstone Inscription Stirs up Indignation." January 17, 1904, II, 5.
———. "Words on Gravestone Offend." April 12, 1912, 6.
Monumental News. "Epitaphs." November 1897, 658.
New York Times. "David Goodman Croly." May 1, 1889, 5.
———. "Obituary Notes." May 3, 1918, 15.
Pittsburgh Telegraph. "Personal." September 30, 1873, 2.
Wallis, Charles L. *Stories on Stone.* New York: Oxford University Press, 1954.
Washington Reporter [PA]. "An Antique Epitaph." January 27, 1875, 1.

And Harry Edsel Smith's Epitaph That Wasn't:

Buszta, John W., Albany Cemetery Association. Letter to author. April 17, 1999.
———. Letter to author. June 15, 1999.
Knickerbocker News [Albany, NY]. "Deaths." September 11, 1942.
New York State Education Department, New York State Archives. Letter to author. January 20, 1999.
State of New York Department of Health. Letter to author. July 14, 1999.

Franklin B. Evans Proves Useful:

Hearn, Daniel Allen. *Legal Executions in New England.* Jefferson, NC: McFarland, 1999.
Louisville Courier-Journal. "Playing with a Skeleton." November 16, 1878, 1.

McEwen's Grave and Reuben's Chair:

Louisville Courier-Journal. "From the News." January 26, 1899, 4.
New York Times. "Strange Burial at Amesbury." January 27, 1899, 1.
Pittsburgh Evening Leader. "How an Eccentric Vermonter Was Buried." January 22, 1873, 3.

An Urban Golgotha:

Louisville Courier-Journal. "A Charnel House." December 20, 1884, 4.
————. "Dead Men's Bones." December 20, 1884, 1.
————. "Nine Skulls on a Shelf." December 26, 1884, 2.

Bones and Brats:

Louisville Courier-Journal. "Juvenile Ghouls." November 16, 1884, 5.

A Legal Question:

Louisville Courier-Journal. "Woman Denied Right to Disinter 8 Bodies." May 5, 1939, II, 5.
New York Times. "Trespassed on Wife's Grave." January 31, 1901, 1.

Body Snatching BS:

Louisville Courier-Journal. "Fiction Eclipsed." December 12, 1884, 2.
————. "A Horrible Story." December 11, 1884, 2.
————. "Pronounced a Hoax." December 13, 1884, 1.

The Animal Kingdom Gets In On the Act:

Louisville Courier-Journal. "Ghoulish Cats." June 27, 1879, 4.

Guardian of the Grave:

Louisville Courier-Journal. "Perhaps." September 11, 1879, 4.

Adapting to Their Environment:

Louisville Courier-Journal. "A Family of Emigrants . . ." November 26, 1879, 3.
Philadelphia Inquirer. "He Liked the Tomb." October 24, 1904, 2.

Playing It Safe:

Louisville Courier-Journal. "A Rosy-Cheeked Corpse." February 16, 1881, 1.

What Smelled Up the Sunday School Library:

Louisville Courier-Journal. "A Corpse in the Church." August 8, 1881, 1.

An Obsolete Occupation:

Louisville Courier-Journal. "Ghastly Yarns." September 4, 1881, 9.

Entrepreneurial Embalmers:

Louisville Courier-Journal. "A Corpse Preserver." November 18, 1883, 10.

Cementation and Paperweights:

Louisville Courier-Journal. "Beats Embalming." October 1, 1886, 5.
————. "Death Seems a Live Subject for the Inventor." June 22, 1896, 3.

An Unorthodox Filing System:

Louisville Courier-Journal. "Took It with Him." February 1, 1885, 2.

How a Person May Be in Two Places at One Time:

Louisville Courier-Journal. "Divided between Two Graves." December 4, 1884, 4.

John W.'s Adventure:

Louisville Courier-Journal. "Called Back to Life." February 26, 1885, 5.

The Suspicious Saga of Joseph Dyer:

Louisville Courier-Journal. "Back from the Grave." November 11, 1885, 1.
————. "Mulhattanism from Maine." November 12, 1885, 5.
————. "The Resurrection Hoax." November 20, 1885, 5.
————. "A Resurrection Story." November 12, 1885, 5.

For the Greater Good:

Louisville Courier-Journal. "Grave Desecrators." August 11, 1887, 5.

Keep Did Not Keep:

Louisville Courier-Journal. "Keep's Body Exhumed." January 18, 1888, 4.
New York Times. "Coroner Robinson's Regrets." February 26, 1888, 9.
————. "Wants the Grave Opened." January 17, 1888, 5.

No Dignity for the Dead:

Louisville Courier-Journal. "Dead-House Horrors." December 14, 1886, 4.

Battle of Wills:

Louisville Courier-Journal. "Buried in a Shoe Box." December 26, 1888, 1.

Sometimes Cigars Are Good for You:

Louisville Courier-Journal. "Passed a Night in a Tomb." February 5, 1889, 2.

A Nasty Necropolis:

Louisville Courier-Journal. "Graveyard Horrors." March 29, 1889, 2.

A Vandalistic Vortex:

Louisville Courier-Journal. "Wrecked a Cemetery." June 19, 1889, 2.

Paying Their Disrespects:

Louisville Courier-Journal. "Fiendish Ghouls." January 23, 1890, 1.
Wilkes-Barre Record [PA]. "The Faction War." January 22, 1890, 1.
————. "Horrible Fiendishness." January 23, 1890, 1.

The Grateful Dead Sing:

Louisville Courier-Journal. "A Remarkable Funeral." February 27, 1890, 8.

And in Related Stories:

Louisville Courier-Journal. "Phonograph Burial." August 20, 1895, 5.
————. "Wed by Dead Man's Voice." February 26, 1900, 1.

The Strange Death of Jessie B.:

Louisville Courier-Journal. "Smiling in Death." April 3, 1890, 7.

Just Making Sure:

Louisville Courier-Journal. "A New Test of Death." December 13, 1890, 2.

The Less-Than-Successful Cremation of Percy R.:

Louisville Courier-Journal. "Burned before Their Eyes." August 15, 1892, 1.
————. "Told in a Few Words." February 19, 1902, 4.

Bizarrely Buried:

Louisville Courier-Journal. "Bible Is Pillow; Hearse, Handcar." February 1, 1925, VI, 6.
————. "Buried in Green Colored Coffin." May 3, 1903, V, 2.
————. "The Voodoo Queen Dead." December 19, 1893, 2.

Would You Like Flies with That?

Louisville Courier-Journal. "Restaurant in a Graveyard." July 10, 1899, 4.

Skeletal Sailors:

Louisville Courier-Journal. "Corpses Washed Away by Rushing Waters." August 12, 1902, 3.

At Least the Slogans Weren't Set to Music:

Louisville Courier-Journal. "Comforting Signs." October 5, 1902, IV, 4.

A Profusion of Problems:

Louisville Courier-Journal. "Family Isolated with Corpse by Flood." March 25, 1903, 1.

That Irresistible Urge to Pinch a Mummy's Nose:

Louisville Courier-Journal. "Noble Mummy Unclaimed." April 17, 1904, IV, 6.

Brokenhearted Businessman:

Louisville Courier-Journal. "Found Dying in His Wife's Tomb." March 24, 1905, 1.

Very Still Life Photography:

Louisville Courier-Journal. "Exhume Body for Photo." January 10, 1908, 4.

A Face Full of Benson:

Louisville Courier-Journal. "Ashes Blow in Face; Faints." March 23, 1910, 4.
New York Times. "Man and Wife Drink Poison." March 13, 1910, I, 4.

Death's Deed:

Louisville Courier-Journal. "Digs Into Grave, Gets Deed from Dead Man." August 20, 1915, 8.

Some People Will Do Anything for $20 Million:

Louisville Courier-Journal. "$20,000,000 Will to Be Sought in Grave." October 26, 1937, I, 11.
———. "Coffin Clew May Settle Huge Estate." August 7, 1937, I, 7.
———. "Hopes of 23,000 Threatened by Man in Huge Estate Case." April 10, 1938, I, 8.
———. "Pennsy Approves Grave Opening in Will Search." August 21, 1937, I, 2.
———. "Searchers Fail to Find Will inside Tomb." October 27, 1937, I, 8.

Vicissitudes:

Louisville Courier-Journal. "Pauper to Be Buried in His $10,000 Tomb." January 19, 1921, 1.

Keeping Them Around:

Louisville Courier-Journal. "Gotham Wretchedness." May 30, 1889, 4.
———. "Man Sleeps With Dead Wife for Two Weeks." May 27, 1935, 1.
———. "Mother's Body Is Kept 7 Weeks." February 16, 1925, 1.
———. "Woman Lives with Dead Body of Spouse for Nearly a Year." September 9, 1937, I, 1.

Weaver, LaMarch. *Tombstones I Have Known*. San Jose, CA: Writers Club Press, 2001.

Once Again on Display:

Louisville Courier-Journal. "Boys Dig Up Skeleton . . ." December 29, 1934, 1.

Home Cooking:

Louisville Courier-Journal. "Maine Man Cremates His Sister in Furnace." June 12, 1938, I, 3.

Mrs. B.'s Illness:

Louisville Courier-Journal. "Killed by Wax Flowers." November 4, 1879, 1.

Train in Vain:

Louisville Courier-Journal. "Face to Face with Death." November 6, 1878, 3.

Amused to Death:

Louisville Courier-Journal. "One Night Not Long Ago . . ." Editorial. December 25, 1878, 2.

Seeing the Mule from the Inside:

Louisville Courier-Journal. "The Mule Died." August 10, 1888, 6.

David H. Loses His Superpower:

Louisville Courier-Journal. "Died of a Rattlesnake Bite." September 19, 1890, 6.

Illustrating the Point:

Louisville Courier-Journal. "'A Man Might Fall.'" December 9, 1890, 2.

Moral: Never Imitate a Circus Freak:

Louisville Courier-Journal. "A Morbid Appetite." April 18, 1891, 11.

Simultaneous Departures:

Hearn, Daniel Allen. *Legal Executions in New England*. Jefferson, NC: McFarland, 1999.
Louisville Courier-Journal. "Husband and Wife, Far Separated . . ." August 29, 1905, 1.
———. "A Strange Coincidence." October 25, 1892, 1.
———. "A Strange Tragedy." October 24, 1892, 2.

In Which Freethinkers Test Their Theories:

Louisville Courier-Journal. "Beside His Daughter." October 4, 1898, 1.
———. "Bodies Were Fully Dressed." December 20, 1896, I, 10.
———. "Chloral May Play a Role . . ." December 14, 1896, I, 2+.
———. "Drowned in a Pond." October 3, 1898, 3.
———. "Father of May Collins Said to Be Dying of Grief . . ." January 23, 1897, 1.
———. "Liquor May Have Stupefied . . ." December 15, 1896, 1.
———. "May Collins' Parents Deny." December 31, 1896, 3.
———. "No Prayer Was Said." December 16, 1896, 3.
———. "Suicide of Free-Thinkers." December 13, 1896, I, 2.
———. "To Earth." December 17, 1896, 2.
———. "Was Not Suicide." December 19, 1896, 3.

What a Trouper:

Louisville Courier-Journal. "Dead on the Stage." February 11, 1897, 1.

The Swan Knows When It Is Dying:

Hornell Evening Tribune-Times [NY]. "Prepares Own Death Notice." December 30, 1919, 5.
Louisville Courier-Journal. "Death Comes as Was Predicted by Victim." May 28, 1911, I, 3.
———. "Dies as He Predicted." March 26, 1898, 6.
———. "Eight-Year-Old Girl Foretells Her Own Death." November 21, 1910, 2.
———. "It Is Futile to Argue with a Woman . . ." Editorial. July 25, 1908, 6.
———. "Man Feels Some One to Die and Is Victim." September 16, 1922, 3.
———. "Man Foretells His Own Death Almost to the Hour, Plans Rites." April 22, 1937, I, 14.
———. "Missed by One Day." September 24, 1899, I, 7.
———. "Names Hour of Death and Dies on Minute." December 31, 1919, 1.
———. "Predicted Death." February 2, 1899, 1.
———. "Search Ends as Fugitive's Death Learned." February 25, 1937, II, 8.

At Least He Didn't Play an Accordion:

Louisville Courier-Journal. "Whistled Until He Died." January 5, 1899, 1.

Whippersnappers, Attempt This Not at Your Domicile:

Louisville Courier-Journal. "Caught Real Bullets." October 30, 1899, 4.

Final Stretch:

Louisville Courier-Journal. "Grew Seven Inches on His Deathbed." April 30, 1900, 4.

Don't Drink Lizards:

Louisville Courier-Journal. "Swallowed a Lizard." July 25, 1900, 4.

A Skeptic with a Good Arm:

Louisville Courier-Journal. "A Girl's Fatal Fun." August 20, 1900, 2.

Insane Clown without a Posse:

Louisville Courier-Journal. "Former Circus Clown Dies in an Asylum." June 19, 1901, 4.

Back to the Old Drawing Board:

Louisville Courier-Journal. "Irony of Fate." June 14, 1902, 4.
———. "Youth Meets Death in Electric Chair He Devised." May 15, 1917, 2.

Aiming for the Apple:

Louisville Courier-Journal. "Rifle, Apple on String Clews . . ." December 13, 1939, I, 1.
———. "William Tell Act." October 27, 1902, 1.

Mabel's Dream:

New York Times. "Dream of Death Came True." October 25, 1904, 9.

Fatal Fear:

Louisville Courier-Journal. "Dies in Jail While Trial Was Pending." November 12, 1904, 10.

The Last Diagnosis:

Louisville Courier-Journal. "Quietly Wrote His Own Demise." February 3, 1905, 8.

It Worked:

Louisville Courier-Journal. "Put Dynamite by Fire to Take the Frost Out." November 9, 1906, 8.

Practical Jokers at Work:

Louisville Courier-Journal. "Burned to Death; Victim of Joke." March 12, 1907, 4.
———. "Jokers Arrested as Victim Dies." November 12, 1927, 16.

Mesmerism or Manslaughter?:

Louisville Courier-Journal. "Calls in Vain to Deaf Ears." November 10, 1909, 1+.
———. "Girl Hypnotists 'In Bad.'" November 15, 1909, 4.
New York Times. "Couldn't Awaken Hypnotist's Subject." November 10, 1909, 1+.

When Modesty Is Not a Virtue:

Louisville Courier-Journal. "Excessive Modesty Causes Death . . ." December 22, 1910, 3.
New York Times. "Kindness Caused Her Death." December 22, 1910, 7.

Bookworm Becomes Worm Food:

Louisville Courier-Journal. "Read Himself to Death." July 10, 1912, 6.

News Flash!

Phoenix Gazette [AZ]. "'It's a Big Story, I Can't Write It . . .'" June 14, 1913, 1.

Boys at Play:

Louisville Courier-Journal. "2 Boys Burn to Death at Stake Playing Indian." August 27, 1923, 1.
———. "Boy Burned at Stake by Playmates Dies." March 11, 1935, 2.
———. "Boyish Banter Ends with Lad's Death." July 20, 1912, 1.
———. "Child Hanged by Boys Playing 'Wild West.'" November 14, 1913, 7.
———. "Indian Play Ends in Death." November 29, 1923, 1.
———. "Playmates Bear Boy They Killed to Grave." March 14, 1935, 1.
———. "Youths Freed in Burning at Stake." January 1, 1924, 3.

Death's Little Ironies:

Indiana Gazette [PA] "Infant Battles Wrong Medicine." June 12, 1933, 9.
Louisville Courier-Journal. "Boy Sickly Entire Life Killed Hour after Cure." May 2, 1937, I, 13.
———. "Escapes Death in Fire; Meets End While Asleep." December 26, 1914, 3.
———. "Man Dies Poor Who Wasted $250,000." July 9, 1928, 1.
———. "Man Dies When Hit by 'Safety First' Sign." July 24, 1925, 1.
———. "The Matron of the Society for the Prevention . . ." Editorial. June 13, 1933, 6.
———. "Reading of Fall, Man Drops Out Window." February 23, 1928, 1.
———. "Six Persons Killed When Train Strikes Buckboard." July 12, 1914, I, 1.
———. "Survives War with 22 Wounds; Killed by Bolt." August 15, 1920, II, 7.
———. "Whims of Fate." May 20, 1925, 6.
New York Times. "*Titanic* Survivor Drowns in Shallow Pond." April 19, 1925, 1.

Death's Door:

Louisville Courier-Journal. "Chops Hole in Door; Trapped . . ." January 6, 1919, 1.

Home Remedy for Lightning Strike:

Louisville Courier-Journal. "Children, Bolt Victims, Buried Up to Necks." July 25, 1920, I, 1.

New York Times. "Lightning Kills Two Children." July 23, 1920, 5.

Dead Man's Hand:

Louisville Courier-Journal. "Old Man Draws Royal Flush and Dies in Chair . . ." October 12, 1921, 1.

Which Does Not Speak Well for His Musical Ability:

Louisville Courier-Journal. "Piccolo's Weird Note Scares Man to Death." December 10, 1922, I, 4.

The Elizabeth Barrett Cook Mystery:

Louisville Courier-Journal. "Cause of Girl's Death Not Found." March 17, 1932, 3.
————. "Consul Says Cook Girl Sent Self Hoax Notes." February 22, 1932, 1+.
————. "Cook Probe Awaits Landing of 2 Ships." February 15, 1932, 2.
————. "Girl Sent Fake Cable, Her Friends Believe." February 19, 1932, 15.
————. "Mystery Deepens in Death of Girl." February 21, 1932, I, 1+.
————. "Mysterious Death of American Girl Puzzles Mother and Fiancé." February 14, 1932, I, 1.

The Moon as Murderer:

Louisville Courier-Journal. "Body of Missing Girl Found in Philadelphia." February 25, 1932, 2.
————. "Death of a Pennsylvania Girl . . ." Editorial. March 16, 1932, 6.
————. "Lured to Her Death by Moon Madness." Magazine Section, March 27, 1932, 6.

Leave 'Em Laughing:

Louisville Courier-Journal. "Reporter Almost Passes Out . . ." November 15, 1937, II, 3.

Final Communications:

Louisville Courier-Journal. "2 Commit Suicide in Hotel Rooms." July 29, 1929, 12.
————. "Actor Turns on Gas, Joins 'Big Timers.'" November 10, 1930, 3.
————. "Blonde Refuses to Be Rice Pudding." August 11, 1936, 5.
————. "Bridge Expert Found Dead of Gas Fumes." February 23, 1939, I, 9.
————. "Broker Killed in Fall from Window." June 21, 1933, 2.
————. "'Exit, Laughing' Wrote Man before Ending Life." March 26, 1917, 5.
————. "Farewell Notes Foil Suicides." August 16, 1929, 1.
————. "Small Talk." April 26, 1878, 3.
————. "Suicide Boast Proves Untrue." December 29, 1929, II, 4.
————. "Suicide's Note on $5 Bill." May 22, 1912, 6.
————. "Woman, 'Luxury,' Kills Self." February 20, 1935, 4.

New Orleans Times-Picayune. "Strange Double Tragedy . . ." December 20, 1909, 1.
———. "Suicides in Phone Booth." March 19, 1908, 1.
New York Sun. "A Philosopher Kills Himself." March 11, 1887, 2.
New York Times. "A Victim of Perpetual Motion." November 24, 1882, 5.
Phoenix Gazette [AZ]. "One Jim Smith Less." February 1, 1913, 1.

Location Is Everything:

Louisville Courier-Journal. "Bank Cashier Commits Suicide in Cemetery." November 18, 1913, 8.

Crowd Dis-pleaser:

Louisville Courier-Journal. "Waiting to See Him Die." August 22, 1880, 1.

Cats Are Not the Only Ones with Nine Lives:

Louisville Courier-Journal. "Suicide and Philosophy." November 4, 1880, 3.
New York Times. "Crazed from Religious Mania." October 28, 1880, 2.

Corpse and Corset:

Louisville Courier-Journal. "One Way to Die." August 3, 1889, 4.

A Lifetime Membership in the Suicide Club:

Louisville Courier-Journal. "50 Enrolled in Suicide Club." May 17, 1931, I, 4.
———. "All But One." April 9, 1890, 4.
———. "In Lake County, Indiana . . ." November 29, 1893, 1.
———. "Member of a Suicide Club." November 20, 1895, 1.
———. "Member of Suicide Club Takes Poison in Saloon." June 2, 1902, 4.
———. "One More Fool Dead." October 4, 1892, 7.
———. "Some Strange Suicides." August 24, 1890, 12.
———. "To Ashes on a Funeral Pyre." July 18, 1892, 4.
———. "Was Elected to Die." September 7, 1903, 4.
New York Times. "One of the Suicide Club Gone." November 8, 1891, 5.

Foolproof:

Louisville Courier-Journal. "Some Strange Suicides." August 24, 1890, 12.

Sort of Like a Maypole, but Not Really:

Louisville Courier-Journal. "Some Strange Suicides." August 24, 1890, 12.

Gag Me with a Spoon:

Philadelphia Inquirer. "Tried Something Original." November 12, 1891, 1.
Pittsburgh Press. "Success in Suicide." January 6, 1892, 6.

Getting a Grippe:

Louisville Courier-Journal. "Mad with Pain." February 19, 1892, 2.

Suicide by Hair:

Louisville Courier-Journal. "Suicide in a Bath Tub." June 1, 1892, 7.

Death Gets a Twofer:

Louisville Courier-Journal. "Suicide Causes Two Deaths." June 14, 1894, 2.

Not Civic Minded:

Louisville Courier-Journal. "Suicide in the City Reservoir." August 3, 1894, 2.

Death of a (Well-Dressed) Salesman:

Louisville Courier-Journal. "Dead in an Easy Chair." December 13, 1895, 5.

Season's Greetings:

Louisville Courier-Journal. "A Cool Suicide." December 30, 1897, 1.

A Musician to the End:

Louisville Courier-Journal. "Suicide with a 'G' String." June 3, 1898, 2.

Napoleon Leaves a Challenge:

Louisville Courier-Journal. "Magazine Writer Commits Suicide." August 15, 1902, 2.

An Honest Effort:

Louisville Courier-Journal. "Tried His Best to Carry Out Programme." January 9, 1903, 3.

Consideration for the Working Class:

Louisville Courier-Journal. "Suicide Wouldn't Mess Hotel Room." July 10, 1904, II, 4.
New York Times. "Hotel Guest Leaves a Grim Jest Behind." June 28, 1904, 3.

Party Poopers:

Louisville Courier-Journal. "Actress' Suicide Gives Grim Fillip . . ." April 26, 1937, I, 1+.
———. "Girl Killed Self to Find Peace, Note Reveals." May 2, 1937, I, 13.
———. "Guests Arrive for Party, Find Hostess Suicide." April 25, 1937, 1+.
———. "Kills Himself in Presence of Guests." January 14, 1906, II, 5.

———. "Man Kills Himself at Party in His Honor." December 22, 1922, 9.

———. "Man Sips Poison on Dare, Is Dead." January 2, 1929, 1.

Come, Sweets Death:

Indianapolis Journal. "Queer Idea of a Woman." June 21, 1903, I, 4.

Aping the Master:

Louisville Courier-Journal. "Cuts Her Throat after Playing Sixth Symphony." July 22, 1907, 1.

Better Late Than Never:

Louisville Courier-Journal. "Killed Herself by Eating Needles." July 31, 1907, 7.

Photo Finish:

Louisville Courier-Journal. "Feelings Expressed on His Photographs." August 9, 1908, I, 4.

Long Way Down:

Louisville Courier-Journal. "Jumps Down Smokestack; Dead Since Christmas." April 12, 1910, 4.

The Turn of an Unfriendly Card:

New Orleans Times-Picayune. "Upon Turn of a Card." March 23, 1911, 3.

Maine Tragedy:

Louisville Courier-Journal. "Widow Kills Herself and Boy to Keep Promise." February 13, 1911, 1.

Courteous:

Louisville Courier-Journal. "Suicide Warns Family Not to Strike Matches." January 7, 1914, 5.

I Trust You See the Irony:

Louisville Courier-Journal. "Dwarf Uses Littlest Caliber Bullet . . ." October 25, 1919, 1.

None Other Would Do:

Louisville Courier-Journal. "Goes 3,000 Miles to Use Graveyard." December 17, 1920, 9.

Who Could Have Seen That Coming?

Louisville Courier-Journal. "Doctor Circles Heart for Man to Shoot Self." August 15, 1921, 7.

"What Fools These Mortals Be":

Louisville Courier-Journal. "Man Hangs Self at Foot of Puck Statue." October 26, 1922, 2.

An Unintended Consequence:

Louisville Courier-Journal. "Suicide's Gas Near Fatal to Another." December 22, 1923, 3.

Unartistic Use of a Chisel:

Louisville Courier-Journal. "Man Drove Chisel into Head, Belief." December 30, 1923, I, 4.

Advance Notice:

Louisville Courier-Journal. "Man Writes Death Message; Kills Self." September 14, 1924, VI, 4.

In the Days before Reality TV Shows Made Everyone Famous:

Louisville Courier-Journal. "Tragedy of the Talented Beauty Who Failed to Find Fame, Riches, or Love." Magazine Section, March 6, 1927, 4+.
New York Times. "Writer, Bankrupt and Ill, a Suicide." March 14, 1925, 15.

Too Much Joy:

Louisville Courier-Journal. "Woman, Fearing Her Happiness at Peak, Kills Self . . ." October 27, 1928, 1.
———. "Woman Kills Self on Wedding Day." October 26, 1928, 1.

A Concerned Husband:

Louisville Courier-Journal. "Doctor, Using Mirror, Sees Wife End Life . . ." January 17, 1928, 1.

The Vengeful Pie Clerk Carries Out His Threat:

Louisville Courier-Journal. "Man Weds Widow of Brother, Suicide." August 9, 1930, 1.
New York Times. "Ending Life by Gas, Writes Reactions." April 27, 1930, I, 27.

Suicide of a Cartoonist:

Louisville Courier-Journal. "Artist Writes Satiric Obituary, Kills Self." May 21, 1931, 1+.

New York Times. "Ralph Barton Ends His Life with a Pistol." May 21, 1931, 1+.

Seemed Like the Thing to Do:

Louisville Courier-Journal. "Girl Sips Poison, Man Follows, Dies." December 30, 1931, 1.

A Real Stumper:

Louisville Courier-Journal. "6 'Perfect Crimes' Baffle Detectives." December 19, 1934, 12.
——. "Woman Dead of 60 Ax Wounds Held Suicide." December 11, 1934, 5.

Hey, What's in the Box?

Louisville Courier-Journal. "Man Uses Spider as Instrument of Suicide." June 2, 1935, I, 1+.
——. "Poisonous Spider Not Blamed for Man's Death." June 4, 1935, 5.
——. "'Spider Bite' Held Overdose of Drug." June 3, 1935, 1+.

Another First:

Louisville Courier-Journal. "Mobile Television Transmitter Picks up Girl's Suicide Leap." June 24, 1938, I, 1.

Politely Declined:

Louisville Courier-Journal. "Man Sticks to Suicide Plan." August 19, 1938, I, 5.

No Prank:

Associated Press. "Body Hanging from Tree Mistaken for Halloween Decoration." *CNN.com,* October 28, 2005. http://www.cnn.com/2005/US/10/28/mistaken.suicide.ap/index.html.

Rising from a Pond:

Pittsburgh Leader. "Another Ghostly Visitor." July 28, 1876, 4.

Pounded by a Poltergeist:

Louisville Courier-Journal. "Killed by Spirits." October 29, 1884, 2.

Ghost on the Tracks:

Louisville Courier-Journal. "Queer Pranks of a Ghost." January 14, 1883, 2.

Rachel Is Lonesome:

Louisville Courier-Journal. "A Lonesome Corpse." November 12, 1883, 5.

Did the Dead Disrupt the Democrats?

"Daniel J. Hayes." CityofAnsonia.com. City of Ansonia, CT, 2014. http://www
.cityofansonia.com/filestorage/3322/209/227/Chief_Hayes.pdf .
Louisville Courier-Journal. "A Sable-Robed Spook." November 14, 1884, 5.

Be Careful What You Read:

Hartford Daily Courant. "Killed at Pratt & Whitney's." December 26, 1884, 2.
Hartford Daily Times. "A Fatal Accident at Pratt & Whitney's." December 26, 1884, 8.
Louisville Courier-Journal. "Ghost Stories." January 18, 1885, 14.

The Phantom of Cotuit Gets Close and Personal:

Louisville Courier-Journal. "Ghost Stories." January 18, 1885, 14.

Spook on the Streets:

Louisville Courier-Journal. "The Ghost Walks." December 26, 1885, 1.

Drastic Measures:

Louisville Courier-Journal. "His Wife's Ghost." April 27, 1887, 3.

Scared to Death:

Louisville Courier-Journal. "Death Caused by Fright." August 18, 1896, 9.

Haunted Honeymoon:

Louisville Courier-Journal. "Visions of Dead Wife . . ." December 24, 1923, 1.
New York Times. "Marriage Lasts 74 Days." December 22, 1923, 8.

Snow on Fire:

Louisville Courier-Journal. "Avengers Burn Body of Snow." December 26, 1923, 1.
———. "Child of Crazed Killer of 6 Dies." December 29, 1923, 1.
———. "Grave Opening Laid to Ghost Tradition." December 27, 1923, 3.
———. "Madman Slays Wife, Three Other Women . . ." December 23, 1923, I, 1+.
New York Times. "Exhume and Burn Murderer's Body." December 26, 1923, 1.
———. "Slays Five and Self in Murder Frenzy." December 23, 1923, 1.

The Haunted Women's Club:

Louisville Courier-Journal. "New York Not without Ghosts." February 26, 1928, V, 3.

Headstone:

New York Times. "A Child's Head Petrified." December 29, 1885, 1.

Head Injury Hijinks:

Louisville Courier-Journal. "His Skull in His Pocket." April 11, 1880, 5.
———. "Set Back Forty Years by a Blow on Head." March 15, 1904, 4.
New York Times. "Strange Experience of Clem Wallis." November 11, 1894, 21.

Oh, Rats!

Arizona Republican [Phoenix]. "Badly Bitten by Rats." February 23, 1892, 1.
Louisville Courier-Journal. "Attacked by Rats." January 13, 1889, 11.
Washington Reporter [PA] "A Queer Battle." March 31, 1875, 7.

Buried on the Installment Plan:

Louisville Courier-Journal. "A Disjointed Case." July 21, 1878, 3.

Dubious Doctors:

Louisville Courier-Journal. "Bogus Diploma Buchanan Captured." September 11, 1880, 3.
———. "The Bogus Diploma Man Again." January 21, 1885, 5.
———. "The Bogus Pill Vendor." March 25, 1881, 3.
———. "Bogus Sheepskins." June 10, 1880, 1.
———. "Buck's Bound." August 25, 1880, 1.
———. "Diplomas to Lunatics." March 7, 1880, 2.
———. "Dr. Buchanan Sentenced." December 7, 1880, 3.
———. "Dr. Buchanan, the Notorious Manufacturer . . ." Editorial. October 15, 1881, 4.
———. "Philadelphia." September 29, 1883, 4.
———. "Pittsburgh." August 21, 1880, 4.

Phantom Limb:

Louisville Courier-Journal. "His Buried Hand Itched." August 17, 1915, 2.
———. "Pain from an Amputated Foot." February 22, 1886, 6.
———. "Pain from Severed Limb." July 9, 1882, 5.
Pittsburgh Leader. "Sympathy between a Living Body and a Severed Arm." July 18, 1874, 3.

Giving the Finger:

Louisville Courier-Journal. "Left the Butcher a Memento." August 12, 1883, 2.

Why It Is Not a Good Idea to Do Home Experiments on Someone's Brain:

Louisville Courier-Journal. "Living yet Dead." January 23, 1884, 7.

Silent John:

Louisville Courier-Journal. "Willfully Dumb." December 7, 1884, 12.

A Stripper Would Have Been Preferable:

Louisville Courier-Journal. "Rat Pie for Tammany Braves." July 12, 1889, 6.

When Diamond-Studded Watch Fobs Are No Longer Good Enough:

Louisville Courier-Journal. "Human Skin Tanned." June 2, 1889, 9.

Reddington Returns:

Louisville Courier-Journal. "Back from the Dead." November 28, 1889, 5.

I Prescribe a Honey Glaze at 350 Degrees:

Louisville Courier-Journal. "Advocates Cannibalism." August 15, 1890, 2.

Speaking of New England Cannibals:

New York Times. "John Smith, Cannibal." June 15, 1879, 1.
———. "A Wonderful Man Named Smith." June 11, 1879, 5.

If You Must Crucify Yourself, Get Help:

Louisville Courier-Journal. "Boys Nail Companion to Improvised Cross." April 23, 1911, I, 5.
———. "He Crucified Himself." March 21, 1891, 6.
———. "Nailed to Cross and Tortured." April 24, 1910, IV, 2.

Will Weirdness:

Louisville Courier-Journal. "12-Word-Will Probated." December 16, 1937, I, 4.
———. "Actress, Dying at 80, Refuses to Be Known as Wife or Mother." February 10, 1933, 4.
———. "Bars Mother-In-Law from Arranging His Burial." April 5, 1923, 1.
———. "Because He Received Many Years Ago . . ." June 30, 1914, 2.
———. "Leaves $100,000 to Chauffeur, Widow $1." March 17, 1923, 1.
———. "Legacy of Hate." May 2, 1936, 4.
———. "Legacy of Hate Will Is Upheld." December 11, 1936, III, 8.
———. "A Peculiar Will in Court." November 1, 1892, 3.
———. "Recommends That Son-In-Law Hang Himself." November 19, 1908, 2.
———. "Rhymed Will Gives Estate to His Widow." June 3, 1922, 1.
———. "Spinster, 64, Requests Extra Pillow in Grave." April 30, 1922, VI, 12.
———. "Warns Son Not to Visit Her Grave." January 19, 1903, 4.
———. "Will Orders Family Portraits Destroyed." May 15, 1938, V, 12.
———. "Will Tells Wife to Kill Herself, Too." March 21, 1926, II, 16.

————. "Wills Glass of Beer to Those at Funeral." August 10, 1905, 4.

————. "Woman in Will Asks 2 Feminine Friends to Live with Widower." August 7, 1922, 2.

New Orleans Times-Picayune. "Nickel a Week Is Allowed Husband." November 1, 1912, 2.

Women Have Their Terrifying Little Secrets:

Louisville Courier-Journal. "What Was the Awful Secret?" January 23, 1898, II, 4.

New York Sun. "Terrible Secret." January 17, 1898, 6.

A Professor Revolts:

Louisville Courier-Journal. "Plotted to Burn." June 24, 1898, 2.

————. "The Professor Convicted." February 19, 1899, II, 5.

Yankee Practicality:

Louisville Courier-Journal. "Married a Babe to Save an Estate." April 6, 1901, 6.

Creature Comforts:

Louisville Courier-Journal. "Pennsylvania Men Who Built Mansions for Animals." July 14, 1901, III, 2.

Ominous:

Louisville Courier-Journal. "Smoke Cigarettes; Win a Coffin." July 28, 1903, 4.

Battle Royale in a Lighthouse:

Louisville Courier-Journal. "Fights Six Days with Maniac." August 15, 1905, 4.

Superstitious, Eh?

Louisville Courier-Journal. "Prefers Fourteen to Thirteen-Year Sentence." November 8, 1905, 4.

Time Capsule:

Louisville Courier-Journal. "Reminder of Past Day." September 13, 1907, 4.

Do Not Resuscitate—Please:

Louisville Courier-Journal. "Resuscitation Test Was Not Attempted." December 23, 1908, 1.

New York Times. "Cannot Revive Executed Man." December 9, 1908, 1.

Sing or Swing:

Greenville Evening Record [PA]. "Velka Ankarich Receives Pardon." April 18, 1912, 3.
Kane Republican [PA]. "May Escape Noose by Ability to Sing." April 17, 1912, 2.
Louisville Courier-Journal. "Voice Keeps Noose from Neck." April 26, 1912, 6.

Unorthodox Innards:

Louisville Courier-Journal. "Woman Would Auction Boarder's Body . . ." August
  7, 1915, 2.

Who Needs to Hire Lawyers When We Can Always Dream?

Louisville Courier-Journal. "Saw Will in Dream." June 26, 1916, 5.

A Cheap Way to Remove a Tattoo:

Louisville Courier-Journal. "Man Uses Train to Cut Off Tattooed Arm." December
  20, 1922, 2.

Surrounded by Razors and Throats:

Louisville Courier-Journal. "Escaped Lunatic Works as Barber." November 14, 1923, 1.

Finger of Fate:

Louisville Courier-Journal. "Maniac Utters Curse; Victim Drops Dead." February
  24, 1935, I, 1+.

Just Like Howard Hughes, Sort Of:

Louisville Courier-Journal. "House Where Love-Sick Man Lay in Bed 50 Years
  Burns." November 24, 1936, I, 16.

Musical Saw:

Louisville Courier-Journal. "Actor Plays Tune as Surgeons Cut Off Leg." December
  7, 1937, I, 2.
New York Times. "Plays Harmonica as Leg Is Amputated." December 7, 1937, 26.

Those Final Moments:

Hearn, Daniel Allen. *Legal Executions in New England.* Jefferson, NC: McFarland,
  1999.
———. *Legal Executions in New Jersey, 1691–1963.* Jefferson, NC: McFarland, 2005.
———. *Legal Executions in New York State.* Jefferson, NC: McFarland, 1997.
Louisville Courier-Journal. "Danced before Death." February 10, 1888, 5.
———. "Gunman in Chair Blames 'Bad Wolf.'" July 3, 1935, 2.
———. "The Hangman's Day: He Dies Cursing Creation." August 11, 1883, 2.

————. "He Died Laughing." May 11, 1883, 2.

————. "How They Face Death in the Electric Chair." Magazine Section, March 22, 1931, 2.

————. "Refusal to Sign His Right Name Deprives Man in Shadow of Chair of His Last Consolation." January 28, 1920, 1.

————. "Show White Feather at End." September 1, 1920, 12.

————. "Welcomed Death." June 28, 1904, 2.

Pittsburgh Leader. "Capital Punishment Down South." July 31, 1876, 3.

The Denmead Horror:

Louisville Courier-Journal. "Beats Charlie Ross." March 15, 1887, 2.

————. "They Starved to Death." March 12, 1887, 5.

————. "Too Horrible for Belief." March 11, 1887, 2.

National Police Gazette. "Dead in a Den." March 26, 1887, 6.

New York Times. "The Denmead Heir." March 23, 1887, 5.

————. "Denmead's Ghastly Hovel." March 12, 1887, 2.

————. "The Denmeads in Court." March 13, 1887, 14.

————. "A Long Lost Son Appears." March 22, 1887, 5.

————. "New Brunswick Excited." March 10, 1887, 2.

————. "No Case against the Denmeads." March 16, 1887, 5.

————. "No Proof of Neglect." March 18, 1887, 5.

————. "A Sickening Revelation." March 11, 1887, 2.

Trenton Times [NJ]. "Denmead's Fortune." March 12, 1887, 4.

The Lost Is Found:

Louisville Courier-Journal. "Ellenville, N.Y." March 13, 1879, 1.

Brutes of Husbands:

Hearn, Daniel Allen. *Legal Executions in New England.* Jefferson, NC: McFarland, 1999.

Louisville Courier-Journal. "Brained His Wife." December 26, 1891, 1.

————. "Brevities by Wire." January 9, 1890, 2.

————. "Drank His Wife's Blood." February 12, 1886, 5.

————. "Herman Hanged." February 13, 1886, 4.

————. "His Life Taken by Law." February 4, 1893, 9.

————. "Murder in a Prison." March 6, 1898, I, 3.

————. "Slashes His Throat, Admits Slaying Wife." March 18, 1920, 1.

————. "A Tragic Story from Buffalo." November 5, 1885, 4.

Perpetrating an Eyesore:

Louisville Courier-Journal. "A Frightful Crime." January 7, 1887, 2.

————. "A Mangled Body." January 6, 1887, 5.

————. "The Missing Leg Found." January 8, 1887, 2.

New York Times. "Nowlin Pleads Not Guilty." January 8, 1887, 5.

————. "A Young Murderer Hanged." January 21, 1888, 3.

Conscience Makes Cowards of Us All:

Louisville Courier-Journal. "Coward Conscience." March 13, 1887, 12.
New York Times. "Examining Bohle's Body." January 30, 1887, 3.
——. "A Mystery Soon Solved." January 28, 1887, 5.
——. "Twenty Years for Unger." February 20, 1887, 3.

A New Jersey "Burker":

Hearn, Daniel Allen. *Legal Executions in New Jersey, 1691–1963*. Jefferson, NC: McFarland, 2005.
Louisville Courier-Journal. "Fiendish Crime." May 10, 1892, 2.

Old Habits Die Hard:

Louisville Courier-Journal. "Deeds of a Fiend." December 9, 1893, 4.
——. "Expert Testimony." December 14, 1893, 2.
——. "A Juror Becomes Insane." December 19, 1893, 1.
——. "The Meyer Jury Discharged." December 22, 1893, 5.
——. "Murder Plotted in Prison." October 10, 1895, 3.
——. "Trial of Dr. Meyer." December 15, 1893, 2.

Schmidt Out of Luck:

New York Times. "150-Page Query in Schmidt Trial." January 31, 1914, 3.
——. "$10,000 Fund for Schmidt." January 23, 1914, 2.
——. "Alienists Pass on Schmidt." October 21, 1913, 10.
——. "Alienists to See Schmidt." November 21, 1913, 5.
——. "Arrest Dentist as Schmidt's Aid in Coining Plant." September 16, 1913, 1+.
——. "Chain of Murders Schmidt's Plan." September 20, 1913, 1+.
——. "Coroner Derided in Schmidt Case." September 29, 1913, 5.
——. "Doctor Not Sure Schmidt Is Insane." September 22, 1913, 18.
——. "Dr. Jelliffe Says Schmidt Is Insane." December 23, 1913, 11.
——. "Ends Schmidt Inquiry." November 11, 1913, 9.
——. "Find Third Flat Hired by Schmidt." September 18, 1913, 1+.
——. "Find Woman Dummy Who Aided Schmidt." February 4, 1914, 4.
——. "Find Woman's Body in Bundle in River." September 7, 1913, II, 11.
——. "Hans Schmidt Dies in Chair." February 19, 1916, 12.
——. "Hans Schmidt Dies Today." February 18, 1916, 12.
——. "Hans Schmidt Must Die." February 10, 1910, 7.
——. "Hear Schmidt's Appeal." October 28, 1915, 14.
——. "Holds Schmidt Is Sane." November 22, 1913, 22.
——. "John D. Not to Serve at Murder Inquest." October 1, 1913, 5.
——. "Jury Discharged in Schmidt Case." December 31, 1913, 1.
——. "Jury Indicts Schmidt." October 11, 1913, 5.
——. "Muret Denies Plan to Accuse Schmidt." September 27, 1913, 9.
——. "Nearer to Solving the River Murder." September 10, 1913, 3.
——. "New Reprieve for Schmidt." January 12, 1916, 10.

———. "Plans for Schmidt's Trial." October 5, 1913, III, 12.

———. "Priest Is Shamming, Dr. MacDonald Says." December 27, 1913, 6.

———. "Priest Slayer Had an 'Order' to Kill." December 20, 1913, 10.

———. "Priest Slayer Puts Hope in Alienists." December 9, 1913, 6.

———. "Reprieve to Hans Schmidt." January 13, 1916, 8.

———. "River Murder Traced to Priest Who Confesses." September 15, 1913, 1+.

———. "River Yields More of Woman's Body." September 8, 1913, 2.

———. "Say Schmidt Is Insane." December 24, 1913, 18.

———. "Say Tombs Doctor Aids Schmidt's Side." January 29, 1914, 6.

———. "Schmidt Amazes His Native Town." September 17, 1913, 2.

———. "Schmidt and Muret Indicted as Coiners." September 24, 1913, 20.

———. "Schmidt Brought Woman to America." September 21, 1913, 1+.

———. "Schmidt Case to Jury Today." February 5, 1913, 10.

———. "Schmidt Eccentric before Coming Here." December 18, 1913, 6.

———. "Schmidt Examined by State Alienists." September 25, 1913, 7.

———. "Schmidt Fails to Save Muret." October 29, 1913, 20.

———. "Schmidt Gets a Delay." October 15, 1913, 8.

———. "Schmidt Hearing Abroad." October 25, 1913, 3.

———. "Schmidt Hurls Coins at Crowd." October 4, 1913, 5.

———. "Schmidt in Sing Sing." February 1, 1914, 18.

———. "Schmidt Is Guilty in the First Degree." February 6, 1914, 1.

———. "Schmidt Jury Complete." December 10, 1913, 10.

———. "Schmidt Jury Not Agreed; Locked Up." December 30, 1913, 1.

———. "Schmidt Must Die, Court of Appeals Says." November 24, 1915, 6.

———. "Schmidt Must Die; Loses Final Appeal." January 8, 1916, 5.

———. "Schmidt Planned Murder." December 25, 1913, 11.

———. "Schmidt Purposed to Kill for Money." September 23, 1913, 5.

———. "Schmidt Ready for More Deaths." September 19, 1913, 1+.

———. "Schmidt Resents Plea of Insanity." December 17, 1913, 6.

———. "Schmidt Seeks Clemency." April 25, 1914, 10.

———. "Schmidt Told Girl She Was Doomed." December 12, 1913, 5.

———. "Schmidt Trial Nears Close." January 28, 1914, 18.

———. "Schmidt Trial Put Off." January 10, 1914, 11.

———. "Schmidt Trial Under Way." January 22, 1914, 20.

———. "Schmidt's Defense Opens." January 27, 1914, 5.

———. "Schmidt's Doctor Testifies at Trial." December 13, 1913, 13.

———. "Schmidt's Father Here to Save Him." December 11, 1913, 20.

———. "Schmidt's Story Untrue." May 31, 1914, III, 3.

———. "Schmidt's Trial Goes Over." November 20, 1913, 5.

———. "Sends Muret to Prison." October 30, 1913, 5.

———. "Still Fight for Schmidt." February 7, 1914, 3.

———. "Tell Queer Things That Schmidt Did." December 19, 1913, 20.

———. "Think Leg Found Is River Victim's." September 11, 1913, 4.

———. "To Argue Schmidt Appeal." October 24, 1915, II, 15.

———. "To Retry Schmidt on January 12." January 1, 1914, 8.

———. "Trace River Victim by Sale of Pillows." September 9, 1913, 2.

———. "Tried to Insure His Victim's Life." December 16, 1913, 20.

———. "U.S. Agents Search Schmidt Evidence." September 16, 1913, 1+.

———. "Would Examine Schmidt Family." September 26, 1913, 9.

A Locked-Room Mystery:

Boston Globe (morning edition). "Doors, Windows Found Locked, but Laundry-man Is Slain in His Shop." March 12, 1929, 18.

Fort, Charles. *The Complete Books of Charles Fort*. New York: Dover, 1974.

New York Sun. "Queer Murder in Black Belt." March 11, 1929, 9.

New York Times. "Hunt On in Harlem for Tenement Slayer." March 11, 1929, 27.

———. "Laundry Owner Slain at Work in His Shop." March 10, 1929, I, 24.

New York Times-Herald. "Harlem Laundryman Slain in Locked, Bolted Shop." March 10, 1929, 20.

Sifakis, Carl. *Encyclopedia of American Crime*. New York: Facts on File, 1982.

It Pays to Get to the Point:

Louisville Courier-Journal. "Operator Wired For Help . . ." November 20, 1903, 1.

The Martha Stewart of Murder:

Louisville Courier-Journal. "Burned Piecemeal." February 11, 1903, 1.

———. "Chopped Husband's Body to Pieces . . ." February 9, 1903, 1.

———. "Told in Dots and Dashes." May 31, 1903, I, 5.

New York Times. "Death Claims Kate Taylor." November 24, 1907, I, 3.

———. "How She Watched a Murder." May 25, 1904, 2.

———. "Woman Guilty of Murder." May 31, 1903, I, 12.

The Legal Conundrum of Harrison Noel:

Houston Post-Dispatch. "Daly Slayer Indicted in Six Minutes." September 10, 1925, 1.

———. "Harrison Noel Liberty Probes Are Scheduled." September 9, 1925, 1.

———. "Kidnaper Leads Police to Slain Child." September 7, 1925, 1+.

———. "Posses Hunt Maniac Who Stole Child." September 6, 1925, 1+.

———. "Resignation of Asylum Head Asked." September 13, 1925, 2.

New York Times. "$5,247 for Noel Victim's Widow." December 3, 1925, 8.

———. "1926 Murder Indictment Dropped." May 6, 1973, 72.

———. "Alienist for Defense Examines Young Noel." September 24, 1925, 19.

———. "Alienist for Noel Calls Thaw Insane." October 2, 1925, 16.

———. "Alienists to Swear Noel Is a Lunatic." September 30, 1925, 14.

———. "Ask Resignation of Asylum Doctor." September 12, 1925, 32.

———. "Case against Noel Finished by State." November 11, 1925, 25.

———. "Court Directs Noel Plea of Not Guilty." September 22, 1925, 15.

———. "Court Rules Today on Noel's Sanity." September 21, 1925, 6.

———. "Declare Asylum Turned Noel Away." September 11, 1925, 4.

———. "Defense Alienists Call Noel Insane." November 14, 1925, 17.

———. "Denies Clemency for Noel." December 2, 1925, 14.

———. "Denies He Allowed Noel to Be Paroled." September 13, 1925, 7.

———. "Doctors Examine Noel in Prison." September 15, 1925, 8.

———. "Dr. Thompson to Sue." October 7, 1925, 7.

———. "Dr. Thompson Won't Quit Asylum Post." September 17, 1925, 25.

———. "Hopelessly Insane, Noel's Experts Say." October 1, 1925, 31.

———. "Jury Dooms Noel to Death as Slayer . . ." November 17, 1925, 1+.

———. "Kidnaps Little Girl in Montclair after Killing Auto Driver." September 5, 1925, 1+.

———. "Lawyer Holds Noel Is Legally Insane." September 19, 1925, 16.

———. "Lawyer to Appeal the Noel Verdict." November 18, 1925, 25.

———. "Lawyer's Son Questioned in Kidnapping . . ." September 6, 1925, 1+.

———. "Mrs. Noel Aids Fund for Negro." September 17, 1925, 25.

———. "Mrs. Noel on Stand at Murder Trial." November 13, 1925, 21.

———. "Murder Indictment Found against Noel." September 10, 1925, 1+.

———. "Noel Hears Demand for Death Penalty." October 4, 1925, 21.

———. "Noel Is Held Sane and Must Be Tried." October 9, 1925, 2.

———. "Noel Is Sentenced to Die in January." November 24, 1925, 16.

———. "Noel Legally Sane, Alienists Testify." September 25, 1925, 6.

———. "Noel Loses Second Appeal." December 10, 1925, 3.

———. "Noel Pleads Guilty to Kidnapping Child, but Denies Murder." September 8, 1925, 1+.

———. "Noel Trial Goes On Today." November 12, 1925, 27.

———. "Noel's Counsel Asks Clemency for Slayer." November 25, 1925, 5.

———. "Noel's Father Will Fight to Save Son . . ." September 9, 1925, 1+.

———. "Noel's Last Appeal Goes to High Court." February 23, 1926, 10.

———. "On Trial for Life, Noel Is Apathetic." November 10, 1925, 27.

———. "Oust Dr. Thompson from Noel Asylum." September 18, 1925, 17.

———. "Sanity Test Judge Visits Noel in Cell." October 6, 1925, 19.

———. "Youth of 20 Kidnapped and Killed Girl . . ." September 7, 1925, 1+.

Death Row Dramas:

Louisville Courier-Journal. "Artist Is Denied Permit to Paint Sing Sing Chair." July 12, 1920, 1.

———. "Execution Held Up for Prison Show." December 14, 1928, 1.

———. "Fatal Drop." March 31, 1883, 2.

———. "Man Would Die in Murderer's Place." March 12, 1924, 12.

———. "Murderer Given Death Sentence on Second Trial." February 24, 1910, 1.

———. "Shorten Lives So That Kin's Grief May Be Dulled." December 18, 1916, 2.

———. "Took a Seat." December 18, 1894, 1.

———. "Vermont Justice." November 20, 1881, 2.

New York Times. "Twice Guilty of Murder." February 24, 1910, 7.

The Pennsylvania Witchcraft Murder, or: I'm Charmed, I'm Sure:

Colangelo, Drema. Emails to author. December 1, 2005.

Demos, John. "Underlying Themes in the Witchcraft of the Seventeenth Century New England." From *Religion in American History.* Eds. John M. Mulder and John F. Wilson, Englewood Cliffs, NJ: Prentice-Hall, 1978.

Evans, Elizabeth. "Not Since Hex Trial Has York Seen Such Attention." *York Dispatch* [PA]. September 23, 2002.

Indiana Evening Gazette [PA]. "Lockard in New Life Try." March 13, 1937, 2.

Maxwell-Stuart, P. G. *Witchcraft in Europe and the New World, 1400–1800.* New York: Palgrave, 2001.

New York Times. "Ask 'Witch Doctor' about Girl's Death." December 2, 1928, 2.

———. "Bars Witchcraft as Murder Defense." January 9, 1929, 3.

———. "Boy Denied Joining in 'Witch Killing.'" January 11, 1929, 25.

———. "Charm Book Throws Light on 'Witch' Trial." January 6, 1929, I, 25.

———. "Convicts Boy of 14 for 'Witch Murder.'" January 12, 1929, 3.

———. "Death of Five Babies Laid to Witch Cult." December 4, 1928, 14.

———. "Farmers Fleeced through 'Black Art,'" December 3, 1928, 27.

———. "Fear of Witchcraft Leads to Murder." December 1, 1928, 3.

———. "'Powwow' Doctors Use Faith and Prayer." December 9, 1928, I, 19.

———. "Prisoner Told Him, 'I Got the Witch,'" January 8, 1929, 3.

———. "Third Witch Killer Convicted at York." January 13, 1929, I, 3.

———. "Witchcraft Trio Face Trial Today." January 7, 1929, 31.

———. "'Witch' Killer Guilty, Sentenced for Life." January 10, 1929, 1+.

Riverside Daily Press [CA]. "Will Rogers Asks Why Sentence Boy for Bringing Up?" January 12, 1929, 1.

Star and Sentinel [Gettysburg, PA]. "Hex Slayer Seeks Pardon." February 22, 1936, 1.

York Dispatch [PA]. "Aims to Put Teeth in Law to End Quackery." December 6, 1928, 24+.

———. "Another Link to Rudy Murder Chain . . ." December 4, 1928, 22+.

———. "Blame Trio for Murder." December 14, 1928, 42.

———. "Find Curry Boy Guilty of First Degree Murder." January 11, 1929, 32+.

———. "Hess, 'the Dupe,' Guilty of Second Degree Murder." January 14, 1929, 20+.

———. "'I Got Witch, Fault Is Mine,' Said Blymyer." January 8, 1929, 22+.

———. "Insanity Experts Say Blymyer Is Mentally Weak." January 9, 1929, 20+.

———. "Killer Hess May Know His Fate before Sunset." January 12, 1929, 16+.

———. "Life Term for Blymyer; Curry Now Faces Jury." January 10, 1929, 20+.

———. "Many More Months before York Lives Down Its 'Spook' Reputation." December 14, 1928, 52.

———. "More Ministers Talk of Witchcraft Folly." December 17, 1928, 20.

———. "Murder Farmer to Get Lock of Hair . . ." November 30, 1928, 36+.

———. "Physicians Will Not Prosecute Quacks." December 21, 1928, 40+.

———. "Six Questions and Replies Sufficient to Hold Three Witch Slayers . . ." December 5, 1928, 24+.

———. "Slayer in Witchcraft Crime Is Suspected of Killing Gertrude Rudy." December 1, 1928, 16+.

———. "Thirty-Four Will Testify in Witch Murder Case." January 2, 1929, 18.

———. "Unfavorable Publicity Resented by Yorkers." December 5, 1928, 24.

———. "Witchcraft Led to the Killing of Irwin Heagy." December 10, 1928, 22.

———. "Witch Murder Case Counsel Is Named By Court." December 2, 1928, 20+.

———. "Witch Slayer Blymyer Seeks a Separate Trial." December 21, 1928, 40.

———. "Witch Slayers Each Enter Plea of 'Not Guilty.'" January 7, 1929, 18.

———. "York Medical Society Would End Quackery." December 20, 1928, 28.

———. "York Pow-Wow 'Cures' Investigated by State." December 10, 1928, 22.

George's Attention to Grammar:

Louisville Courier-Journal. "Sees Humor in His Crime." May 20, 1908, 2.
New York Times. "Murder and Suicide to Stop a Wedding." May 20, 1908, 1.
———. "Sterry Will Fight Is On." August 4, 1909, 7.
———. "To Bury Sterrys Together." May 21, 1908, 5.

An Unimaginative Hiding Place:

Louisville Courier-Journal. "Kills Himself When Crime Is Discovered." September 3, 1909, 1.

Dead Man Waiting:

Louisville Courier-Journal. "Bill Would Revive Legally Dead Man." March 11, 1922, 9.
New York Times. "Kills Old Minister in Village Street." July 16, 1908, 1.

Helen Helps Harry Conquer His Phobia:

Louisville Courier-Journal. "Crazed Butcher Slays Woman." October 17, 1927, 1.
New York Times. "Derided by Woman, Kills Her in a Fury." October 17, 1927, 1+.
———. "Husband Threatens Slayer of His Wife." October 18, 1927, 9.

A Disgruntled Employee:

Hearn, Daniel Allen. *Legal Executions in New York State*. Jefferson, NC: McFarland, 1997.
Louisville Courier-Journal. "2 Women, Man Cut to Pieces." July 11, 1927, 1.
———. "Girl Believed Slain by Ax of New York Man." July 12, 1927, 1+.
———. "Man Convicted in Woman's Ax Death." November 4, 1927, 2.
———. "Man Is Indicted in 2 Ax Murders." July 15, 1927, 3.
———. "Severed Limbs Found in Bundle." July 10, 1927, I, 1.
———. "Woman Identifies Slaying Suspect." July 14, 1927, 1.

Homework and Hatchets:

Louisville Courier-Journal. "Mother Arrested on Clew Son Furnished." March 18, 1931, 1.
New York Times. "Add to Diller Evidence." March 20, 1931, 18.
———. "Freed in Husband's Death." March 26, 1931, 2.

A Creepy Story:

Louisville Courier-Journal. "Hermit with Long White Beard Leads Scouts to Murder Scene." July 11, 1932, 1.
———. "Man Arrested as 'Hermit,'" July 12, 1932, 10.
Philadelphia Record. "Aged Suspect Held in Mystery Slaying." July 12, 1932, 3.
———. "Check Slain Man on Dental Charts." July 15, 1932, 3.

Wittels, David C. "Fantastic Hermit Leads Scout Aides to Murder Victim." *Philadelphia Record*. July 11, 1932, 1+.

The Jeweler Digs Holes for His Wife—and Himself:

Louisville Courier-Journal. "Body of Missing Woman Is Found." September 17, 1932, 1+.

———. "DuBois Calls Wife a Suicide." September 18, 1932, I, 1+.

———. "Hair Is Clew as Woman Missing." September 16, 1932, 8.

In the Days before Craigslist:

Indiana Gazette [PA]. "'Mail Bride' Tells Her Story." August 30, 1934, 2.

———. "Murderer Is Happy Now." June 22, 1934, 9.

Louisville Courier-Journal. "Girl Cleared of Killing." August 31, 1934, 1.

———. "Ohio Girl, 20, Kills 'Mail Order' Fiancé." June 19, 1934, 1.

Grumpy Old Men:

Louisville Courier-Journal. "Man, 75, Given Life for Killing His Friend, 83." September 1, 1935, I, 11.

———. "Man, 81, Killed by Nail Driven in Head." June 14, 1935, III, 2.

3-X: A Madman ahead of His Time:

Louisville Courier-Journal. "Another Shot Found in Motor as Madman Marks 7 for Death." June 20, 1930, 1+.

———. "Ex-Foreign Agent is Nabbed in 3-X Case." July 10, 1930, 7.

———. "Police Patrol Town for Madman-Slayer." June 19, 1930, 1+.

———. "Slayer Says He's Through." June 22, 1930, I, 3.

———. "Veteran Says He Met Maniac." June 23, 1930, 1+.

———. "Woman Found Dead in Abandoned Coupe." July 6, 1930, I, 1.

———. "Youth Is Suspect in Maniac Murders." June 26, 1930, 24.

New York Times. "2,000 Police Patrol Queens in Wide Hunt . . ." June 19, 1930, 1+.

———. "3-X Notes Writer, Demented, Is Taken." August 17, 1930, I, 8.

———. "'Best' Clue Fails in Queens Slayings." June 25, 1930, 6.

———. "Court Aide Is Held in 3-X Murders." August 23, 1930, 2.

———. "Brooklyn Man Shot in Auto as Police Hunt Queens Slayer." June 20, 1930, 1+.

———. "Ex-Policeman Held in 6 Auto Hold-Ups." November 22, 1930, 19.

———. "Find New 3-X Note a Fake." August 6, 1930, 14.

———. "Freed in Queens Killings." July 10, 1930, 30.

———. "Hear Queens Slayer Is Posing as Woman." June 23, 1930, 6.

———. "Hunt for Suicide as Queens Slayer." July 6, 1930, II, 2.

———. "Insane Man Hunted in Second Killing." June 18, 1930, 27.

———. "New Clue Found to Queens Slayer." June 26, 1930, 12.

———. "New Death Threat Ends 3-X Silence." June 29, 1931, 9.

———. "New Threat Laid to Queens Slayer." June 24, 1930, 27.

———. "Officials Doubt 3-X Suspect's Tale." June 3, 1936, 46.

———. "Police Sifting Clue in Queens Murders." July 7, 1930, 21.

———. "Queens Police Alert after New 3-X Note." October 17, 1931, 3.

———. "Question Girl in Murder." June 15, 1930, I, 13.

———. "Secretary to Harvey Gets New 3-X Call." June 29, 1930, I, 19.

———. "Self-Styled Killer Phones to Harvey." June 27, 1930, 9.

———. "Slayer Now Warns Brother of Victim." June 21, 1930, 6.

———. "Suspect Seized in Queens 3-X Murders . . ." June 2, 1936, 1.

———. "Witnesses Clear Engel, 3-X Suspect." June 4, 1936, 10.

Three Victorian-Era Orphan Girls:

Louisville Courier-Journal. "Female Fiends." January 11, 1887, 5.

St. Paul Daily Globe. "Girl Assassins Let Go." April 26, 1887, 1.

Postcards from a Killer:

Boston Evening Transcript. "Hickey Confesses to Murdering Two Boys." November 29, 1912, 1.

———. "Hickey Is Sentenced." December 23, 1912, 3.

———. "Hickey Will Not Testify." December 17, 1912, 3.

———. "Think Murderer in Boston." November 18, 1912, 3.

Fond du Lac Daily Commonwealth [WI]. "Insanity a Ruse." December 5, 1912, 1.

Marion Daily Star [OH]. "Remarkable Case of Dual Personality." December 14, 1912, 7.

New Orleans Picayune. "Drink Is Blamed by Boy Murderer for Killing Two." November 30, 1912, 1.

———. "Evidence against Hickey." December 19, 1912, 15.

———. "Have Clew to Man Who Murdered Boy." November 19, 1912, 6.

———. "Hickey Is Guilty of Murder of Boy." December 22, 1912, 3.

———. "Hickey to Be Tried December 16." December 3, 1912, 15.

———. "Indicted for Murder of Joseph [sic] Boy." November 21, 1912, 3.

———. "Murderer Still Writes Police." November 18, 1912, 3.

———. "Mutilated Body of Child Found." November 17, 1912, 2.

———. "Police Asked to Question Hickey of Other Crimes." December 2, 1912, 1.

———. "Relates Story of His Many Crimes." December 1, 1912, 12.

New York Times. "Boy's Chum Picks Hickey." December 1, 1912, 15.

———. "Hickey Escapes the Chair." December 22, 1912, 8.

———. "Hickey in Custody on Murder Charge." November 20, 1912, 10.

———. "Hickey Is Indicted as Slayer of Boy." November 21, 1912, 3.

———. "Hickey Killed Man and Murdered Boys." November 30, 1912, 7.

———. "Kruck Boy's Death." December 13, 1902, 2.

———. "Murderer of Boys May Be in Custody." November 18, 1912, 8.

———. "Newsboy Murder Mystery." December 14, 1902, I, 12.

———. "Newsboy Murdered in Central Park." December 12, 1902, 16.

———. "Plans New Hickey Trial." December 26, 1912, 1.

———. "Seek a Jersey Man as Slayer of Boy." November 19, 1912, 1.

———. "Slayer of Youths Killed One Here." November 17, 1912, 1.

———. "Slew Only Three, He Says." December 6, 1912, 6.

KEVEN McQUEEN is an instructor in the Department of Eng.
Eastern Kentucky University. He is the author of numerous boo.
including *Horror in the Heartland: Strange and Gothic Tales from the
Midwest, Creepy California: Strange and Gothic Tales from the Golden Sta.
The Kentucky Book of the Dead, Murder and Mayhem in Indiana*, and *The
Axman Came from Hell and Other Southern True Crime Stories*.